JORDAN B. COOPER

The Doctrine of God

First published by Weidner Institute: A Division of Just and Sinner Publications 2023

Copyright © 2023 by Jordan B. Cooper

All rights reserved. No part of this publication may be reproduced, stored or transmitted in any form or by any means, electronic, mechanical, photocopying, recording, scanning, or otherwise without written permission from the publisher. It is illegal to copy this book, post it to a website, or distribute it by any other means without permission.

From the Weidner Institute

A Division of Just and Sinner Publications

Ithaca, NY 14850

JustandSinner.org

First edition

ISBN (paperback): 978-1-952295-60-7
ISBN (hardcover): 978-1-952295-61-4

This book was professionally typeset on Reedsy. Find out more at reedsy.com

Contents

Volumes in this Series	iv
1 Introduction	1
2 The State of the Current Discussion	9
3 Divine Simplicity	47
4 Divine Immutability	86
5 Divine Atemporality	125
6 Divine Impassibility	155
7 The Challenge of Social Trinitarianism	185
8 Conclusion	216
Bibliography	221

Volumes in this Series

1. Prolegomena: A Defense of the Scholastic Method (Released 2020)
2. The Doctrine of God: A Defense of Classical Christian Theism (Released 2023)
3. Theological Anthropology: An Augustinian Approach (Upcoming)
4. Christology: Jesus's Person and Work (Upcoming)
5. Justification: Salvation as Forensic Declaration (Upcoming)
6. Union with Christ: Salvation as Participation (Released 2021)
7. Law and Gospel: In Scripture, History, and Contemporary Theology (Upcoming)
8. The Church and Sacraments (Upcoming)
9. Eschatology (Upcoming)

1

Introduction

Among the most contested points of the scholastic tradition today is the ancient commitment to what is often referred to as "classical theism." Throughout the nineteenth century, various philosophers and theologians questioned the accepted orthodoxies of past ages, arguing that the doctrine of God which had developed in the Western world, especially in the late medieval era through St. Thomas Aquinas, was more indebted to Greek philosophical constructs than to Scripture itself.[1] This led to the development of alternative proposals as models for understanding the God of Scripture.

Roman Catholic philosopher of religion Brian Davies has characterized two basic approaches to theology proper which are definitive of the core divide arising from the nineteenth century and continuing today.[2] First is classical theism, which strongly differentiates the changeless God from a continually shifting creation, understanding him via the way of either analogy or negation. This tradition extends from Augustine to Aquinas, throughout both the Roman Catholic and Protestant traditions in the post-Reformation era. In contrast to this, Davies identifies another strand of thought as "theistic personalism," which characterizes a move away from

---

[1] For example, Dorner, *Divine Immutability*.

[2] Davies, *Philosophy of Religion*, 2–16.

the majority Christian perspective in the past, which is claimed to have borrowed from pagan philosophers. This move depends largely upon the Hellenizing thesis, which was especially prominent in the early twentieth century and purports that Christianity went through the gradual process of losing characteristics of its Hebraic roots, being engulfed in the foreign concepts of Hellenism. In contrast to the classical approach, these authors argue that God is defined, scripturally, as ultimate personality, sharing many characteristics of his creation which were denied by earlier thinkers who sought to distance God from any idea of mutability.

A more recent proposal, drawing on Davies's work, was offered by Baptist author James Dolezal, who refers to these moves away from classical theism as "theistic mutualism."[3] Despite the many differences of authors who are placed under that label, there is a common strand of thought in which the relationship that the believer has with God is a mutual one. It is not only the human creature that is changed through his or her personal interaction with the triune God, but God himself changes in one way or another. In other words, it is both God and man who, in some way, are dependent upon that mutual relationship in order to be who they are. While classical philosophy would characterize God as pure actuality, theistic mutualism posits that God himself has potentiality which has yet to be actualized, and can be through his creaturely interactions.

The Variety of Theistic Mutualisms Today

It is important in such a discussion to differentiate between various thinkers who may be more broadly united in their rejection of classical tenets of theology proper. Certainly, many Evangelical theistic mutualists in particular may be quite offended by the categorization of their own work as existing within the same ideological framework as the heirs of Protestant liberalism, who are sometimes their chief theological opponents. Evangelical

---

[3] Dolezal, *All That Is in God*, 1–8.

Baptist theologian Bruce Ware, for example, has been one of the most outspoken critics of the more radical position of open theism. Nonetheless, despite Ware's critique of the open theist approach to divine foreknowledge, he affirms their insistence upon the reality of change within the divine nature, thus placing himself firmly within the theistic mutualist frame of thought. To be fair to such divisions among theistic mutualists, it behooves us to further break down mutualist approaches into multiple categories under that same broader umbrella. Here, I identify four.

The first group to be identified here as critics of classical theism are those who affirm process theology.[4] Though, again, many differences exist among these thinkers, there is broad agreement as to the conviction that God himself is in a historical process of change and self-realization. The rise of Hegel's idealism is at the root of these conceptions, in which history itself is continually being driven toward its *telos* through a process of self-actualization. For Hegel, God was conflated with the world as the "world Spirit," who progressed through the process of thesis, antithesis, and synthesis. Though not many theologians adopted the entirety of Hegel's system, popular thinkers such as Danish theologian Hans Martensen adapted parts of his thought to their approaches to Christian theism. Following Hegel, the most important figures for the development of process theism in the twentieth century were Alfred North Whitehead and Charles Hartshorne. These authors adopted becoming, rather than being, as the foundational metaphysical principle, in contrast to the essentialist approach of Greek thought. This conviction led to the development of unique concepts of God's relationship to the world, divine mutability, and the preeminence of free will (both in God and the creature).

The second group of thinkers is similar to the approach of Hegel and Whitehead in a number of ways, while remaining its own distinctive theological school. This is what is broadly labeled "the theology of hope."[5] In some ways, the beginning of this school can be identified with Karl

---

[4] Cobb and Griffin, *Process Theology*.

[5] Moltmann, *Theology of Hope*.

Barth, whose actualistic ontology shaped a significant portion of the thought process of the most significant authors categorized with this label. However, the founding of the movement itself can more particularly be associated with Jürgen Moltmann. In his book *The Theology of Hope*, Moltmann argues that eschatology is not to be treated, as it often has in classical dogmatics, as the last of many doctrinal topics; it is instead the lens through which all theology must be viewed. This future-oriented theology had a profound impact upon twentieth-century theology, being adopted in various ways by Carl Braaten, Robert Jenson, and Wolfhart Pannenberg (among others). Why such a move is significant for the present purposes is that eschatology is not merely identified as the end for which humanity was created, but is instead definitive of God's own being. God is not the timeless and changeless essence proposed by earlier thinkers, but is changeable and future to himself.

Third, and perhaps even more divergent from classical thought, is the movement classified as "open theism," which arose from within Evangelicalism in the beginning of the twenty-first century.[6] Like the previous theologians addressed, these authors—such as Clark Pinnock, Gregory Boyd, and John Sanders—argue for a form of the Hellenization thesis, believing that classical theistic ideas are incommensurate with the scriptural witness. Generally less philosophically rigorous than the writers previously mentioned, open theists base their arguments primarily within what they conceive to be a straightforward reading of the biblical narrative. It is contended that concepts such as divine immutability and divine impassibility do not sufficiently account for God's consistent changing of mind or action in response to his creatures. In order for personal relationships to be real, they argue, God must be mutable and cannot be atemporal. In fact, for the open theist, God's foreknowledge is based upon probability rather than an absolute apprehension of future actions. These claims serve, for open theists, to answer the problem of evil, as well as to allow for libertarian freedom for creatures without divine interference.

The fourth group of theologians classified here are those who are

---

[6] Pinnock, *Most Moved Mover*; Sanders, *God Who Risks*; Boyd, *God of the Possible*.

broadly considered Evangelical theologians who have criticized classical formulations of the divine essence and attributes, while also dismissing the denial of divine foreknowledge as taught by the open theists.[7] Thinkers who affirm such an approach arise from a variety of Protestant perspectives, including Reformed, Lutheran, and Baptist. Of some controversy in recent years has been a debate within the Orthodox Presbyterian Church surrounding a proposal from K. Scott Oliphint in his book *God with Us: Divine Condescension and the Attributes of God*. In this book, as well as in the rest of his corpus, Oliphint is critical of Thomism generally, and subsequently its formation of the doctrine of God. This leads Oliphint to offer a proposal which differentiates between God in himself, who is immutable and simple, and God as he has condescended to humanity, thus taking upon himself various covenantal attributes which are changeable. John Frame and Bruce Ware offer similar ideas wherein they affirm both continuity and discontinuity with the classical tradition in their adaptation of personalistic theism. Beyond the Reformed tradition, Lutheran authors such as Steven Paulson, Gerhard Forde, and Oswald Bayer contend for a Lutheran system which is devoid of classical metaphysics, including in their formulation of the doctrine of God. More philosophically inclined Evangelicals such as William Lane Craig and John P. Moreland have similarly argued against the use of Greek ontology in expositing God's nature and attributes.

While each of these four groups of thinkers differs from the others in rather significant ways, each of them rejects classical theism for an approach which allows for some kind of mutuality in the God-human relationship. This flows, for each of them, from a contention that the Hebraic conception of divinity as taught in Israelite religion differs from the God described by the Greek philosophers. The developed Western approach to the divine attributes, especially as taught by Aquinas, is a divergence from this Hebrew conception of divinity, and is thus to be—in some form—rejected.

---

[7] Richards, *Untamed God*; Oliphint, *God with Us*.

Defining Classical Theism

The present volume serves as both a critique of these mutualist approaches and as a positive construction of classical theism, especially as formulated in the Protestant scholastic tradition. While some of the volumes in this series are more specifically Lutheran, especially in areas where the Reformed-Lutheran divide is most apparent, the conclusions reached here are simply those of the catholic tradition, which was appropriated by both branches of the Reformation.[8] From John Owen to Francis Pieper, despite significant theological differences in sacramental theology and Christology, there is a unified consensus that the patristic and medieval churches were correct in their basic convictions surrounding God's nature and attributes. In order to proceed with this defense of classical theism, for the purpose of this work, that phrase itself must be defined.

In spite of some criticisms, to be a classical theist does not mean that one is an Aristotelian rather than a Platonist, or that every category developed by Aquinas is a necessary one for theology (though I tend to think his categories are generally better than the alternatives). The Western theological tradition need not be committed solely to the use of one particular philosopher's categories, as if the classical theistic tradition did not exist prior to the thirteenth-century recapturing of Aristotle. Figures such as St. Anselm, Thomas Aquinas, and Duns Scotus all construe God's essence in a way that is generally consistent, despite differences on particulars. Thus, the definition of classical theism used here is not meant to be so narrow as to necessitate the use of certain philosophical terminology and categories. Instead, for the purposes of the present project, classical theism is defined by the belief in four specific propositions regarding the divine nature.

The first of these propositions is that God is simple. To affirm the simplicity of God is to say that God's essence is not distinct from his attributes, or properties. It is divine simplicity which has received the most criticism or dismissal out of hand as either incoherent or absent from the

---

[8] That is not to say that my Lutheran emphases do not come out throughout the discussion.

scriptural witness. The second is that God is immutable. This term affirms that God is unchanging, not merely in his purposes or faithfulness, but in his being. Though God's interactions with his creation are real,[9] they do not cause change to the divine nature itself. Third, God is atemporal. God is not everlasting merely in the sense that he has an infinite duration of life from the past and into the future, but he exists in an eternal present. Fourth, God is impassible. The divine nature in itself does not and cannot experience suffering, as that is uniquely part of creaturely existence. According to the definition used in this work, affirmation of these four propositions constitutes classical theism.

The Argument of This Book

This work is the second volume in my multi-book project A Contemporary Protestant Scholastic Theology. The first covered the subject of theological method, affirming the usefulness of the categories of classical philosophy, as well as their historical pedigree within the theology that arose from the Reformation. This volume will not retread all the necessary ground in that work, so it is recommended that one read that volume prior to this, especially if one is not familiar with the philosophical terminology employed here.

This work begins with an overview of some of the most important theologians and published works involved in these contemporary debates. For the sake of my own limitations, I have not chosen to interact with figures involved in all of the four different strands of mutualism as exposited above. Though there may be some mention throughout the text of Hegel and Whitehead's process theism and of open theism, these are not going to be engaged significantly. Instead, I have chosen to focus attention on proponents of the theology of hope, as well as on some of the more Evangelical challenges to the classic divine attributes. It is these two groups

---

[9] However, as will be seen, it can in an orthodox sense be said that God has no "real relations" with creatures.

which have made the most significant impact within churches committed to the historic Reformation traditions. The literature review includes a discussion of classical theistic proponents, theologians of hope, and Evangelical personalists.

Following this overview, the next four chapters discuss each of those divine attributes mentioned above: simplicity, immutability, atemporality, and impassibility. Each doctrine is defined in its classical formulation, using the medieval scholastic textbooks, such as Aquinas's *Summa Theologia* and *Summa Contra Gentiles*; and the continued use of Aquinas's categories by both Lutheran and Reformed authors, including seventeenth-century scholastic thinkers like Johann Gerhard and David Hollaz, along with early twentieth-century writers from both traditions, including Francis Pieper and Herman Bavinck. Scholars who specialize in earlier Protestant scholasticism are used, such as Richard Muller and Robert Preus, to further define such ideas. Following an exposition of the scholastic approaches, critics of each of the classical divine attributes are engaged, and responses are offered in defense of classical theism. In a following chapter, classical theism is discussed in connection with Trinitarian theology, as contemporary social trinitarian models are demonstrated as insufficient formulations for the church, in favor of an essentialist schema. In the conclusion, the practical implications of such a divergence are discussed for the contemporary church.

2

The State of the Current Discussion

The literature reviewed here is that belonging to three of the aforementioned schools of thought surrounding theology proper and the value of classical theism. First are post-Barthian thinkers who, in various ways, contend that eschatology is in some sense determinative of God's being. The three authors addressed from that perspective here are Robert Jenson, Wolfhart Pannenberg, and Carl Braaten. Second are those thinkers who consider themselves to be Evangelicals, but strongly reject the Thomistic approach to the Godhead as a Hellenizing departure from the scriptural teaching concerning God. The theologians mentioned in this regard are Jay Wesley Richards and John Frame. The third group of thinkers discussed here are those who are contemporary proponents of the classical theism defined by the acceptance of the four major tenets of the present work—simplicity, immutability, atemporality, and impassibility. The authors included in this category are James Dolezal and Stephen J. Duby.

Post-Barthian Theologians

There is no clear way to demarcate this first group of theologians, as they are not part of a unified theological movement as one might have said about neo-orthodoxy in the era of Barth. Nonetheless, these theologians arise within a post-Barthian context with similar themes in their overall thought, as well as in their understanding of God in particular. The three thinkers here—Robert Jenson, Carl Braaten, and Wolfhart Pannenberg—are all adherents of the historical critical method, while also retaining a strong adherence to the basic truth claims of Christianity in opposition to nineteenth-century liberalism. They all are, to some degree, indebted to the theology of hope, as they argue for a doctrine of God by which he is defined, in some sense, by his own future. Similarly, they are critical of the traditional Western doctrine of God, especially in the medieval period, by which God's essence and attributes are treated separately from, and prior to, his triunity. For these authors, God's essence is to be found precisely *within* his triunity, rather than ontologically prior to it.

Robert Jenson

Robert Jenson is undoubtedly among the most significant theologians within the last century, having a strong impact on both systematic and ecumenical theology across geographic and denominational boundaries. Throughout his life, Jenson held positions at Luther College, Luther Seminary, Oxford University, St. Olaf College, and finally Princeton Seminary. Among his many theological writings, Jenson's most important works were his two-volume *Systematic Theology* (1997–99) and his contributions to *Christian Dogmatics*, which served as a theological textbook at various Lutheran seminaries. Along with several other dogmatic books and essays, Jenson contributed to the ecumenical movement in founding the Center for Catholic and Evangelical Theology along with its regular journal *Pro Ecclesia* in 1991. Though Jenson was deeply committed to the catholicity of the

Reformation, and of Lutheranism in particular, he was consistently critical of medieval approaches to God's essence and attributes. Below is an exposition of two places in which he explains this reformulation of Christian theism: his contribution to *Christian Dogmatics*, and volume one of his *Systematic Theology*.

Christian Dogmatics

The dual volume *Christian Dogmatics* was a project that involved a number of Lutheran thinkers in an attempt to provide a systematic theology from a Lutheran perspective which engages the theological questions and disputes of the late twentieth century. First published in 1984, these volumes were a collaborative effort among six Lutheran thinkers: Carl Braaten, Robert Jenson, Gerhard Forde, Philip Hefner, Hans Schwartz, and Paul Sponheim. What is relevant for the purposes of this study is the second locus, "The Triune God," written entirely by Jenson, being based in part on his book *The Triune Identity*. This summarization of Jenson's thought on this topic is immensely clear, and it provides a basis for the primary themes emphasized throughout his work on the topic.

In order to understand Jenson's positive Trinitarian construal of the divine identity, it is imperative that one grasp his adoption of the Hellenizing thesis and subsequent critique of classical theism. In his treatment of the Nicene Trinitarian formulation, Jenson sets up the gospel and Greek views of divinity as complete opposites. He refers to Hellenistic theology as "an exact antagonist of biblical faith,"[10] and both the Greek and Hebraic views of divinity as "fundamentally incompatible."[11] This divergence, for Jenson, largely arises from the questions which each tradition asked historically, and the theology emerged from answering such questions.

An explanation of the Greek conception of deity is divided, for Jenson,

---

[10] Jenson, *Christian Dogmatics*, 1:115.

[11] Ibid.

into five essential characteristics. First, Greek thinkers contended with the problem of time. In particular, they asked the question, "Can it be that *all* things pass away?" in light of the continual flux of history with its unexpected turns.[12] It was this uncertainty of a changing world which led to the conviction that an unchanging, timeless reality must exist, which reality is identified with God. Jenson characterizes the Greek deity's defining attribute as "immortality, immunity to destruction."[13] Second, the Ionians wrestled with the comprehensibility of events in human history. God was used to give meaning and direction to seemingly random occurrences. Third, the Greek philosophers were committed to the unity and singularity of an unchanging being behind the Homeric anthropomorphic deities. Fourth, God is separate from ordinary human experience. Daily life is a continual series of changes, and thus if something which is unchanging exists, it stands behind, rather than within, one's worldly experience. This leads to what Jenson identifies as Hellenistic theology's fifth and final distinctive characteristic: as one never encounters timelessness or changeless reality in earthly occurrences, in order to find this underlying source of stability, one must reason to God's existence and attributes. In such a schema, God is known not through historical revelation, but by analogy with created things, and the process of negation from attributes of things which are temporal and mutable. In other words, in this apophatic theology, God is known not so much by what he is, but by what he is not.[14]

Hebrew theology developed in a completely different set of circumstances, for Jenson. The concern of the Jewish people was not that of the relationship between change and constancy, but of identity—both theirs and Yahweh's. For Jenson, God in the Old Testament is not known by his essence or timelessness, but instead by his historical acts. For the people of the Old Covenant, God was identified with one particular act: the Exodus. God was known to the Israelites not via negation or analogical predication abstracted

---

[12] Ibid., 116.

[13] Ibid.

[14] Ibid., 117.

from the material world, but through his concrete manifestation of love and redemption in delivering the Jewish people from slavery by an oppressive people.[15] The exodus is, for Jenson, "the chief content of Israel's creed."[16] Such an identification of God through his redemptive acts continues in the New Testament, wherein God is identified as "whoever raised Jesus from the dead."[17] Proposing an actualistic ontology as he draws upon Barth, Jenson contends that the resurrection is not merely revelatory of God's eternal identity, but it *constitutes* it. These Old and New Testament identifications of God by divergent redemptive acts do not, importantly, divide the God of both Testaments. It is essential for a proper understanding of Yahweh that it is the same God who delivered the Israelites that brought Jesus back to life from the dead.[18] Jenson further expands upon this theme of divine identity in his exposition of the Trinity.

Jenson is critical of those theologians who begin any talk of God with an exposition of the divine attributes rather than the Trinitarian persons. For him, this is a capitulation to the Hellenistic concept of God over which a Trinitarian Christian formula is placed.[19] A properly Christian dogmatics must begin, instead, with the divine identity expressed in Trinitarian relations. As he explains such a Trinitarian identification of deity, Jenson is radically Christocentric. He writes: "God, we may therefore identify, is what happens with Jesus," and perhaps even more bluntly that "God 'is' Jesus."[20] While at first glance, such statements may appear to be a collapse of divine personalities into the Son, he continues his discussion of divine identification by acknowledging a second divine identity which is "what will come of Jesus and us, together."[21] God is future to himself, being identified

---

[15] Ibid., 90.

[16] Ibid.

[17] Ibid., 91.

[18] Ibid.

[19] Ibid., 118.

[20] Ibid., 100.

[21] Ibid.

not only with Jesus's accomplished acts, but with his eschatological end. This future is identified as the Spirit, which is further said to be "Jesus' spirit."[22] In view of God's being defined by his redemptive acts for his people, Jenson contends that there is a "temporally three-point identification of the gospel's God," identified as Father, Son, and Spirit.[23] Throughout his work, Jenson identifies the Trinitarian persons with the past, present, and future. Jenson's definition of God is best encapsulated by his own summation of his work, in which he writes: "God is the universally transforming event between Jesus the Israelite, and the transcendence he called to as 'Father,' and their Spirit among us."[24] The foundational claim of Jenson's Trinitarian proposal is that divine timelessness is a foreign construct, which should never have been appropriated into the church's speech regarding the divine nature. Jenson's formulation of the Trinity is dependent upon his unique approach to God's relationship to time. Jenson's proposal essentially stands or falls on the veracity of his construal of God's temporality.

Systematic Theology: The Triune God

Thirteen years after his contribution to *Christian Dogmatics*, Jenson released the first volume of his *Systematic Theology*, giving it the subtitle *The Triune God*. There is not any substantial change to the content of his previous contribution to the topic in this volume, and several of the same themes are reiterated here, such as his reaffirmation of the Hellenization thesis, criticism of divine atemporality, and the importance of divine identity as constituted by the resurrection of Christ. This text is, however, more expansive than the last, as Jenson provides clarification and a defense of his approach.

In his prolegomena, Jenson affirms his opposition to the use of Greek philosophy as it has been appropriated within Christian thought. He

---

[22] Ibid., 101.

[23] Ibid., 101.

[24] Ibid., 190.

opposes any attempt at theologizing which views the truths of Plato or Aristotle as a "unilateral judge of the whole," thus elevating such figures above the prophets and apostles.[25] The problem, in Jenson's view, is that Greek thought has been given the label "philosophy," allowing for the impression that these metaphysical convictions were, in themselves, some kind of areligious enterprise to be adopted universally, without regard to specific theological commitments. One should instead approach Greek metaphysics as "simply the theology of the historically particular Olympian-Parmenidean religion."[26] As may be expected here, Jenson is critical of the strong distinction between natural and special revelation, as if the former is a neutral ground of philosophical agreement between Christians and pagans.[27] Such a claim does not mean that theology should not engage in continual conversation with philosophy, as Jenson himself demonstrates familiarity with a variety of philosophical movements and arguments. What he does mean, however, is that one must approach something like Greek philosophy not as a distinctive enterprise from theology, but as a set of competing theological commitments.

As in the previous work, Jenson sets up this contrast between Hellenistic thought and divine revelation in his exposition of the essence and attributes of God. This is especially clear in his treatment of the concept of "being." The very notion of being, in Jenson's view, is not a necessary discussion in view of the gospel itself, but became a topic which the church had a need to address simply due to the ideology of the Greco-Roman world.[28] In keeping with his previous claims, Jenson is clear to assert that the concept of being itself is inherently theological, especially as the concept in its Greek formulation posited a timeless unchanging reality as the ground of all things.[29] This conception, for Jenson, ultimately had the goal of positing some sort of inner

---

[25] Jenson, *Systematic Theology*, 1:9.

[26] Ibid., 10.

[27] Ibid., 7.

[28] Ibid., 207.

[29] Ibid., 208–09.

ground of commonality between humanity and the gods, thus accounting for the possibility of communion between the two different sorts of entities.

For Jenson's proposal, it is important to understand what exactly being is in this Hellenistic context. He denotes three concepts which are definitional of the idea. First, being is "immunity to time," or permanence.[30] It is this idea which gets the most attention throughout Jenson's corpus, and it is addressed in a later chapter in the present work on divine atemporality. Second, being is without change, but is instead pure form. Jenson refers to this as "transcendence over time's surprises."[31] This gives assurance that despite the unknowability of the future, there is some unchanging and sure ground upon which we can rely. Finally, being is that which is understood through the mind's eye. When one views an object, its being (or form) can be grasped without reference to its past or future.[32] It is in response to this that Jenson contends for an approach to the triune God which denies that his eternality can be defined as "immunity to time," as is foundational for this Hellenistic conception of being.[33] What Jenson formulates as the Hebraic view of God is, for him, a "fundamental challenge to the Greeks' metaphysics."[34] In response, Jenson describes an alternative approach to that of the Greek philosophers.

Among the most important distinctions (or perhaps the *most* central) is that the Hellenists devised their idea of being in order to affirm commonality between humanity and the divine. Christianity, in contrast to this, firmly upholds a creature/Creator distinction which is never to be bridged.[35] Jenson is not entirely critical of the classical theistic tradition at this point, as he affirms that Aquinas's distinction between essence and existence is a radical departure from Aristotle. For Aristotle, created things are all

---

[30] Ibid., 209.

[31] Ibid.

[32] Ibid., 210.

[33] Ibid.

[34] Ibid.

[35] Ibid., 212.

form and matter composites, so that anything devoid of matter is divine. In contrast to this, Aquinas strongly rejects some sliding scale of divinity that includes spirits, and instead posits the reality that angelic beings are both without matter and fundamentally distinct from God. Aquinas then locates the fundamental differentiation between God and creation not in the possession of matter, but instead in his distinction between essence and existence. For Thomas, all created things can be described as having both a distinctive essence, and existence as an element which is added to that essence, thus resulting in an instantiation of that form. For God, however, his essence *is* his existence. This means that God's distinction from creatures consists in his identification as the only *necessary* being, in contrast to creaturely contingency. This Thomistic solution is called, by Jenson, "one of intellectual history's most powerful and tantalizing ideas."[36]

While Jenson recognizes the genius of Thomas's solution here, he contends that it nonetheless remains flawed. Jenson's primary critique of all Western treatments of God as developed within the Thomistic tradition is in its discussion of any divine essence as such. For Jenson, there is no divine essence to be exposited *behind* the Trinitarian persons; instead, God's essence *is* his triunity. Jenson draws heavily upon Gregory of Nyssa in this discussion (as he does throughout his corpus) in arguing that the divine being is the mutual act of Father, Son, and Spirit.[37] This act, for Jenson, is referred to as an "infinite" one, which is again a strong contrast to Hellenism. For both Plato and Aristotle, no object, whether God or anything else, could be described as infinite, as this would leave a thing without any boundaries to define it from other objects. Therefore, to be infinite would simply be to have no form at all. It is precisely this idea that Jenson is critical of, affirming that deity can be defined as "temporal infinity."[38] This temporal infinity is not God's existence apart from time, but instead defines him as existing without any personal limitation to himself. This infinity, and eternality,

---

[36] Ibid., 213.

[37] Ibid., 214–15.

[38] Ibid., 216.

is defined by God's faithfulness, being defined by his giving and receiving through anticipation of his own future in the Spirit.[39] Jenson summarizes his proposal thus: "The temporal infinity that opens before us and so embraces us as the triune God's eternity is the inexhaustibility of one event. That event is the appropriation of all other events by the love actual as Jesus of Nazareth."[40] This brings us to the last point discussed here in this work of Jenson's: God as event.

It is here in his summary of the distinction between his view and that of the Greeks that Jenson is most clear. In a rather startling statement, Jenson writes: "the one God is an event; history occurs not only in him but as his being."[41] Rather than God's being as distinct from history external to himself, such a history is, for Jenson, identical with the divine essence. One must then inquire as to exactly what Jenson means at this point. Is such a history to be identified with *ad intra* Trinitarian relations, or with the *ad extra* works with reference to creation? Jenson has a twofold answer here. First, the foundational event with which God is to be identified is "what happens between Jesus and his Father in their Spirit."[42] This may, at first glance, appear to be an affirmation of God's self-identity within the *ad intra* operations. Note, however, that Jenson references not the *Logos*, but the incarnate Son Jesus. As he clearly explains elsewhere, there is no *Logos asarkos* for Jenson.[43] The second element of the act which constitutes the divine being is that "God is what happens to Jesus and the world."[44] God's being is constituted by his acts within the world, thus denying any significant distinction between the *ad intra* and *ad extra* operations of the triune persons. There is much more to be said on this point, as this is revisited in later chapters.

---

[39] Ibid., 217.

[40] Ibid., 221.

[41] Ibid.

[42] Ibid.

[43] Jenson, "Logos Asarkos," in *Revisionary Metaphysics*, 119–23.

[44] Jenson, *Systematic Theology*, 1:221.

THE STATE OF THE CURRENT DISCUSSION

Robert Jenson: Concluding Summary

In each of these two works, along with his many essays and books, Jenson remains highly critical of the formation of classical theism. It is apparent throughout these works that Jenson is well acquainted with the writings of Thomas Aquinas and other scholastic sources, meaning that throughout he is careful to offer several clarifications to defend the Thomistic approach from accusations of being a complete collapse of Christian theology into Greek philosophy. Nonetheless, despite such qualifications, Jenson affirms the basic tenets of the Hellenization thesis. For Jenson, the Greek philosophical construct of divinity is contradictory to the biblical Hebraic view. These Greek ideas persisted from the patristic era throughout the Middle Ages—especially in the Western church. His contrast between these two schools of thought consists in a differing approach to the divine attributes, the relationship between God and the world, and the relationship between God's essence and the triune persons.

Perhaps the chief three concerns for Jenson's theology proper are these: his rejection of divine atemporality, his Trinitarian emphasis in which the Trinitarian persons are ontologically prior to the divine essence, and his narrative approach both to theology as a whole and to his construction of the doctrine of God. Though more extensive criticisms are given later in the present work, there are two primary problems with Jenson's view, which also remain among several other theistic mutualists. First, Jenson's approach to God's relationship with time necessarily results in time itself having ontological priority over God himself. If God is future to himself in his Spirit, regardless of language of God's not being limited by time, there remains a sense in which God's being coheres within a greater schema: that of past, present, and future. Second, In Jenson's approach, God is not self-sufficient, as his being consists—at least to some degree—in his external operations within creation. Thus, God needs something other than himself in order to be who he is. Though Jenson recognizes this criticism and offers some preliminary responses to it, his arguments remain inadequate. These ideas are explained in further chapters on each of the four primary affirmations of classical theism.

Carl Braaten

One would be remiss to speak of Robert Jenson without also mentioning his lifetime friend and co-laborer Carl E. Braaten. Like the former author, Braaten was devoted both to the Lutheran tradition and to the ecumenical movement of the latter half of the twentieth century. The two authors cooperated in the formation of the Center for Catholic and Evangelical Theology and of *Pro Ecclesia*. They also served as co-editors for the *Christian Dogmatics* volumes mentioned previously. Like Jenson, Braaten adopted certain elements of the theology of hope as it emerged from Jürgen Moltmann and Wolfhart Pannenberg, which impacts his approach to the doctrine of God. This is particularly clear in an early work of Braaten's titled *The Future of God: The Revolutionary Dynamics of Hope*, which is a kind of mini dogmatics text utilizing the eschatological-orientedness of Moltmann in a Lutheran doctrinal framework. Though an older work, the text remains in print, and several of Braaten's contentions continue in their impact upon modern Trinitarian thought.

This work was written in the late 1960s, in which theology was moving out of the so-called "death of God" phase into one which emphasized the need for eschatology, not merely as an afterthought or final subject of dogmatics, but as the beginning of all theological reflection. As Braaten summarizes this era, he states that "[t]he new place to start in theology is at the end—eschatology."[45] This shift was brought on three primary factors. First, Albert Schweizer's study of Jesus led to the conclusion that the Messiah viewed himself as an apocalyptic prophet, thus shifting scholarship surrounding the historical Jesus and his self-consciousness. Second, Pauline scholars (Ernst Kaseman being perhaps the most notable) began to recognize the distinctly eschatological nature of the apostle's thought. The eschaton was not to be

---

[45] Braaten, *Future of God*, 9.

seen as one theme among many, but as a core around which other ideas were built. Third, and finally, theologians in the era that followed Barth, Tillich, and Bultmann moved away from an existentially influenced view of the gospel as allowing for an open future, to one which viewed both God and human salvation through the lens of historical process. Like Jenson (whom Braaten mentions here),[46] Braaten belongs to this final group of thinkers, and in his system, he formulates a doctrine of a God who is similarly involved in historical process.

As the title suggests, Braaten repeatedly refers to Christian eschatology with the phrase "the future of God."[47] Such a statement does not merely denote that God has destined a future for his creation, but God is future to himself. Like Jenson, Braaten is critical of the classical conception of divine immutability as a holdover from ancient Greek thought. For Braaten, this problematic notion is exemplified in mysticism, which is an "unhistorical way of thinking."[48] For the mystic, reality is to be found not in the ordinary events of historical life, but in an unchanging ground of being which lies behind experience. In such a view, salvation is achieved not by entering into eschatological history, but by escaping history altogether. Braaten suggests that such a view has a strong presence within Christian history both through the Hellenization of Christian thought (Origen being the primary culprit),[49] and by a literalist interpretation of the early chapters in Genesis.

For Braaten, the biblical narrative of the fall is a mythological story, meant to convey the reality and universality of sin along with the consequences of such a violation. In his view, the patristic era faltered in interpreting the story of prelapsarian Adam through the lens of Platonic essences. For the Platonist, there is a static unchanging perfect reality (the forms) of which all earthly elements are a mere reflection as an imperfect copy. In Braaten's view, the church fathers viewed the pre-fall state in the same manner, as some kind

---

[46] Ibid., 13.

[47] Ibid., 25.

[48] Ibid., 43.

[49] Ibid., 44.

of perfect realm which humanity has fallen away from, and now must regain. The problem here is that the goal is not eschatology, but the restoration to a protological state. The future-oriented theology of hope cannot coexist with a notion that humanity's final goal is to revert to something which is past.

Here is where the key to Braaten's proposal is clearly articulated. He rejects essentialism as a hindrance to the biblical understanding of both God and man. In this schema (one which the present project is written to defend), a thing is defined by something that it is in the present tense. These notions of Platonic essences or of salvation as an act of restoration to a primeval reality are rejected as Greek impositions. Unlike Bultmann, however, Braaten is not willing to affirm the existentialist dogma that "existence precedes essence," as such assumes that one's being is created by self-determination apart from any transcendental identification whatsoever. Both existentialism and essentialism commit the same basic error in Braaten's view; they are "antihistorical thinking."[50] Hope offers a way forward, beyond these errors, in a historically informed manner. In Braaten's approach, hope is more than a theological axiom or one among other virtues, but it is ontologically determinative. The essence of something "is neither in its past nor in its present but in its future."[51] This future-determined metaphysic is the necessary starting point for Braaten's view of the divine nature.

The first place in which Braaten's futurism has a clear impact upon his theology proper is in his rejection of classical natural theology. While patristic, medieval, and Reformation thinkers all argued that natural reason was capable of determining the existence and (some) attributes of God through the contemplation of creation, such a view is dependent upon an unchanging God with eternal attributes that can be rationally deduced. Such an exercise, for Braaten, is due to the syncretistic collapsing of Jesus, the divine Word, into the Platonic Logos. This Logos, or divine reason, forms a universal basis for a rational comprehension of God which exists

---

[50] Ibid., 46.

[51] Ibid., 46.

apart from God's historical revelation in Christ, or in the history of the people of Israel.[52] Braaten thus rejects what has been historically understood as natural revelation. He is not, however, willing to simply echo Barth's "nein!"[53] but instead proposes a modified natural theology. There is, in Braaten's view, an acute awareness within the human person of both a lack of unity in the cosmos as well as an internal awareness that such a unification of all things is somehow longed for—something like Calvin's *sensus divinitatis* eschatologized. In other words, even apart from knowledge of the historical revelation of God in the risen Christ, one cannot escape the question of God.[54] This internal knowledge does not, however, constitute proof of God which can only be demonstrated from God's "self-revelation in Jesus of Nazareth."[55] The reason why such a move is made is that Braaten identifies God with the Christ-act. Thus, apart from that, he cannot be known.

As he has argued for the ontological primacy of the future, Braaten explains that God's being is to be identified with his "eschatological power."[56] God's essence is found in his own future, which is explained as the kingdom of God. God is both identical with his kingdom (along with the judgment and salvation it brings) and with his promises. God, as one who both gives promises and is identified with those promises, is defined by his own future fulfillment of his word. This word, for Braaten, is the Logos himself, not as an eternal manifestation of "a stationary God," but as both these promises and their fulfillment.[57] The necessary question is raised at this point by the reader as to exactly what specific promises Braaten has in mind. Here, like Jenson, Braaten centers his argument on the resurrection. He identifies Christ's resurrection as God's own self-definitional moment. In the resurrection, God identified himself with the person of Jesus, and such a definition was

---

[52] Ibid., 61.

[53] Barth, *Natural Theology*, 67.

[54] Braaten, *Future of God*, 63.

[55] Ibid., 64.

[56] Ibid., 69.

[57] Ibid., 70.

retroactive in determining the divine identity.[58] The orthodox notion of the preexistence of Christ (the *Logos Asarkos*) is a "later symbol" identifying the reality of God's retroactive self-identification with the resurrected Jesus.[59] Any denial of Christ's preexistence would be problematic in view of an essentialist metaphysic. However, if the essence of a thing is identified with its future, and if God's future is identified with the resurrected Christ, then Christ can still, for Braaten, be explained as being of "one substance" with the Father. Braaten also acknowledges that he borrows some from adoptionism at this point, but contends that he is consistent with the New Testament witness in doing so.[60] Though some of the phraseology differs, there is fundamental agreement between Jenson and Braaten here. For both, God's essence is not to be found apart from creation, but in and through his historical acts, especially in the definitive act of the resurrection.

What Braaten does here is collapse the ontological Trinity into the economic Trinity,[61] so that the divine economy determines God's own being. If God were immutable, in Braaten's view, this would make the realm of history merely a place of revelation of eternal static truths or divine decrees. In contrast to this, history "is the means by which God reaches new decisions, makes up his mind, and alters the trend of things."[62] The relationship between God and his creatures is one of mutuality, wherein God both alters the world and is himself internally affected. This impact upon God of the world's happenings consists not only in changes to the divine mind, but also in the suffering of God. As may be expected, Braaten rejects divine impassibility, defining a God with such an attribute as "stone cold in his heart of hearts toward the suffering of his creatures."[63] In contrast

---

[58] Ibid., 73.

[59] Ibid., 74.

[60] Ibid., 90.

[61] This has been the case in much twentieth-century theology following Karl Rahner's claim that the economic Trinity is the ontological Trinity.

[62] Braaten, *Future of God*, 93.

[63] Ibid., 90.

to this, God suffers alongside his creatures.

Throughout this work, Braaten conceives of the divine nature as defined not by an unchangeable divine essence which is shared amongst three eternal persons, but as God's triune acts within history. Whether any kind of ontological Trinity exists behind such acts is, for Braaten, simply not the concern of the theologian. Braaten defines the Trinity instead as "the identity of God's future under the different modes of his appearance to the world."[64] God the Father manifests himself through the resurrection of the Son and in the sending of the Spirit at Pentecost. These different manifestations of God's triune persons are not reflections of an eternal reality outside of such a history with the world. It appears here that God creates his own triune being through his decisions in his historical acts *ad extra*, referring God's triunity, for example, to an act of "self-determination," in its revelation in the Christ event.[65] Nearly everything in this treatment is also mentioned in Jenson's work, though he has developed such an ideology further than Braaten had at this point. In particular, while Braaten does include the Spirit in his treatment, Jenson is far more clear in his explanation of the Spirit's role as the future of God in defining the divine nature. The third figure here, Wolfhart Pannenberg, repeats many of these same ideas.

Wolfhart Pannenberg

Committed both to the Lutheran tradition and to the historical-critical method, Wolfhart Pannenberg was among the most important academic theologians in the latter half of the twentieth century. Pannenberg studied under Barth, and while adopting a largely Barthian approach to revelation, he rejected the absolute negation of nature as a valid realm of divine revelation. Throughout his writing, Pannenberg emphasized the importance of history for theology—especially the event of the resurrection of Christ—

---

[64] Ibid., 108.

[65] Ibid., 108.

and exposited his doctrine of God in light of this. Pannenberg's Trinitarian thought is most clearly expressed in his magnum opus: his three-volume *Systematic Theology*. It is this explanation of the doctrine of God which is explored here.

In many ways, Pannenberg appears as a middle ground in discussions related to philosophy and theology. Though initially a Barthian by conviction, Pannenberg slowly began to recognize the lack of philosophical rigor in Barth's system, and began—like some of the older dogmaticians—to incorporate metaphysics into theology once again. Similarly, Pannenberg contended for extensive interaction between the disciplines of science and history with that of theology. Well acquainted with the history of both theology and philosophy, Pannenberg presents a doctrine of God which distinguishes itself from classical theism, while retaining elements of the theology of the patristic and Protestant scholastic eras. There are extensive references throughout Pannenberg's corpus to Quenstedt, Hollaz, and Gerhard, whom he generally represents accurately and sometimes sympathetically. It is for this reason that any interaction between the classical approach to God (especially in the scholastic tradition) and modern views must take Pannenberg's critiques into account.

Like Braaten, Pannenberg is both critical of the older arguments for God's existence derived from natural theology, and yet desires to retain a significant element of the natural theology tradition. For Pannenberg, the arguments which underlie Aquinas's (and others') proofs are not convincing to the modern mind, as significant doubts have been raised as to their validity since the time of the Enlightenment. However, Pannenberg is not willing to say that there is *no* knowledge of God apart from the direct revelation found in Sacred Writ. He affirms the innate knowledge of God as taught by the scholastics (though with some qualifications), while rejecting the concept of the acquired knowledge through philosophical proofs.[66] What the arguments on divine existence do demonstrate, for Pannenberg, is the enduring and inescapable reality of the question of God throughout human

---

[66] Pannenberg, *Systematic Theology*, 1:107.

experience. Pannenberg summarizes his view thus:

> But in this process of experience, and the awareness of God that it brings, we do not have primarily the natural theology of the philosophers. What we have is the religious experience of God by means of a sense of working and being of God in creation. There has not been a philosophical natural theology from the beginning of creation. But in the history of humanity there has always been in some form an explicit awareness of God which is linked to experience of the works of creation.[67]

With this in mind, Pannenberg does, however, make (rather compelling) philosophical arguments for the existence of the infinite in his book *Metaphysics and the Idea of God*. Though this concept does not offer proof of a personal God, it does demonstrate that belief in God is not irrational, as it aligns with both human experience and aspects of reality which are philosophically demonstrable.

It is this concept of the infinite, as argued for in the book previously mentioned, which is at the core of Pannenberg's conception of God as it arises throughout his *Systematic Theology*. Definitionally, God's infinity is his distinction from all finitude and that which is "limited and transitory."[68] This distinction between God and creation is not to be read, however, as an argument that God is defined purely by opposition to the finite. Instead, infinity is truly expressed not merely in opposition to the finite, but in his transcending his own "antithesis to the finite."[69] In other words, God's infinity involves his interaction intimately within that which is other than himself. In this way, Pannenberg is able to reconcile the often asked

---

[67] Ibid., 117.

[68] Ibid., 397.

[69] Ibid., 400.

question as to how God is simultaneously immanent and transcendent. Divine transcendence (as infinity) is found precisely in God's immanence. His infinity overcomes the division between the finite and the non-finite. Pannenberg recognizes the logical difficulty posed by such a contention, but contends that this contains a "paradox" which is unresolved.[70] This view of the infinite ties Pannenberg to Jenson who, similarly, argues for the primacy of this conception in opposition to Greek thought, which does not identify God himself as infinite. Pannenberg's view is a bit more explicitly Hegelian than is Jenson's, whereas Jenson is more strictly biblical and patristic in his language.[71]

As Pannenberg explains further his view of the essence of God, he (like Jenson and Braaten) argues for the ontological priority of the divine persons over a unified divine essence. In his exposition of the unity of the divine essence, Pannenberg rejects the Eastern approach regarding the Father as the fount of divinity, as well as the Augustinian perspective which identifies the Spirit with the mutual love of the Father and Son, as inadequate proposals.[72] In particular, Pannenberg is critical of the idea that the Father himself is the source of the divine essence for the other two persons, as this—in his view—necessitates a kind of subordinationism. Instead, the divine essence must not be founded upon the unilateral action of one divine person, but of the mutuality of perichoretic relations.[73] There is a reciprocity of divine identification, wherein the Father does not merely define the identity of the other two persons, but is also himself defined by them. The Father begets the Son, and in turn, the Son grants his kingdom to the Father, and in doing so, they are distinguished from one another, and mutually receive divine

---

[70] Ibid.

[71] Pannenberg makes this connection between his approach to infinity and the Hegelian schema of thesis (finitude), antithesis (infinity), and synthesis (a transcendence over antithesis to the finite). Ibid.

[72] Ibid., 342.

[73] Ibid., 385.

life and authority.⁷⁴ In short, God's triunity does not flow forth from a derivation of essence or personhood from the Father to the Son and the Spirit; rather, God's essence *is* his triunity, and this triunity is defined by mutual reciprocity among the divine persons.

Like the other two authors mentioned above, Pannenberg adheres to "Rahner's rule," in identifying the economic and immanent Trinities with one another. What this appears to do, in his formulation, is make God's own essence in some way dependent upon something external to himself. If God is defined primarily by his infinity, and this infinity necessitates an overcoming of the antithesis between infinite and finite, then an external finite creation is necessary for God to be who he is. This is further evidenced in his conception of divine reciprocity, which is constituted not by eternal relations apart from the *ad extra* work of creation, but in the redemptive-historical reality of the Son's giving the kingdom to the Father. Pannenberg says, for example, that the "rule or kingdom of the Father is not so external to his deity that he might be God without his kingdom."⁷⁵ Pannenberg attempts to clarify this further by acknowledging that creation is an act of divine freedom rather than necessity. However, he is still left in the same conundrum as Robert Jenson. Both figures identify God's own essence with—in some sense—the divine economy, but simultaneously back away from the seemingly logically necessary corollary to this that creation is necessary to God, thus denying divine aseity. This is a problem which is yet to be resolved in these systems.

There is much more to be said regarding Pannenberg's system, especially with reference to the particular divine attributes. That, however, will remain the task of further chapters as the specific claims of classical theism are evaluated in light of modern criticisms. In this brief overview here, there are four primary points to be noted in Pannenberg's thought. First, Pannenberg rejects the traditional arguments for God's existence, but retains the Protestant concept of internal knowledge of God or a *sensus divinitatis*.

---

⁷⁴ Ibid., 312.

⁷⁵ Ibid., 313.

Second, divine infinity is an overarching theme for one's understanding of God. Third, Pannenberg prioritizes the divine persons over the unity of essence. Finally, Pannenberg argues for God's mutability in his conflation of the economic and immanent Trinities, thus making the divine economy part of God's own essence.

Post-Barthians: Conclusion

The three figures above are among the most significant Christian thinkers within the latter half of the twentieth century, and their unique formulations of the divine essence and attributes continue to impact theologians today. Though each comes from a slightly different perspective, there are several areas of agreement among these dogmaticians. First, all three argue against classical theism as developed in Thomas Aquinas and the scholastic tradition as an imposition of Greek conceptions on the biblical witness. Second, all three thinkers give ontological priority to the distinction of persons over the unity of the divine essence. Third, all reference the idea of infinity as a core tenet of their theology proper. Fourth, they all have an eschatological emphasis, not simply with regard to human redemption, but in reference to God's own being. Finally, consistent with this last point, they argue that the redemptive economy informs God's identity and essence. Some of these points have been echoed by Christians of other traditions, including some popular Evangelical authors.

Evangelical Theologians

The second category of works and authors are those who write within the Evangelical tradition who seek both to retain elements of the classical theistic approach while also arguing for incompatibility between certain tenets of philosophical theism and the scriptural witness. Several figures could be mentioned here, such as Bruce Ware, Scott Oliphint, William Lane Craig, and J. P. Moreland (along with many others). Here, two of many examples of theologians in this stream are discussed. First is John Frame, and second is Jay Wesley Richards. The reason for the first inclusion is not due to any particularly insightful commentary or originality in argumentation from John Frame, but in the fact that he has a significant influence upon the Reformed tradition, along with Evangelicalism as a whole. Also, Frame has specifically responded to the rise of classical theism within the Reformed tradition, and has done so with suspicion. His responses to James Dolezal's recent work on the subject help to demonstrate what Evangelical theistic mutualists view as the primary divide between their approach and that of more classically minded thinkers. Richards's work is included here due to its extensive presentation and nuanced disagreements with the scholastic perspective. Richards approaches the subject from a philosophical perspective, analyzing God's essence and attributes with the aid of modal logic and contemporary essentialist thought.

John Frame

John Frame is one of the most influential authors in the contemporary Evangelical Reformed community, having published a comprehensive *Systematic Theology*, along with dozens of articles and other books. Frame arises from the neo-Calvinist tradition, being particularly influenced by Abraham Kuyper and Cornelius Van Til. Often interacting with philosophy, Frame is generally critical of classical Greek thinkers, and in particular their influence on the development of medieval thought.[76] Though these themes are apparent throughout his writing, Frame's rejection of classical thought has become especially clear since James Dolezal has named Frame as a significant proponent of theistic mutualism. Frame has responded to these criticisms in an essay published on his website titled, "Two Models

---

[76] See Frame, *Doctrine of God*.

of Divine Transcendence: Pure Being vs. Divine Lordship."[77] This article helpfully outlines the difference between Frame's view and that of classical theistic approaches.

Frame defines this difference as two divergent understandings of divine transcendence. The first is the philosophical concept in which God is defined as "pure being," and the second is the Christian theological claim of God as Lord over creation. These are not, for Frame, two aspects of the single transcendent God, but diametrically opposed views on the divine nature. Frame echoes the basic sentiments of the Hellenization thesis.

The overview of Greek thought that Frame offers begins with Plato's understanding of being. For Plato, there is a chain of being, wherein some things are more or less real than others. Frame writes that Plato views all being, other than God, as "metaphysically defective," having less being than their source. It is this question of both being and non-being which undergirds the thought of the Greeks, from the pre-Socratics like Parmenides and Heraclitus. For Parmenides, all is pure undifferentiated being; change is an illusion and an impossibility as it, in his view, would contend that non-being could become being. For Heraclitus, being is to be found in becoming, as a process of continual change rather than the kind of static permanence as taught by Parmenides. Plato's view then stands, for Frame, in the middle of these thinkers, as he differentiates between degrees of being, thus allowing for both change and permanence. This Platonic perspective, in Frame's view, is not connected in any significant way to the beliefs of Christianity. Such metaphysical questions of being and non-being are simply not those of the theologian.

Here is where Frame argues, as may be expected, for the Hellenization thesis. He acknowledges that the early Christian apologists, such as Justin Martyr and Athenagoras, cite Plato and connect Yahweh to the deity identified with pure being in the philosophers. He then cites Plotinus's impact on Christian theologians alongside of this as another example of an unfortunate Greek-Hebraic synthesis. Frame cites the common connection

---

[77] There are no page numbers in this essay, hence the lack of references in this section.

between the Greek view of God and God's covenantal identification as "I AM," as found in most (all?) early and medieval Christian thinkers, and denies such metaphysical connections. Like many other thinkers who adopt the Hellenizing thesis, Frame argues that God's name identifies his relationship to the people of Israel only, and has no metaphysical implications.

Frame defines the distinction between Plato and the Christian view of God in three points. First, Plato's construction of the forms is impersonal, in opposition to the relational God of Scripture. Second, for Plato, there is a great chain of being in which God is at the top. In Frame's reading of Plato, this denies the Creator/creature distinction, which is a key theme of Christian theology, and especially of the Reformed tradition. For Plato, both God and man are, in some way, of the same kind. Third, Frame contends for the incoherence (though more through mere assertion than actual argumentation) of the relationship between being and non-being in Greek thought in general. The concept of Platonic being, therefore, makes God unintelligible.

These criticisms, for Frame, remain with Plato's student Aristotle. Frame argues that the same dilemma of being and non-being was a core element of the construction of Aristotle's system, leading him to a conception of God as the source of being and motion. He is both pure being and the unmoved mover. It is because of the influence of Aristotle on Thomas Aquinas that divine simplicity became such an important element of Christian theism. God, as understood by Aquinas, is pure actuality. Frame argues that this creates a tension in Aquinas between absolute divine simplicity as confessed by Aristotle, and the fact that God interacts relationally with the world external to himself. In Frame's view, Aquinas attempts to marry together two divergent understandings of God which cannot be reconciled. Further, Frame argues that Aristotle and Aquinas both conflate the creature and Creator by arguing that they are to be distinguished by degrees of being, again contending that for Aristotle, created things are metaphysically defective.

It is in contrast to this Greek-Christian synthesis (which defines almost the entirety of the Christian tradition) that Frame argues for a personalist approach to God rather than a metaphysical one. He purports that Scripture hardly speaks in such metaphysical categories, instead explaining God as covenantal Lord. This priority of relational categories then results in a redefining of the classical attributes of God. Divine simplicity is defined as the fact that God "thinks and acts as a whole, not as a combination of potentially conflicting thoughts, impulses, and qualities." In other words, God's simplicity means that he does not contradict himself. Such is simply not divine simplicity in the classical sense. He offers similar revisions of the attributes of impassibility, immutability, omnipresence, and immensity. Frame's proposal is not one of both continuity and discontinuity between the Greek and Christian traditions, but of absolute distinction. He confesses simply that "The Prime Mover of Aristotle is not the God of the Bible."

What one finds in Frame is a simplification of the same claims of absolute discontinuity between the Hellenic understanding of God with regard to the questions of being, change and permanence, and unity and multiplicity, and the covenantal Redeemer as taught in the Old and New Testaments. The arguments themselves are, frankly, extremely weak and hardly worth a response. However, it is mentioned here because of Frame's broader influence within the Reformed and Evangelical worlds. Though without the academic rigor or complexity of thought as the post-Barthian authors cited above, Frame's essay demonstrates that several of the same claims are echoed within various Christian communities, from theologians who otherwise are in almost complete disagreement. These critiques of classical theism, however, have also been made apparent in other academic Evangelical theologians who offer a more substantive proposal. Among those is Jay Wesley Richards.

Jay Wesley Richards

In his book *The Untamed God*, Jay Wesley Richards explores the primary themes of classical theism and attempts to provide a view of God's essence and attributes that retains some of those themes, while also offering critiques of Aquinas's formulations. Richards is well versed in both theology and the philosophy of religion, and this volume is an attempt to bridge the discussions within the two related disciplines. In doing so, Richards uses the mechanism of modal logic as developed in contemporary analytic philosophy throughout the work, and uses that to express a modified version of divine immutability, simplicity, and perfection. Richards's view, though an attempt at preserving elements of classical theism, ultimately diverges from the four tenets of classical theism as described in the present work.

Richards defines what he views as the central commitments of a classical Christian view of God as threefold. First is the principle of biblical normativity, by which it is acknowledged that what is revealed about God's essence and attributes in Scripture is primary.[78] Second is what Richards refers to as the principle of perfection, or the conviction that God is "maximally great."[79] This idea has its foundation in Anselm's ontological argument, but it has been emphasized far more extensively by contemporary analytic philosophers, especially as they have redefined the ontological argument in modal language. The third principle, for Richards, is the sovereignty-aseity conviction.[80] This idea is the conviction that God is not dependent upon anything outside of himself for either his essence or existence. To be clear, Richards does not follow this principle in an absolute sense in that no properties of God (which he believes exist separately from the divine essence itself) can be changed by anything external to the divine nature. For Richards, real mutuality in relation to creation means that God's accidental properties do change in response to objects outside of himself. In the manner in which Richards has redefined the themes of classical theism, every author mentioned in this chapter would then be categorized as an adherent to classical theism in some sense.

The continued exposition of his proposal is dependent upon Richards's adoption of essentialism. What this term means in this context is not what I

---

[78] Richards, *Untamed God*, 31.

[79] Ibid., 33.

[80] Ibid., 33–34.

refer to throughout this series as *real essentialism*. Instead, Richards contends for a newer form of essentialism which is not dependent upon the categories of either Plato or Aristotle, but of modal logic. In this new essentialism, all things are composed of properties. These properties are divided into two categories: those which are essential to something, and those which are accidental. This is defined within the context of possible-world semantics. If something necessarily has some specific properties in all possible worlds, then those properties are essential. If there is a possible world in which these properties differ while the subject remains the same, those are its accidental properties.

In this way of formulating metaphysics, essences are bundles of properties, whereas in classical essentialism, properties flow out of an essence (which is ontologically primary). It is also worth noting that the term "property" is extensive in its meaning in analytic philosophy, such that nearly everything is categorized as a property. Such categories have profound implications for how one speaks of the classical divine attributes. For Richards, God's creation of the world, for example, is a property. He has the property of being Creator, which he did not have before.[81] In the incarnation, God the Son now has the property of having a human nature, which was not true of him prior. Every interaction that God has with his creation therefore adds some kind of property to God which he did not contain previously. The implications of this, then, are that God cannot be simple in any absolute sense, as he has a number of additional properties, just as he has actions. Immutability also cannot be upheld in an ontological sense, as God is constantly in a process of gaining new properties or losing properties (when a relation changes). Within this conceptual schema, therefore, either God remains static and unengaged with creation, or he has changing properties. Richards opts for the latter.

Richard's view demonstrates the fundamental weaknesses for analytic philosophy in its use for the exposition of theology proper. The particularities of categories in Thomistic thought, especially with regard to the distinction

---

[81] Ibid., 200.

between act and potency, are not present here, and thus one is left with either an impersonal God, or a composite and changing one with various sets of properties. The dilemma is solved within Aristotelian categories with a distinction between active and passive potency.[82] Passive potency is the potentiality that exists in an object, which can be actualized by objects external to it. Active potency is the potential of an object to actualize the potentiality of external objects. In classical theism, God has the latter but not the former. This then retains the truths of both 1) God's own unchangeable nature, as one who is ontologically self-sufficient, and 2) a real and active interaction between the triune God and his creation. If God's interaction with creation, whether it involves a change to him or to created objects, is all lumped together in the broad category of "properties" (as is the case in analytic philosophy), then God must, in some sense, be composite.

In view of his rejection of these classical distinctions, then, Richards redefines simplicity, immutability, and atemporality. In his explanation of divine simplicity, he confesses the truth inherent in the topic that God is not composed of elements more fundamental than himself (though, as will be argued in the next chapter, that much seems difficult for Richards to affirm with his actualist commitments).[83] He rejects, however, the idea that God's properties are identical with his essence, and that God's properties are coextensive. This, again, is necessitated by the broad use of the concept of property. Within his categories, to confess otherwise would mean that God's creation or the incarnation is identical with God's essence, which idea Richards rightly rejects. With regard to immutability, Richards similarly diverges from the classical understanding. He contends that God has essential properties which are unchangeable. These are identified as God's perfections: omnipotence, eternity, freedom, faithfulness, and the like.[84] However, God has accidental properties, including his free relation

---

[82] Feser, *Scholastic Metaphysics*, 39.

[83] Richards, *Untamed God*, 217.

[84] Ibid., 199.

to the world, which are subject to change.[85] Thus, in some sense God is immutable, but in another, he is mutable. This confession of mutability also leads to a reformulation of the relationship between God and time. Richards refers to those who hold to a lack of succession in God as "eternalists."[86] This perspective, in Richards's view, leads to a static approach to God as one who cannot truly relate to the time-bound events of creation. Instead, God must have knowledge that is subject to change through the successive actions of creatures, thus negating God's atemporality in the strict sense.

Richards's work offers a philosophically informed critique of classical theism, while he himself attempts to retain what he views as the positives of the classical tradition. There is no question as to Richards's mastery of analytic philosophy, and his modal logic is robust. However, what the book ultimately demonstrates is the inherent lack of precision in categories within analytic philosophy itself. His new essentialist convictions lead Richards to modify every classical incommunicable attribute of God in one way or another, and it is the contention of this book that such modifications are unwarranted and without theological or philosophical benefit over against the classical tradition. It is these modifications which James Dolezal and Steven Duby are critical of in their work.

Modern Defenders of the Classical View

The contemporary theological landscape has seen an explosion of publications in defense of classical theism. With the renewed interest in Protestant scholastic thought, translations of previously unavailable works, and the popularization of Aquinas through Edward Feser (among others), the church is in a renaissance of classically informed theology proper. As just one example of this (and there are many), in 2021, *Christianity Today* named Baptist theologian Matthew Barrett's defense of classical Trinitarianism

---

[85] Ibid., 201.

[86] Ibid., 203.

Simply Trinity as its "Theology and Ethics Book of the Year."[87] Seminaries from Baptist, Presbyterian, Anglican, and Lutheran traditions are beginning to incorporate medieval and post-Reformation scholastic treatments of God's nature into their curricula.[88]

With all of these publications, it is a bit difficult to narrow down the available texts for a literature review like this. Though there are several texts could have been discussed, I have chosen only two. The first is James Dolezal's *All That Is in God*. Though not a dense academic work, this book has exposed many to the problems with modern currents in Evangelical theology, which has become disconnected from the historic affirmations regarding simplicity and immutability associated with classical Christian theism. Due to its popularity and influence, Dolezal's book is a helpful starting point for anyone looking into the current debates. The second text is Steven J. Duby's *God in Himself,* which presents an exposition and defense of divine aseity from Scripture, history, and philosophy.

James Dolezal

Dolezal's book presents a challenge to many of the most well-known Evangelical treatments of the doctrine of God in recent years. This alone has made Dolezal's book rather controversial, as he does not hesitate to criticize figures who are among the most influential in Evangelicalism. Some have accused Dolezal of hubris for daring to offer correctives to such respected Evangelical authors.[89] I contend that the real hubris belongs not to Dolezal, but to twentieth-century Evangelicals who depart from nearly two thousand years of consistent writing on the doctrine of God. This depends, of course, on the accuracy of the thesis of this text, which is that many current Evangelicals do indeed depart from a historic doctrine of God.

---

[87] Reynolds, "2022 Book Awards."

[88] For an example of this, the *Journal of Classical Theology* has an editorial team with representatives from Lutheran, Anglican, Baptist, and Presbyterian seminaries alike.

[89] Frame, "Scholasticism for Evangelicals."

It is in this text that Dolezal uses the "theistic mutualism" label to identify an approach to theism that differs from the classical one. He defines this mutualism as "a symbiotic relationship in which both parties derive something from each other."[90] Dolezal is clear that he does not simply mean some kind of relationship where there is a synergistic dependence such that the two parties are equal powers that mutually constitute one another. He speaks instead of a relationship in which God derives *anything* from the creature. In Thomas's language, a mutualist view contends that there is some potentiality in God which is actualized by the creature in relation with him. For Dolezal, this is a challenge to God's aseity, and it is only the classical view that preserves complete divine independence.

In the text, Dolezal explains mutualism largely through the loss of two primary classical doctrines: simplicity and immutability. Along with these two ideas, he also engages social trinitarianism, modified conceptions of eternity, and other related errors regarding the doctrine of God. In each of these areas, Dolezal points to the importance of preserving God's aseity, which these modern approaches do not do. For Dolezal, aseity comes to the forefront as the central issue that is challenged by modern approaches. For example, Dolezal argues the following regarding immutability: "If there is nothing in God's existence or life that is given to Him by the creature, and if He is not the cause of Himself because He is pure being, then it follows that He cannot undergo change."[91] As he grounds immutability in God's aseity, so does he also connect a denial of simplicity with a denial of God's absolute independence.[92] As the biblical text continually points to a God who is in no way dependent upon his creatures, any proposal that negates aseity must be rejected.

One of the most helpful aspects of this text is that Dolezal provides some historical reasoning for the loss of classical theism within Evangelical theology. Classical theology depended upon realist metaphysical categories

---

[90] Dolezal, *All That Is in God*, 1.

[91] Dolezal, *All That Is in God*, 17.

[92] Ibid., 75.

in order to define these doctrines. With the Enlightenment, and the rise of modern philosophy more generally, these classical categories were rejected or misunderstood, as their ontological foundations were no longer taken for granted. So, for example, while classical simplicity denies any distinction between essence and accidental qualities in God, nineteenth-century theologians began to interpret divine simplicity instead as the idea that "God lacks material parts."[93] With such an interpretation, simplicity is no longer a clear statement regarding how one speaks about God in general, but instead is simply an affirmation of God's immateriality. Similarly, theologians begin to speak of God's immutability not as an absolute ontological statement, but one about divine self-consistency. God always remains God, yet he is in some sense relationally mutable. These misreadings of classical sources have permeated Evangelical theology for the last hundred years, so that theologians have failed to grasp what is really at stake in these discussions.

Dolezal's formulation of theism is largely derived from Thomas Aquinas. He speaks consistently of God as pure act.[94] Further, along with Aquinas, Dolezal argues for an identification between God's essence and his existence. This is commensurate with Dolezal's earlier work *God without Parts*, which treats simplicity from a Thomistic approach. What Dolezal demonstrates here is that these Thomistic commitments are no anomaly in Protestant thought, but that they have consistently been used by Reformed thinkers. These basic commitments of classical theism are affirmed in the Westminster Confession of Faith along with the London Baptist Confession of 1689. More detailed explanations appear in the writings of Stephen Charnock, Herman Bavinck, and many others. While thinkers like John Frame are heavily critical of the Thomistic elements that appear in classical theistic writings, Dolezal demonstrates that there is perfect consistency between Aquinas and the Reformed scholastics on the divine attributes.

Lest one assume that Dolezal's writing is solely dependent upon medieval

---

[93] Ibid., 64.

[94] Ibid., 11.

philosophy, he consistently cites Scripture throughout this work. As a Protestant adherent to *sola Scriptura*, Dolezal affirms that doctrine should be drawn from Holy Scripture rather than natural reason alone. While recognizing that terms like actuality, potency, ontological immutability, and aseity are not explicitly biblical, Dolezal shows that the content implied by the use of these terms is. If Scripture truly teaches that God is *a se* (which Dolezal demonstrates to be the case), then this necessitates that God is also simple and immutable.

Dolezal's book is a wake-up call to Evangelicals. The manner in which God was explained with regard to his existence and attributes within twentieth-century Evangelicalism is not consistent with the early church, the medieval church, or the heirs of the Protestant Reformation. These discrepancies have gone unnoticed for too long, and Dolezal forces his readers to think seriously about these issues. It is not only the Protestant liberals in the line of Schleiermacher who have been formed by post-Enlightenment rationalism; this philosophy has impacted the Evangelical church in some essential ways. Here, Dolezal reveals some serious problems with Evangelicalism in its totality. While these problems can be traced at least as far back as the Second Great Awakening, the Evangelical Christianity which prevailed in the Western world in the twentieth century was divorced from history, without strong theological or practical ties to the ancient church. Along with recovering a better doctrine of God, Dolezal also calls the church to recapture its own historical roots.

Steven J. Duby

Steven Duby currently serves as an Associate Professor of Theology at Grand Canyon University. He has now published numerous books related to these debates on classical theism, touching on topics such as divine simplicity, Christ's relationship to the Father, and God's aseity. The work under discussion here is *God in Himself: Scripture, Metaphysics, and the Task of Christian Theology*. This work is an exploration of natural revelation, theological language, and the nature of God. He provides an account which is consistent with the Protestant scholastics, in opposition to many contemporary theologies.

One of the primary topics of Duby's book is the recapturing of natural theology within a Protestant context. In his analysis, Duby contends for a significant amount of overlap between the medieval and later Protestant traditions regarding natural knowledge of God. For Thomas, natural knowledge of God is that which is derived from rational causal analysis. As the intellect perceives the created world, it is driven by logic to search for a cause of the various effects one experiences. This leads to the conclusion of an unmoved mover as first cause.[95] Duby affirms Thomas's argument here, but is careful to say that the knowledge gained by reason is an indirect one. It does not, in the fullest sense, show what is "proper to God."[96] Some of the attributes of God associated with classical theism are rationally deduced, but one cannot claim the same regarding the divine economy or God's triune self-revelation. It is here that the Reformed orthodox (and Lutherans, I may add)[97] speak not only of this derivative knowledge of deity, but of an internal implanted knowledge of God that is *a priori*. Both aspects of natural theology are revealed by God as means by which humans are to recognize their need for divine mercy.[98]

This affirmation of natural theology in Duby's work is a strong contrast with Karl Barth and those following his lead in rejecting natural theology altogether. As Duby rightly sees, the rejection of natural theology is nearly always tied to a dismissal of a classical understanding of God for a perspective in which God is defined in some manner by his redemptive acts. This begins with Barth's conflation of the electing God with Jesus Christ.[99] For Barth (according to some readings), God determines his own being through his

---

[95] Duby, *God in Himself*, 76–77.

[96] Ibid., 94.

[97] Weidner, *System of Dogmatics*, 1:216–18.

[98] Duby, *God in Himself*, 129.

[99] Ibid., 47.

act of election in which he chooses what God he will be.[100] Duby cites Robert Jenson and Bruce McCormack as two theologians who continue in this same trajectory. Jenson conflates God with his historical acts, and McCormack argues that there is no God *in se* apart from his decision to become incarnate *pro nobis*. While Duby acknowledges that in a classical approach to simplicity there is no difference between God's essence and acts, he contends that any approach which makes God's nature contingent upon creaturely interactions is a denial of aseity.

While Dolezal's book diagnoses the problem with regard to specific claims about God's nature (i.e., simplicity and immutability), Duby spends a significant portion of his work on the topic of the incarnation.[101] The reason for this is that the theologians mentioned above in this present work reformulate God on the basis of the incarnation. While Dolezal counters Evangelical theistic mutualists, Duby is more focused on the Barthian arguments against classical theism. In opposition to Jenson, Duby contends that the economy is the means by which the Christian encounters God, but that the economy does not thereby constitute the divine being.[102] As Duby contends, this does not depend merely upon philosophical reasoning, but is apparent throughout the New Testament text.

There are five points Duby makes here that I want to highlight which demonstrate the biblical foundations for a classical approach to God's aseity. First, texts like John 1 and John 5:19–30 speak explicitly about an internal triune relationship between Father and Son which is not dependent

---

[100] This is a notoriously difficult issue, as interpreters arise at vastly different conclusions regarding Barth's thought here. Well-known Barth scholars George Hunsinger and Bruce McCormack, for example, disagree on this question. Duby summarizes the difficulty, writing, "It seems to me that one can find in Barth some statements that tend toward a more traditional account of God's aseity vis-a-vis election and the incarnation and other statements which imply that God is constituted as God by his determination to be God for us in the incarnation" (Ibid., 178).

[101] He has expanded upon this more in Duby, *Jesus and the God of Classical Theism*.

[102] Duby, *God in Himself*, 141.

upon God's economic activity.[103] Second, the biblical narrative does not present the incarnation as the sole revelation of God, but as the culminating one. Third, the New Testament assumes knowledge of God the Father's Old Testament actions, which are not always explicitly identified with Christ. Fourth, Paul speaks of the gentiles' natural knowledge of God in Athens. Finally, the entire biblical narrative of creation and God's continued relationship to it is based upon his independence from creation for his own existence.[104] It is through a consideration of these textual concerns, rather than only speculative reason, that Christians have historically not conflated God's being with his economic activities—particularly the incarnation.

Duby also devotes a section of his book to the relationship between theology and metaphysics. Going as far back as Ritschl, Duby identifies the anti-metaphysical strain in Protestant thought from the nineteenth century and remaining in some spheres today.[105] Each of these thinkers adopts the Hellenization thesis to some extent, contending that Aquinas departed from a biblical understanding of a mutualistic God to a metaphysical being. This has the danger, according to Barth, of creating some broader category of "being" which encapsulates both God and creation, thus eliminating the distinction between creature and Creator. A further critique mentioned by Duby here is the contention that the classical view limits divine freedom, and thus God's interaction with creatures. In response to the first claim, Duby argues that the medievals did not speak of being as some kind of broader category, as God is not defined by Aquinas as one being among many. On the second point, Duby constructs a rigorous account that affirms both God's immutability and the freedom of God through the use of Aquinas and Reformed theologians.[106] What Duby offers is a thorough defense of a classical approach in response to Barth and those who follow his line of thought.

---

[103] Ibid., 142.

[104] Ibid., 145.

[105] Ibid., 191.

[106] Ibid., 219–30.

The work of Duby stands alongside of Dolezal's as a call to recapture the doctrine of God as was taught by the medieval scholastics and inherited within the Protestant scholastic movements. Duby presents Jenson, Pannenberg, and Barth with fairness while offering a robust response to their claims. Classical theism, as Duby shows here, is not just an outdated philosophical schema, but instead it remains a theologically, exegetically, and philosophically robust set of propositions.

Conclusion

What has been discussed in this chapter is a small sampling of a field in which an extensive amount of material has been published. The volumes chosen here are representative of some of the major points under discussion. This overview identified several of the major themes that extend through three distinctive schools of thought that continue to drive the conversation in the twenty-first century. First, there are those who are actualists, who contend that to some degree, God's economic actions determine his being. This leads to a complete rejection of the classical doctrine of God. Second, some Evangelical theologians and analytic philosophers have attempted to retain elements of the classical approach while challenging the stronger forms of simplicity, immutability, impassibility, and atemporality. Finally, a growing number of authors have sought to revitalize the classical view by giving thorough responses to the challenges that have been consistently raised for the last century and a half. As I count myself among these authors, I now continue with an explanation and defense of each of these four primary elements of classical theism.

3

Divine Simplicity

The first of the four divine attributes explained here which is definitional to classical theism is God's simplicity, or his nature as non-composite. Flowing out of a concern for God's ontological self-sufficiency and unity within the divine nature, divine simplicity is the contention that God is not composed of parts. "Parts" do not merely denote physical properties, but any qualities whatsoever. There is, in God, no difference between his essence and attributes, or his substance and accidental properties (to use the common Aristotelian phraseology). Such an affirmation constitutes the doctrine in its broadest sense, though in the Western tradition, the further affirmation of an identity between essence and existence as taught in Aquinas became a key tenet in the exposition of the idea.

The Confessionalization of the Medieval Concept

At the time of the Reformation, one of the driving factors in the theological exposition of both the Lutheran and Reformed traditions was the defense of their theology as historic and patristic. The reformers contended that there was no attempt at theological novelty in their dogmatic commitments; they argued to the contrary that "nothing has been received on our part against

Scripture or the Church Catholic" (AC Conc. 5).¹⁰⁷ This commitment to catholicity is especially evident in the early doctrinal formulations of the doctrine of God and of Christology. In the publication of the *Book of Concord* in 1580, three ancient creeds were included at the front as confessions of the Lutheran tradition: the Apostles' Creed, the Nicene Creed, and the Athanasian Creed. Such a commitment to the ecumenical Trinitarian confession and to a two-nature Christology consistent with Chalcedon is also evident in the Westminster Confession of Faith and the Thirty-nine Articles.

Included within what was the standard catholic approach to God is an affirmation of his absolute simplicity.¹⁰⁸ This is evident in Article I of the Augsburg Confession, wherein prior to discussing any debated doctrinal articles, the authors of the document include a concise statement about God's identity and attributes. With their patristic and medieval forebears, the reformers confess a singular divine essence (*una essentia divina*), along with the tri-personality of God as Father, Son, and Holy Spirit (AC I.2–3). The three persons of the Godhead are all coeternal (*coaeternae*), as eternity is inherent to the divine essence as such (AC I.2). It is evident that, at this time, eternality was understood in its Augustinian formulation as atemporality, though that discussion is for a future chapter. What is most significant for the present chapter is that within the brief paragraph which explains the reformers' view of the Godhead, they include his being "indivisible" (*impartibilis*) (AC I.2). This lack of dividable parts as described here is not merely a denial of his possession of physical parts, as the categorization of God as without body (*incorporeus*) already affirmed his lack of physicality (AC I.2). One may contend, however, that the Latin word *impartibilis* only denotes a lack of parts which may be separated from one another, rather than a denial of parts in God at all. That, however, cannot be sustained with the German text, which uses the phrase "ohne Stücke," translated more literally as simply "without parts." While the Lutheran reformers do not

---

[107] Citations of the Lutheran Confessions are from the Triglotta edition unless otherwise noted.

[108] See the excellent exposition of this article in Loy, *Augsburg Confession*, 407–10.

affirm one particular school of thought on simplicity (that of Augustine, Thomas, or Scotus, for example), they are clear in the affirmation of the idea as an essential component in doctrinal exposition of the essence and attributes of God.

The Reformed confessional tradition contains similar affirmations of divine simplicity. The second chapter of the Westminster Confession of Faith summarizes the Reformed view of the divine nature, including a more detailed description of the divine attributes than does the Augsburg Confession. The clearest affirmation of the doctrine of simplicity in this document is the statement that God is "without body, parts, or passions" (WCF 2.1). The Larger Catechism's section on the divine attributes does not have as clear a statement as does the prior document, though the related attributes of God's infinity, all-sufficiency, and immutability are enumerated (WLC Q.7). What is affirmed in these documents agrees with earlier Reformed statements on the topic. The Belgic Confession of Faith, written in 1561, defines God in Article I as "a single and simple spiritual being." The Thirty-nine Articles of Religion in the Church of England contains the phrase later included in the Westminster Confession of Faith that God is "without body, parts, or passions" (39 Art. 1). Like the Augsburg Confession, each of these Reformation documents affirms the simplicity of the divine essence.

It is clear that the entirety of the Magisterial Reformation (Lutherans, Reformed, Anglicans) affirmed the basic elements of the doctrine of God which had been inherited in the late medieval West. At the core of this understanding of the divine nature is God's simplicity, or his non-composite nature. In none of the texts, however, are more specific philosophical commitments discussed or affirmed. Confessional boundaries, then, are broad enough to include a variety of formulations of simplicity, while the basic affirmation that God is without parts is affirmed. It is to the particulars of the exposition of divine simplicity, particularly that of Thomas Aquinas, that the discussion now turns.

Thomas Aquinas's Account

As mentioned already, there are a number of different manners in which divine simplicity can be explained—not just the Thomistic formulation. However, within the Western tradition, from the late medieval period unto the current day, it is Aquinas's model which has predominated, and it is his language which is most often echoed within Protestant scholastic thought. Thus, it is necessary to explain his argumentation in formulation of the doctrine. Divine simplicity is at the center of Aquinas's explanation of God's nature in both the *Summa Theologica* and the *Summa Contra Gentiles*.[109] The explanation here comes from the latter work, though the same basic argument is present in the former.

Thomas's argument begins with a consideration of the nature of composition.[110] If any object is a composite of multiple things, those things which constitute the object are ontologically prior to that object. Water, for example, is a composition of both hydrogen and oxygen, meaning that those two elements are more ontologically foundational than the composite object which they constitute. Were God composite, he would be made up of things separable from his essence, making those things an ontological foundation for God's being. If this were the case, God would no longer be the first being, and thus would not be God. Furthermore, any composite object is by definition dissoluble—such as the example of water used here. The elements of hydrogen and oxygen can be separated from one another, and thus from water, dissolving the united essence which they form. The implication of this is that a composite thing cannot have *necessary* being, but instead *contingent* being (as it is dependent upon a unity of other objects). God, however, is necessary being.

A further problem outlined by Aquinas for a divisible God is that composite objects are put together in unity by something outside of themselves. An object consisting in a unity of multiple objects cannot compose itself, as

---

[109] For an exposition of Thomas's account, see White, *The Trinity*, 239–60.

[110] This argument is in Aquinas, *Summa Contra Gentiles*, 18:1–8.

this is a contradiction. A thing not formed cannot be its own principle of composition. Therefore, if God were composite, some external composer must exist, meaning that God would no longer be the first cause—thus not God. Also, Aquinas argues, if God were composed of parts, his perfection would exist in the addition of goodness contained within these parts, meaning that his own goodness is not of his essence, but derived from multiple other objects, thus denying that God is goodness itself. Unity and simplicity necessarily exist prior to plurality and multiplicity. If God is truly the most ontologically foundational being (or being itself), he must be simple.

This affirmation of simplicity means that, for Aquinas, God is identical with his essence.[111] When any object is not to be directly identified with its essence, its essence must then be something added to it, thus making the object a composite thing. This identification of God with his essence differentiates him from all created things. For any created object, a thing merely *partakes* of an essence, but cannot *be* an essence, as essences are instantiated in various individual objects. An individual person cannot rightly say, "I am humanity," for example, as he or she is an individual within the larger genus of humanity. With ordinary individual objects within a genus, it is the difference between particulars which constitutes their individuality apart from others within the genus.[112] As the divine essence does not have such particularity to divide it from other objects within the same genus (as one cannot have multiple absolutely simple objects with any differentiation from one another), then God cannot be said to be part of a genus at all.

God, being identical with his essence, is also one with his accidents.[113] Or rather, God has no *real* accidental qualities as do creatures. What one perceives as distinctive attributes or qualities of God are viewed as such by limited human creatures, but they are not ontologically distinct in the

---

[111] Ibid., 21.

[112] Ibid., 25:1–10.

[113] Ibid., 23.

divine nature. Like other points Aquinas makes, this distinction between substance and accidents is taken from Aristotle, who distinguishes between what a thing is and what properties a thing may have which are separable from it. A human may grow, get a haircut, change locations, or put on a new outfit and still retain the same human essence. Yet these various accidental properties have changed. God, as one who is immutable, cannot have accidental properties which are distinguishable from his essence, as he does not experience change as do contingent objects. Further, if one were to contend that God is a mixture of substance and accidents, this would then lead back to the problems addressed previously with any understanding of God as composite.

Aquinas's arguments depend largely upon his adoption of Aristotle's differentiation between act and potency.[114] In Aristotle's conception, all things that exist are a composition of both act (what they are or are doing) and potency (what something has the potential to be or do). This is a logical necessity if any object is to be capable of change, in opposition to ancient Greek thinkers like Parmenides who deny any change in the world as pure illusion. For Aquinas, God—as a simple being—cannot be composed of act and potency. He has no potentiality to be something which he is not already. Therefore, God is pure act (*actus purus*). There is no potentiality in God which is yet to be actualized. For there to be potency means that there is something which can both be or not be, depending upon the actualization of such a potency. Were this true in any sense of God, then God himself would not be a necessary being. Therefore, God is purely actuality. It is important to note here that Aquinas is not negating real interaction between God and creatures. The criticisms of Aquinas often portray the Thomistic God as a static, immovable force who is incapable of any real interaction outside of himself (which *is* basically true of Aristotle's God). When Aquinas speaks about potency here, he references *passive* potency, or the potential for God to change. What he does not deny, however, is that God possesses *active* potency, meaning that God changes that which is outside of himself

---

[114] Ibid., 16.

in continual interaction with his creation.

Along with his use of several of Aristotle's distinctions regarding the unmoved mover, Aquinas adds another important facet to this discussion of divine simplicity: the relationship between essence and existence.[115] It is this idea which brings Thomas beyond Aristotle's categories in a significant way. Aristotle's idea of simplicity largely revolves around the definition of God as pure form. The Greek philosopher's approach to ontology is often referred to as hylomorphism, meaning that all things are a composite of both form and matter. God, as an immaterial being, is form without matter. The problem, from a Christian perspective, of a definition of simplicity which centers on immateriality is that there are spiritual beings who exist as pure form without also being divine (the angelic and demonic realms). Lest one adopt a gnostic approach to emanations of quasi-divine beings, the Christian must make a clearer distinction between immaterial things. It is here that Thomas's distinction between essence and existence is crucial. The essence of something is the *nature* of an object, or what a thing is. The existence of a thing is the *that* of an object, or *that it is*. Existence is something added to an essence, resulting in its instantiation in reality. One could conceive a world in which, for example, dogs were a mere theoretical idea of a fictional creature, never having been instantiated in reality. In God, however, there is no distinction between his essence and his existence. There is no conception of a possible world without God. He is, by definition, a (and the only) *necessary* being.

These are the central claims of Aquinas regarding divine simplicity. First, God is not a composite object, but instead a unity, as the ontological foundation for all other things. Second, God is identical with his essence, and is therefore not a genus. Third, there is no division between his substance and his accidental properties. Fourth, God is not a mixture of act and passive potency, but is pure actuality. Fifth, and finally, God's essence and existence are identical. These same five tenets are adopted by Protestant scholastics in the post-Reformation era.

---

[115] Ibid., 22.

Johann Gerhard

While affirmations of divine simplicity can be found in Melanchthon, Chemnitz, and Hunnius (among others), it is Gerhard who provides the first extensive treatment of the doctrine from the Lutheran tradition in his *Loci Theologici*.[116] In his volume on the nature of God and the Trinity, Gerhard affirms a strong natural theology, reiterating many of Aquinas's arguments for God's existence, along with citations from Aristotle. As an adherent of the classical theistic tradition as mediated through Thomas, Gerhard places the confession of divine simplicity in a central position as he explains the nature and attributes of God.

Gerhard begins his discussion of the topic of divine simplicity under the heading "What God Is." Gerhard asks, first, whether God can be defined and answers in the negative. He gives four reasons for this answer, which each portray his philosophical commitment to the Thomistic concept of deity. First, God cannot be defined because he has no genus. Without a genus, a thing cannot have a proper definition. Gerhard's reasoning for denying God's existing within a broader genus is his rejection of univocity as proposed by Scotus. Were God part of a genus, he would be in the same order of things as other objects, and thus univocal predication would be possible between God and creatures. Gerhard cites Aquinas in defense of this point, noting that it is impossible for "being" (which God is identified with) to be placed in any broader categories.[117] Gerhard further argues that everything which has a genus is both finite and composite. Neither of these things can be predicated of God, who is both infinite and non-composite. Here, Gerhard denies six distinctions in God: that of matter and form, of substance and accidents, of act and potency, of genus and difference from other objects within that genus, of nature and individual substance, and

---

[116] Preus, *Post-Reformation Lutheranism*, 2:71–74.

[117] Gerhard, *God and Trinity*, 92.

of essence and existence.[118] Gerhard reiterates all five points cited above as definitional to Aquinas's exposition of divine simplicity in the *Summa Contra Gentiles*.

Gerhard's second reason why God cannot be defined is in God's perfection. Gerhard identifies God's perfection in his characterization as the "supreme being" along with "sheer and purest act."[119] In order for something to have a definition, Gerhard argues, something must be prior to that object by which it is to be defined. If one adopts Aristotle's definition of man as a rational animal, for example, humanity is defined by two essential realities outside of, and ontologically prior to, itself: rationality and animality. God, as the first being, gives definition to things outside of himself, and cannot be thus defined by anything external, or anything other than himself. In support of this point, Gerhard makes an analogy between God as pure being, and the undefinable nature of prime matter.[120] Gerhard does not cite solely Thomas here on this subject, but he also affirms the Eastern language of God's being beyond essence through a citation of John of Damascus.[121] Both Thomas's conception of God as being itself, and the Eastern contention that God is "beyond being," are orthodox ways to preserve the truth of God's transcendence.

The third argument in Gerhard as to why God cannot be defined is that God is uncaused. To define something (in a proper sense) is to identify either its essence or its cause. Gerhard has already demonstrated at this point why God's essence is undefinable. Similarly, one cannot define God through a causal agent, as he himself is the first cause. Therefore, he cannot be defined

---

[118] Ibid., 93. Interestingly, Gerhard uses the Greek terms οὐσία and εἶναι, rather than the more common Latin *ente* and *essentia*.

[119] Ibid.

[120] Prime matter is a concept explained by Aristotle within his hylomorphic system. For Aristotle, all things are composites of matter (the stuff that makes them up) and form (the thing that they are). "Prime matter" is matter without any form whatsoever. If there is no form, there can be no definition, as any definition would identify the form that matter takes. Gerhard clearly affirms hylomorphism here in the same manner as does Thomas.

[121] Gerhard, *God and Trinity*, 93.

by something outside of himself.

In his fourth and final argument that God cannot be defined, Gerhard cites earlier authorities on the topic. One does not find here, however, a collection of citations merely from church fathers, but also from Greek philosophers. He cites Pythagoras, Simonides, and Plato as early attestations of God's undefinable nature. Along with the ancient Greeks, he offers citations from both Eastern and Western fathers that testify similarly to God's inability to be fully comprehended. None of this means, however, that God cannot be known in *any* sense. This is where the distinction between archetypal and ectypal theology is essential.[122] Only God has comprehensive knowledge of himself (archetypal theology). No human, as a finite being, can have such knowledge of the infinite God, as such would require an infinite knowledge (which is the possession only of God). Further, as a simple essence, God is identical with his knowledge; thus, to know God comprehensively is to be God.

None of this means that the believer is left only with the apophatic method, so that the Christian is bound to contemplate divine unknowability through the negation of positive affirmation and thought. Instead, Gerhard points to the fact that though God cannot be defined according to his infinite essence, he *can* be defined according to the titles which he has revealed to creation. Some truths about God can be explained by philosophers, such as his immateriality, omnipresence, and atemporality, and his function as the first being.[123] However, natural knowledge is imperfect, and the Christian view of God is to be approached by means of Scripture rather than the dim light of reason. In view of Scripture, then, Gerhard identifies five necessary aspects of a Christian exposition of God: his essence, his essential attributes, his tripersonality, his external works, and the benefits that he gives.[124] It is only the first two of these five aspects of God's identity which can be known through reason, as the others are given solely by God's self-

---

[122] Weidner, *System of Dogmatics*, 1:4.

[123] Gerhard, *God and Trinity*, 95.

[124] Ibid., 97–98.

revelation in Scripture. In view of these points, Gerhard then offers the following definition of God:

> God is an utterly simple spiritual essence; infinite; of limitless goodness, wisdom, and power; just; and truthful—namely: the Father, who from eternity begot His Son, His image, and who created and preserves all things through the Son in the Holy Spirit; the Son, who was begotten of the Father from eternity, who in the fullness of time assumed human nature and in it carried out the work of redemption; the Holy Spirit, who proceeds ineffably from the Father and the Son from eternity, who was poured out visibly upon the apostles and still today is sent invisibly into the hearts of believers, and who through the preaching of the Gospel gathers the Church from the whole human race and sanctifies it to the glory of God's name and the eternal salvation of those who believe.[125]

There are a few points of note in this definition. First, it is apparent that divine simplicity is not mentioned as one among a list of attributes, but is identified first as at the core of Gerhard's understanding of God's essence. Second, Gerhard is thoroughly Trinitarian in his understanding of God. Though affirming the commonalities between the Greek philosophical conception of divinity and the Christian God, Gerhard does not in any way ignore the vast differences between the monadic deity of the Greeks and the living triune God. For Gerhard, God cannot in any real way be defined apart from his Trinitarian existence as Father, Son, and Spirit. Third, God is not to be understood in abstraction to the Christian, but in and through his redemptive actions. Gerhard includes in this definition both the immanent Trinitarian *ad intra* relations and his economic *ad extra* works of redemption

---

[125] Ibid., 98.

toward his fallen creation.

It is important to grasp this distinction between God's incomprehensible essence and God's definable names which is at the heart of Gerhard's thought. For Jenson, the scholastic tradition is mistaken in its prioritizing of questions of the divine being over those of divine identity—especially in God's identity with Christ's resurrection. What this results in, for Jenson, is the conflation of these two realities, so that there is no incomprehensible divine essence behind the Trinitarian economic acts. Or, in Torrance's terms, there is no God "behind the back of Jesus Christ."[126] Gerhard's affirmation of this classical doctrine of God's simplicity and self-sufficiency does not in any way undermine the redemptive historical context in which the divine identity is grasped by faith. For the believer, it is absolutely true that God is indeed "whoever raised Jesus from the dead," or for the Old Testament Israelite, "whoever redeemed us from Egypt."[127] God is known by humanity through the concrete manifestations of his condemnatory judgment (via the law) and his redeeming action (via the gospel). However, the epistemological question should not be equated with the metaphysical. God is known *to us* by his *ad extra* acts, but this does not constitute his immanent identity as the triune infinite and simple God.

God's Simplicity and Infinity

As mentioned previously, the Thomistic account of divine simplicity is not the only manner in which the doctrine has been exposited with theologians committed to the classic doctrine. While Thomas's account focuses on the question of metaphysical composition and causality, others have noted the necessity of God's simplicity as a corollary to his infinity. This is especially relevant in conversation with the post-Barthian critics of absolute simplicity, as they make infinity a core commitment in their exposition of the nature of

---

[126] Torrance, *Christian Doctrine of God*, 243.

[127] Jenson, *Systematic Theology*, 1:44.

God. As Jenson notes, infinity was not an operative concept in either Platonic or Aristotelian thought, but became central to the Trinitarian thought of the Eastern church fathers. Yet this concept of infinity, like that of metaphysical composition, implies God's unity and simplicity. The relevance of this is that simplicity is not *only* connected to an adoption of earlier metaphysical schemas, but also flows out of other biblical commitments.[128]

In was undoubtedly Duns Scotus who made this connection most clear in the Western church, as God's infinity grounded nearly every statement about God's nature for the late medieval thinker.[129] In Scotus's defense of God's singularity (of which simplicity is an outgrowth), he argues that this commitment, while revealed in Scripture, can also be rationally demonstrated through the nature of infinity.[130] Out of seven arguments posited for God's unicity, five of them arise from the nature of infinity: those of the intellect, will, goodness, power, and infinity considered in an absolute sense.[131] While these arguments will not be reiterated here, the heart of Scotus's thought on the matter is that infinity necessitates God's self-identical singularity. This means that Scotus affirms that some kind of simplicity and unity must exist within God if his infinity is as central to his essence as is Scotus's claim.

This Scotian argumentation is apparent within some post-Reformation thinkers, including the confessional Lutheran theologian Francis Pieper. Pieper's *Christian Dogmatics* is not philosophical in orientation, but exegetical, though he is committed generally to the conclusions of Lutheran orthodoxy as developed in the seventeenth century. He does not set forth a treatment of the subject from premises of composition, essence, and existence, or from the nature of being. Instead, he contends that simplicity

---

[128] On this note, it is also worth reminding the reader that Aquinas's own key distinction between essence and existence was his own development, rather than an adoption of some earlier non-Christian source.

[129] Greeley, "Divine Simplicity," in Minich, *The Lord Is One*, 214–43.

[130] Scotus, *Philosophical Writings*, 84.

[131] Ibid., 83–85.

arises out of the biblical confession of God's infinity. Pieper argues that God is infinite in that he transcends time and space (he cites 1 Kings 8:27 and Ps. 90:2, 4).[132] God's infinity defines him as divine over against creation, which is finite. If God were composed of parts, these parts would by definition be finite. With this being the case, the infinite God would then contain finitude as part of his being. As the creature/Creator distinction is defined by this division between infinity and finitude, the attribution of something finite to God results in a conflation of the divine with the creature. God, therefore, cannot be composite, and his essence and attributes are "absolutely identical."[133]

Something must be said here regarding Pieper's definition of infinity, as one may scoff at the argument that something infinite cannot be composed of finite things. After all, an infinite series of finite numbers is certainly a mathematical possibility. What Pieper means by God's infinite nature here is not that of a mere infinite series of finite objects. Instead, Pieper is speaking God's *ontological* infinity. Pieper defines God's infinity as "the idea that God in His being and activity is in no way bound by the limitations of time and space."[134] This is contrasted with the finitude in created objects, which is their being subject to "the limits and boundaries of their being and activity."[135] Were God's attributes not identical to one another and to his essence, then each of these attributes would be limited by their not being the other attributes. In other words, the divine attributes themselves would have both limits and boundaries, thus being finite (i.e., created things). To further defend this proposition, Pieper argues that scripturally, not only is God referred to as infinite, but so are his attributes (such as God's understanding in Ps. 147:5).[136] Thus, infinity of essence and infinity of attributes result in

---

[132] Pieper, *Christian Dogmatics*, 1:428.

[133] Ibid., 428.

[134] Ibid., 441.

[135] Ibid.

[136] Ibid.

an absolute identification between the two.[137]

While certainly there is a logical rigor to Pieper's argumentation, his presentation throughout the *Christian Dogmatics* on this point is scripturally grounded. Simplicity is not proposed based on some kind of foreign philosophical system, whether ancient or otherwise, but as the consistent reading of truths clearly explained in the scriptural text. Pieper recognizes, certainly, that Scripture at other times speaks of the divine nature as if the attributes were separable from him or from one another. This is not, however, a contradiction in the text. Instead, Pieper refers to human knowledge of God as that which is "mediated," or given as accommodation to the limitations of the human intellect.[138] Creaturely knowledge of God is fragmentary, and thus allows for human speech about God as if he had distinct attributes, though with a recognition that these things are not properly true of God in the absolute sense. Pieper recognizes the distinction between archetypal and ectypal theology, which is essential to any proper exposition of the divine attributes. This leads us then to the first area of defense regarding simplicity: the biblical data.

Simplicity in Scripture

It is this contention of divine simplicity which is at the heart of the Hellenization thesis. It is this doctrine, perhaps more than any other, which is accused of lacking any biblical support, being a thorough conflation of the Aristotelian immovable singularity and the triune God of Christianity. As discussed in the previous chapter, this doctrine is consistently rejected by post-Barthian thinkers, as well as Evangelical theistic mutualists, as a Greek imposition. The argument that simplicity is a philosophical rather

---

[137] As Scotus argues in his defense of monotheism, the conception of infinity necessarily leads to a singular manifestation of the infinite, as the existence of multiple objects which are ontologically infinite (whether separate infinite attributes or various infinite beings) is by nature contradictory. Scotus, *Philosophical Writings*, 92–95.

[138] Pieper, *Christian Dogmatics*, 1:429.

than biblical doctrine is not completely without merit, as there is a clear difference between simplicity and something like God's love or goodness, which one can affirm in explicit language through a variety of biblical proof texts. Jenson is correct that the questions of divine identity in relation to the redemptive history of God's people, rather than the strictly metaphysical concerns of the ancient Greeks, are central to the biblical text. Nonetheless, this does not mean that simplicity cannot be demonstrated from Scripture as a necessary corollary to themes of divine aseity, unity, and infinity, of which there is abundant evidence throughout the scriptural text. It is these eternal divine attributes (or God's identity *in se*) which stand behind his actions toward creatures in his covenantal dealings.

As acknowledged above, unlike many other divine attributes, there is no singular scriptural text that says in a sentence that God is non-composite. Perhaps the closest thing to a proof text for the identification between God's essence and attributes is in the well-known statement of the apostle John that "God is love" (1 John 4:8).[139] It is clear that in at least this one instance, God is not separable from one of his attributes (that of love). John does not claim simply that God *has* love, or is *loving* (as may be said of a creature). This is certainly a metaphysical claim regarding the nature of God, though it is to be noted that this statement serves a practical end for John, rather than a speculative one. This practical end is twofold. First, God's nature as love is the basis by which Christians themselves are to love others (1 John 4:7). To know God is to know love, and thus to manifest this divine love within Christian community. Second, God's identification with love undergirds the manifestation of that attribute within the divine economy through the Father's sending of the Son (1 John 4:9). Contrary to the claims of Jenson and others, John does not ground God's self-identity in the incarnation; rather, the incarnation is itself the manifestation and outflow of God's identity *in*

---

[139] Commenting on this passage, Lenski says: "Every attribute, whether it is quiescent like his eternity or his aseity, or energetic like his omnipotence or his love, is nothing but his indivisible essence, his entire being revealed and perceived in one respect" (Lenski, *Peter, John, Jude*, 497).

se.[140] The incarnation is described as a revelation of God's self, and as the means by which the human creature knows divine love. God's economic relations flow out of his immanent identity, though the two are not identical.

The primary way in which theologians have historically argued for divine simplicity is by a consideration of divine aseity. It is argued that if God is truly of himself, or sufficient in himself for his own existence and essence (without any reliance upon things external to himself in order for God to be who he is), he must be a simple essence. If Aquinas's and Gerhard's conclusions above are correct that divine self-sufficiency requires simplicity (which I believe them to be), then one only needs to demonstrate the veracity of God's aseity according to the scriptural text. There are a number of places in which such a conviction can be demonstrated by the biblical authors.

The arguments surrounding aseity often begin with a consideration of the divine names, particularly God's self-revelation as "I AM" in conversation with Moses (Ex. 3:14). Danish Lutheran theologian Petrus Nakskow outlines six implications of this title.[141] First, God exists in an eternal present, unconstrained by the limits of temporality. Second, God is the source of all other essences that exist. Third, God is immutable. Fourth, God is the only being who has existence in himself rather than from another. Fifth, God is not composed of parts, but is identical with his attributes. Finally, God is unique. There is no other being like him. One may scoff at such an extensive description of God taken from such a minimal amount of text as some kind of imposition of Hellenism upon the biblical author by this Danish preacher. Perhaps a dismissal of Nakskow's conclusions would be justified had his contention depended merely upon this verse as isolated from its canonical context. However, as a Christian pastor with a strong insistence upon the inspiration and self-consistency of the entire biblical text, Nakskow recognizes that Scripture itself interprets this Mosaic revelation in a manner consistent with classical theistic convictions. This continual scriptural witness is addressed here.

---

[140] See Duby, *Jesus and the God of Classical Theism*.

[141] Nakskow, *Articles of Faith*, 17.

In contrast to Nakskow, in more recent years, it has been popular for commentators to limit the title "Yahweh" to God in his covenant relations. In this view, this divine title proclaims that God is who he is as covenant Lord, and will do what he pleases with his people Israel. Contemporary Reformed theologian John Frame, for example, rejects any claim to metaphysical affirmations tied to this text as some kind of Platonic search for "pure being," in opposition to the Mosaic revelation of divine lordship and faithfulness.[142] It thus is not particularly relevant to the question of divine simplicity at all, or to metaphysics in general.[143] To identify the difference between these older and newer approaches simply, for Nakskow, "I AM" signifies something about God's immanent being, whereas for Frame, it is instead to be identified with economic relations. There are some things to be said in defense of the classical view.

In contrast to Frame, it is not necessary to claim that Moses was asking questions about "pure being" or the relationship between change and constancy in order for the title "Yahweh" to have metaphysical implications. Proponent of divine simplicity James Duguid, for example, confesses that it would be wrong to read Plato's or Parmenides's conceptions of being into the Mosaic testimony while still contending that "this construction [I AM] does ascribe existence to God's nature in some special way, unconditioned by any other predicate, and the idea that God is in some sense more really and truly existent than other things doesn't seem too far off the mark here."[144] There is no question that God's self-revelation in the Book of Exodus occurs within the context of the redemption of the Israelites from Egypt, rather than as a point of philosophical inquiry. As Melanchthon famously says, "to know

---

[142] Frame, *Two Models*.

[143] Geerhardus Vos takes a similar approach, writing: "In its more philosophic form this may be called the ontological view. It would approach what the schoolmen have tried to express in the doctrine that God is pure being. But this is far too abstract an idea to be suitable here. It would bear no direct application to the need of the Israelites at this juncture. They, surely, had something else and more urgent to do than to lose themselves in speculations anent the mode of God's existence" (Vos, *Biblical Theology*, 118).

[144] "Divine Simplicity in the Old Testament," as found in *Lord Is One*, 11.

Christ means to know his benefits" (*Hoc est Christum cognoscere, beneficia eius cognoscere*).[145] Similarly, the Old Testament saints came to know Yahweh through his acts of covenant mercy and deliverance. One must not portray Moses as some kind of pre-Socratic philosopher attempting to extrapolate the mysteries of the universe so that the people of Israel could establish philosophical schools in Jerusalem to engage in debate with their polytheistic neighbors. The question is whether God, in his economic revelation, is founding that economic reality upon something that is ontologically basic about himself apart from such actions. This is to be contrasted with the claims of authors such as Jenson and McCormack, who argue that God's ontology is in some sense founded upon the economy.[146] Through the continual witness of Scripture, and particularly its witness of itself, there is sufficient reason to believe that Yahweh's revelation to Moses *does* in fact provide a basis for God's aseity.

Steven Duby points to some important corollaries to the divine name Yahweh which also establish God's self-sufficiency. The first (and rather significant) point he makes is that the creation narrative in the first chapter of Genesis is one which contains nothing of any kind of self-actualization of God in the act of creation. God does not need creation, nor is there any struggle present through which he creates.[147] God's portrayal is of a divine potentate declaring orders which are then immediately enacted. This is a strong contrast to the varied creation myths of the ancient Near

---

[145] Melanchthon, *Loci Communes*, 21 in Pauck, *Melanchthon and Bucer*.

[146] Both authors, to some extent, found their arguments on Barth. On that note, the reader may wonder why this work does not engage significantly with Barth, whose writing plays a consistent role in these discussions within much of the literature surrounding the divine essence and attributes. This omission was purposeful, as through my own reading of Barth, I am unsure of exactly what interpretation of his view is correct. Certain statements seem to imply God's aseity in a strict sense, while others appear to identify the divine essence with the Christ-event. I felt that any attempt to untangle this would derail the argument of this book significantly. For now, I will let the Barth scholars continue to debate which interpretation is most proper, and not weigh in myself on these matters.

[147] See the analysis in Kline, *Kingdom Prologue*, 26–30.

East.[148] Second, Duby points to the fact that God expressly states that he does not need human worship, as he is self-sufficient (Ps. 50:9–15).[149] Third, God is described as the one who aids the needy, but is never in any need himself (Ps. 145:14–16). Fourth, the prophet Isaiah contrasts God with creatures by arguing that God does not need counsel from any other, and that he is not impacted by time as is his creation (Is. 40:12–31). In other words, God is self-sufficient, and we are not. Finally, Duby points out the contrast mentioned by Jeremiah that God is distinct from idols due to his independence from creation (Jer. 10:1–16). These testimonies of various Old Testament passages demonstrate that questions of God's self-sufficiency and independence from creation were not totally foreign to the ancient Israelites, nor did they need Greek philosophy in order to consider such questions. Simply to claim that God is independent of creation is itself to make a claim regarding the divine nature which is "metaphysical," regardless of what terminology one chooses to attach to it.

Within the intertestamental period, particularly in the Roman context, there was often a mixture of Hellenistic and Hebraic thought forms in Judaism.[150] Contrary to the often-simplified portrayal of Hebraism as some hermetically sealed ideology without influence from Greek philosophy (prior to its corruption in the patristic era, of course), these two intellectual traditions play a role in the thought world of the New Testament. While Moses may not have had any conception of "being" in its Platonic sense, influential Jewish thinkers such as Philo certainly did, and having such concerns, they read the Old Testament descriptions of God in such a light.[151] Taking a canonical approach to Scripture—believing that the New Testament is the proper interpretation of the Old—one must then ask the question as to how the New Testament fits within these broader developments within Second Temple Judaism. This, in my view, is the key question regarding

---

[148] Duby, *God in Himself*, 145.

[149] Ibid., 146.

[150] Sanders, *Shaping of Christianity*.

[151] Copleston, *From Greece and Rome*, 457–62.

divine simplicity, but also regarding the validity of classical theism as a whole. As the New Testament was written in an intellectual milieu within which classical theism was extant, the authors of its books had every opportunity to both affirm the validity of Hellenistic approaches and to criticize it as inconsistent with Yahweh's revelation in Christ. While this question will be addressed in future chapters in relation to the four aspects of classical theism defended in this work, at present, the topic is limited to divine aseity.

While the linguistic debates regarding the Hebrew language of God's self-identification as "I AM" may not be easily resolved,[152] there is no doubt as to the Greek construction of a similar phrase in John 8. This chapter relays one of Jesus's many confrontations with the Jewish leaders who rejected his messianic claims. After Jesus rebukes the leaders for their lack of faith, he accuses them of having the devil, rather than Abraham, as their father (John 8:44). In response to this, the Jewish leaders in turn accuse Jesus of being demonic, claiming him both to lack genuine Abrahamic lineage (as they called him a Samaritan), and as one possessed by a demonic entity (John 8:48). Jesus, of course, denies such charges, and then points back to the witness of the Father toward the validity of his claims, culminating in his contention that he has the ability to grant eternal life (John 8:52). This is quite the shocking statement to his Jewish interlocutors, who draw the implication from Jesus's words that he claims superiority to Abraham.

It is in response to this that Jesus utters these significant words: "Truly, truly, I say to you, before Abraham was, I am" (John 8:58). The Greek term for "I am" (ἐγὼ εἰμί) is a present active indicative. In these few words, Jesus makes numerous claims about himself and of the identity of God as relevant to this project. First, Jesus identifies himself with the I AM revealed to Moses (Ex. 3:14). Second, in affirming the present tense here, Jesus identifies the validity of the Septuagint's rendering of the divine name in the present

---

[152] The Hebrew can be read either as the present tense, "I am who I am," or as the future, "I will be who I will be."

tense.[153] In a canonical approach, one cannot then limit Exodus 3:14 to God in his future covenantal actions of faithfulness ("I will be who I will be"). Third, Jesus makes a strong distinction between his own atemporal existence and the linearity of the historical time to which Abraham was bound. This is a distinction in being between the divine nature and the human. The divine nature "is," while the human "was."[154] This is particularly relevant to the question of God's relationship to time, which is addressed later. The point in this brief exposition is that in using such language as self-description, Jesus validates an understanding of Yahweh's title which accords with the classical theistic view.

The apostle Paul's famous address at the Areopogus also demonstrates continuity with classical theism in his approach to divine simplicity. Paul introduces God in this message by identifying him with the "unknown God," who is differentiated from various pagan deities. This differentiation is founded in Yahweh's superiority over creation, as he has made all things and is in need of nothing (Acts 17:24–25). It is God who gives "life, breath, and all things" (Acts 17:25). The differentiation between the creature and the Creator as outlined by the apostle here is based upon divine self-sufficiency and creaturely dependence. Divine aseity is further explained by Paul as consistent with some Greek language about Zeus, as Paul cites the poet Aratus's invocation of the Greek deity in which he states: "in him we live and move and have our being" (Acts 17:28). Note that Paul is not opposed to using the language of "being" (ἐσμέν, or literally, "we are") here as descriptive of the difference between humans and the living God. People "are" only insofar as they are in God. God, in contrast to finite things, simply *is*. The true God is not changed by his creatures, as are the deities found in finite human materials such as "gold or silver or stone" (Acts 17:29). God does not receive from his creation, but instead gives to creation its existence

---

[153] The full sentence in the Septuagint is ἐγώ εἰμι ὁ ὤν. This could be translated as "I am the being," or "I am the one who is." It has more strongly metaphysical implications in the Greek rendering than the original Hebrew text.

[154] Adolph Spaeth refers to this as "the antithesis of the finite and Infinite, the creature and the Creator" (Spaeth, *John*, 139).

and sustenance. Though Paul does not state so succinctly that "God is not composed of parts," such a conviction is a necessary corollary to the various points made here regarding God's aseity in contrast to creaturely dependence. Paul simply does not use Greek philosophy in the way one would expect had he had a purely polemical attitude toward philosophical theism, as do some contemporary critics.[155]

Divine simplicity is a confession not only of God's aseity, but also of his unity. The unity of God is at the heart of Israel's understanding of Yahweh as expressed in the Shema—the statement that the Lord is one (Deut. 6:4). This unity of God is expressed in opposition to the polytheistic beliefs of surrounding cultures, particularly within the Isaianic text (Is. 40:18–20, 44:6, 44:9–20).[156] Similar texts are found throughout the book of Deuteronomy (Deut. 4:35, 32:39). This monotheism was central to the development of the Jewish faith throughout the Second Temple period, and is reiterated in several New Testament texts. In John's Gospel, Jesus explicitly refers to the Father as "the only God" (John 5:44), and later as "the only true God" (John 17:3). Paul contrasts the true God with pagan gods, which are not in fact deities at all (Gal. 4:8), and contends that there is one God, just as there is one Mediator (1 Tim. 2:5). The Shema is reaffirmed by both Jesus (Mark 12:29) and James (James 2:19). The affirmation here in James is not only that one God exists (who may perhaps be composed of parts), but that God is one in himself (εἷς ἐστιν ὁ θεό). In other words, the confession of divine oneness is not only a statement about the nonexistence of other deities, but is also descriptive of the unity of God's nature.

The question which naturally arises, and has been debated in recent years with the prominence of social trinitarianism, is how exactly this unity of

---

[155] It is important to note that Paul both uses a robust natural theology and condemns pagans for their idolatry at the same time. One need not have an either/or approach to Greek thought in which it is rejected entirely or accepted as completely consistent with the biblical witness. The key difference between the Greek and Christian understanding of God here is in God's identity with the resurrected Christ through whom he will judge the world (Acts 17:31).

[156] See Wenthe, "Rich Monotheism of Isaiah."

divine essence comports with Jesus's identity with God alongside of the Holy Spirit. St. Paul is aware of this difficulty, and (as Richard Bauckham has masterfully demonstrated) includes Jesus within the Shema itself, as the Jewish confession is reformulated in a Christian theological context (1 Cor. 8:6).[157] The unity of the Son and the Father with the divine essence is also expressed in John's prologue (John 1:1–4) and in Paul's Christological exposition in Colossians (Col. 2:9). The developing Trinitarianism of the early church was not formulated in opposition to a conviction of the unity of God, but *within* that framework. This is why John, for example, speaks of divine aseity belonging to both the Father *and* the Son (John 5:26). The details of this discussion are addressed later in the present work as social trinitarianism is explained, but at this point it is important simply to note that the New Testament authors contend both for unity within the divine nature, and for the inclusion of the Son and the Spirit within the divine identity alongside of the Father (Matt. 28:19).

While, like the texts on divine aseity, these biblical statements surrounding the unity of God nowhere explicitly state something like, "God's essence is identical with his attributes," such a conviction is the most consistent way of understanding the entirety of the biblical witness on this point. This is especially apparent when alternative accounts of divine unity are offered which rely on unity of relations, eschatological unity, or other alternatives (which, again, are discussed in a later chapter).[158] Together, the consistent biblical witness of God's aseity, unity, and infinity ultimately only works if the divine essence is confessed as simple. The biblical data presented here is sufficient to conclude that the doctrine of divine simplicity is more than a foreign philosophical construct, but a doctrine which arises from clear testimonies within the biblical text. This groundwork having now been laid, this chapter now proceeds to answer some objections to this classical doctrine.

---

[157] Bauckham, *Jesus and the God of Israel*.

[158] Hinlicky, *Divine Simplicity*, is an example of an attempt at defining divine unity eschatologically.

Arguments against Divine Simplicity

A number of arguments have arisen in recent years against the classical doctrine of divine simplicity. As there is not sufficient space to cover all of those objections here, I have to limit myself to a few of the more prominent arguments. There are a few points to make as a preface here before beginning, as the reader may wonder about some notable absences in this chapter. One particular challenge to the classical doctrine of God which has arisen within the Lutheran theological context is from a polarization of law and gospel which wrenches divine wrath from divine grace, so that God is opposed to himself. Figures such as Steven Paulson and Oswald Bayer engage in such argumentation, while also professing a voluntarist understanding of the divine will.[159] The reason for the lack of engagement with such ideas here is that these developments surrounding law and gospel and their impact on the doctrine of God are simply too pervasive to be addressed briefly. It is for that reason that this series will include a later volume dedicated specifically to the subject. Second, authors such as Paul Hinlicky in his *Divine Simplicity: Christ the Crisis of Metaphysics* have argued against scholastic views from the perspective of Trinitarian reciprocity and eschatological unity. Similar models are addressed, but in the later chapter on Trinitarianism.

The arguments that are addressed here are threefold. The first is the perspective argued by John Frame and Vern Poythress which arises from a general distrust of Thomism and a Biblicist conception of doctrinal development. The arguments are taken from Poythress's recent book *The Mystery of the Trinity: A Trinitarian Approach to the Attributes of God*, which has received endorsements from some of the most prominent Evangelical theologians writing today. Second, I interact with the philosophically driven argumentation of analytic philosophers like Jay Wesley Richards and William Lane Craig, who criticize Thomas's view. The third argument addressed is that of Alvin Plantinga in his work *Does God Have a Nature?*

---

[159] I discuss this in my book *Lex Aeterna*.

Poythress's Biblicism

There is a trend within some Evangelical scholarship to reject philosophical discourse in the development and exposition of Christian theology. This has tended to be prominent within Reformed presuppositional thinkers who, following Cornelius Van Til, generally reject Thomistic categories for those taken directly from Scripture (or, sometimes, German idealism). This has characterized the writings of many professors associated with Westminster Seminary in Philadelphia, such as Scott Oliphint and Vern Poythress, following the writing of John Frame. After a controversy surrounding these issues at Westminster, Poythress penned the most extensive volume in defense of this approach, in contrast to James Dolezal and others who argue in favor of classical theism as defined by the Thomistic tradition. At almost seven hundred pages, Poythress's book addresses nearly every aspect of the classical attributes of God in its proposal for a more scripturally centered doctrine of God's essence and attributes.

There are a number of places in Poythress's work where Poythress addresses the topic of God's simplicity, and in doing so, he attempts to defend a form of the doctrine while simultaneously denying its classical formulation. In a short and basic definition of simplicity, Poythress writes: "God cannot be decomposed into parts."[160] In this rather odd linguistic shift, Poythress has changed the topic from that of composition to decomposition. He then gives an illustration to demonstrate his point: an apple which is cut up and taken apart. God, Poythress contends, is not like this. He is not material and does not have separable pieces which can be removed from him. He further makes arguments that God is absolute and relies on nothing outside of himself to be who he is.[161] Certainly, Poythress cannot be criticized for concluding that God lacks physical parts, or for arguing that nothing has preexisted God in time or is more ultimate than himself. However, the question to be asked of Poythress is, Is this really simplicity?

---

[160] Poythress, *Mystery of the Trinity*, 69.

[161] Ibid., 71.

While it is to be granted that there are a variety of perspectives under the broader umbrella of simplicity (the Thomistic, the Scotian, and some Eastern Orthodox),[162] Poythress has shifted the question altogether, so that he can claim to affirm a doctrine while redefining the purpose of the doctrine. As far as I have been able to find, the driving question in discussions of simplicity has *always* been "Does God have parts?" rather than "Can God be decomposed?" While the former necessitates the latter, the latter does not assume the former. Poythress's basic denial of simplicity (in its classical formulation) is clearer as he expounds more on the subject.

Poythress's denial of divine simplicity in a classical sense (being the identity between God's essence and attributes) is clear in the following quote:

> The persons of the Trinity indwell one another. They cannot be isolated from one another. They are not separable. It is all mysterious. And so also, the attributes of God have a kind of derivative form of coinherent indwelling. The attributes have a unity in one God. They also have a diversity, in the fact that distinct attributes are not synonymous. This unity in diversity exists because the attributes are coinherent. Each attribute is mysterious, and their relations are mysterious.[163]

The perspective outlined by Poythress here is that there is a kind of perichoresis of divine attributes within the unity of God, such that the divine attributes remain formally (not merely perceptually) distinct, while not strictly separable from one another. This is almost a kind of social trinitarianism as applied to the divine attributes, in which perichoresis takes the place of any unity of essence. In short, this is simply not divine simplicity, and it is disingenuous to reformulate the definition of the term in order to

---

[162] David Bentley Hart, for example, has been an outspoken proponent of divine simplicity while being continually critical of Thomism.

[163] Poythress, *Mystery of the Trinity*, 370.

contend that it is.

The chief reason for Poythress's reformulation of the classical doctrine appears to be a strict Biblicism and skeptical posture toward any philosophical terminology. Poythress contends, for example, that the "history of Western philosophy . . . is largely a history of unbelief."[164] He states that Aristotle's categories are "too treacherous for Christian theology,"[165] and that philosophy as a whole is "spiritual poison."[166] Poythress further clarifies this with three criticisms of the classical theistic position.[167] First, Poythress contends that classical theism has replaced God himself as the theological/philosophical starting point with Platonic or Aristotelian categories. In other words, these categories are more foundational than the triune God for the proponent of classical theism. Second, Poythress contends that the human creature is put in a "godlike" position by having the ability to control the categories by which God is defined. Third, Poythress rejects the way in which analogical language is used within the classical tradition, which leads—in his view—to the seeking of some kind of "deeper" knowledge of God apart from Scripture itself.

Poythress uses the illustration of a two-story house throughout his book to explain his points.[168] The first story of this home is that of mankind, and the second, of God. In the view of the classical theist (according to Poythress's portrayal), this first story only contains pictures that God has placed there, which are representative of goodness and beauty. The ordinary believer is stuck on this first floor, without direct knowledge of God on the second floor, but instead with these simple images. Philosophy is a hidden staircase, by which the trained intellectual can now climb from the first to the second story, thus having real knowledge of God which exceeds that of the ordinary Christian. This is essentially a retelling of Plato's allegory of the

---

[164] Ibid., 71.

[165] Ibid., 593.

[166] Ibid., 455.

[167] Ibid., 482–84.

[168] Ibid., 336–37.

cave wherein ordinary Christians are simply spending their time looking at shadows, while philosophers are able to turn from the shadows to the actual things themselves. Were Poythress's portrayal an accurate one regarding a classical doctrine of simplicity, this certainly would raise serious concerns of a kind of two-tiered Christianity in which philosophers are the superior class.

Two problems arise with Poythress's portrayal here, however. First, a Christian perspective on knowledge of God is not foundationally that of intellectual apprehension, but of trust in the person of Christ, through whom God is personally known. This is confessed by the Protestant scholastics (both Lutheran and Reformed) repeatedly. Lutheran theologians, for example, spend a significant amount of time discussing the reality of infant faith, which would be an impossibility had they had such an intellectualized approach to the knowledge of God.[169] A distinction must be made here between intellectual apprehension of facts and personal trust. The baptized infant knows God in a way that the most studied Platonic philosopher does not, because saving knowledge is a gift given by God's Spirit, rather than a human achievement via philosophical argumentation. Second, Poythress's argument relies on the idea that if God is simple (in a classical sense), then the non-philosophically minded Christian does not have any real knowledge of what God's goodness, for example, is. This is simply false. It is true that the average congregant has likely not considered the relationship between God's essence and attributes, nor of God's attributes to one another, in any depth. Nonetheless, every Christian knows that God is good, and that God loves. This is absolutely *real* knowledge, rather than a mere "picture" divorced from God's true essence dwelling on some inaccessible second story.

An illustration may help here. Consider the chemical formula for water—H_2O. One with scientific knowledge of the composition of water knows that this means that each of water's molecules contains two hydrogen atoms and one oxygen atom. Now, consider the case of two separate

---

[169] Pieper, *Christian Dogmatics*, 3:287.

individuals who have knowledge of water. The first is a scientist who has a comprehensive knowledge of the periodic table of elements, and of various chemical compositions. He can communicate quite clearly about at what temperature water freezes and boils, and the precise reasons why it reacts the way it does in various environments. However, this scientist has actually never tasted pure water. He has lived his life drinking exclusively milk, fruit juice, and soda. The second individual lives in a remote tribe that has not had contact with the modern scientific community, and has itself not discovered the chemical composition of water or other substances. However, she drinks water for daily sustenance, as do the other members of this tribe. In this scenario, which of these two individuals truly knows more about water? Yes, the scientist has more intellectual apprehension about its qualities, but the person with more knowledge of water is the woman in the tribe who has actually *tasted* water for refreshment daily. Similarly, it may be true that the philosopher has more intellectual knowledge of God in one way or another, but it is in faith that one actually tastes of God's love and goodness. In faith, there is no first- and second-story division, but the believer is brought near to God in Christ who is present in faith itself.

This leads to another key element which undercuts Poythress's "two story" criticism: the Christological nature of knowledge of God. Ultimately, all true Christian knowledge of God is mediated through Christ, who is the eternal Son united to a human nature. God himself exercises and displays his infinitely simple essence through the composite humanity of Christ, the God-man. Thus, in Christ, the attributes of goodness, love, mercy, and so forth, which are indivisible within the divine essence in itself, *are* divisible when the Son exercises them *in his humanity*. In other words, the second tier of the home in Poythress's illustration has now been brought into the first floor, and the images displayed on that floor are no mere pictures, but they instead contain God himself. The uneducated believer *does* understand divine goodness, because he or she knows what it means that Christ is good. Contrary to Poythress's criticism, it is not that the philosopher has some unfettered access to the divine nature. If anything, the philosopher is brought to an apophatic state of acknowledging that God is, in some way, unknowable. The pagan philosopher is simply brought to the *deus absconditus* (the hidden God), in need of a place where God has actually made himself known. It is only in Christ, who is *deus revelatus* (the revealed God), that God is truly known.

Poythress's criticisms ultimately rely on a fundamentally different approach regarding the relationship between philosophy and theology than has traditionally been taken among scholastic theologians, whether medieval or post-Reformation. This distrust of philosophy leads to an alternative proposal of simplicity which is, ultimately, not simplicity in any historic sense. Throughout his book, it is apparent that Poythress fails to offer a compelling alternative to the classical ones, and thus has only reaffirmed my conviction that the classical categories still provide the best explanatory framework for the communication of God's essence and attributes as described in the biblical text.

Challenges from Analytic Philosophy

While criticisms arise, on the one hand, from those who are skeptical of philosophy as a whole, others have instead criticized the classical view of simplicity for philosophical reasons. This is the case specifically with modern analytic philosophers who view the Thomistic approach as incoherent. Examples of such critics include Jay Wesley Richards, William Lane Craig, and Nicholas Wolterstorff. Like Poythress, these authors argue that divine simplicity does point to something true about the divine nature, but it must be—in some way—reformulated for the contemporary world. Here, two arguments are addressed. First is that of William Lane Craig, and second is that of Jay Wesley Richards.

Though Craig has addressed this issue in numerous talks, interviews, and blog posts, the clearest explanation of his arguments against simplicity is laid out in his *Philosophical Foundations for a Christian Worldview* (with J. P. Moreland). In this work, Craig and Moreland present three basic arguments against the classical understanding of divine simplicity. First, they contend that the idea that God's properties are identical with one another is "patently false."[170] They cite omnipotence and goodness as examples of two completely different properties, which cannot be conflated merely as distinctions in the human mind with no ontological basis in God. Second, Craig and Moreland argue that if God has an exact identity with his essence, then his actions are also identical with his being. If his being is unchangeable, this means that all of his actions are necessary. If this is true, it appears to inevitably lead to fatalism. Things could not be other than they are. This leads either to creation itself being a necessary act, or to a denial that God has any real relations with creatures.[171] Third, Moreland and Craig argue that Aquinas's identification between essence and existence is incoherent, as existence itself is not a "thing." One cannot just say that *"exists* just exists."[172] The first and third of these problems are addressed here first, followed by the more complicated question of God's simplicity and fatalism.

The first problem to be addressed here is the unity between God's various properties. The criticism of Craig and Moreland is essentially the same as that of Richards, as discussed in the previous chapter. All three of these thinkers use the terminology of "properties," rather than substance and accidents (which form the Thomistic language surrounding simplicity). Property, as used in analytic philosophy, is a broad concept which causes several difficulties with regard to the relationship between God and his attributes. For example, Richards contends that paternation, spiration, and filiation are all separate properties, as is "being triune," which therefore makes any conflation of properties and essence inherently non-Trinitarian, and therefore non-Christian.[173] Craig and Moreland have a similar critique. They point to an example of an object which both retains a singular identity and has distinctive properties: the morning star. This popular example, taken from Frege's distinction between sense and reference, notes that it is

---

[170] Craig and Moreland, *Philosophical Foundations*, 588.

[171] Ibid., 588–90.

[172] Ibid., 589.

[173] Richards, *Untamed God*, 217.

in fact the same star (referent) which is identified with two different phrases (senses). As Moreland and Craig point out, a classical theist could use this distinction to identify how an object could be one but yet have different modes of perception on the part of the human creature. There is no actual difference between the object as the morning star or evening star, but only in how and when humans perceive and identify the object. This idea is rejected by Craig and Moreland, who argue that *"being the morning star* and *being the evening star* are distinct properties both possessed by Venus."[174]

The arguments of Richards, Craig, and Moreland all depend upon the validity of the category of "property" as is used in contemporary analytic philosophy as the proper one to use when defining divine simplicity. If such categories are the proper ones in which simplicity is to be placed, then these authors are correct in arguing for simplicity's incoherence. This is especially true of the identification of being the morning and evening stars as properties. Venus, as an object, is the same object when it is morning and when it is evening. While, yes, it is true that Venus does move in its orbit, the identification of Venus with morning and evening simply has to do with the time at which the object is perceived on earth. If human perception and linguistic identification are "properties" of an object, then certainly God has properties. However, this is simply not what the doctrine of simplicity means, as it identifies what is true of God as he is in himself rather than how he is perceived by creatures.

An important distinction must be made here between *passive potency* and *active potency*. Passive potency is the potentiality which a thing has that can be actualized. For example, the potentiality of a ball to be thrown becomes actualized when someone picks up the object and throws it. The potentiality of such change to an object is passive potency. God, as immutable, does not have such potentiality. This is especially true as this potency is actualized by something external to it, whereas God—as pure act—cannot be actualized by something outside of himself. Such an idea impedes upon his aseity. Active potency, however, is the capacity of an object to activate the potentiality of

---

[174] Craig and Moreland, *Philosophical Foundations*, 588.

something *outside of itself*. James Dolezal notes that, when speaking of the divine nature, "classical DDS [doctrine of divine simplicity] does not deny that God possesses active potency in some sense."[175] God can, and does, interact with the universe, as he actualizes potentiality within persons and objects. This does indeed differ from the kind of active potency in creatures, wherein creatures have a further actualization within themselves as they interact with external objects. Such is not true of God. The point of the distinction being made here is this: Not every act of God or new relation in the world can or should simply be described as a "property" which then makes up a part of God. The mere flattening out of all divine attributes and activity as simple properties (though yes, there is the important distinction between Cambridge properties and intrinsic properties)[176] simply does not reflect the necessary distinctions and ideas presented in a classical formulation of God's simplicity. This is why Craig and Moreland's argument regarding Venus's definition as both morning star and evening star does not work. Such identification would be an instance of active potency, as the change is within the human perception, whose potency to identify and name Venus has been actualized in two diverse manners.

A further point must be made regarding the claim that divine simplicity is unintelligible. This assumption underlies both the first and third arguments that Craig and Moreland put forward. They note, for example, that omniscience and goodness are obviously two different qualities, and common sense thus militates against a strict identification of God's attributes with one another and with the divine essence. This same thought underlies the argument that to identify God with his existence is to say that exists exists (which sounds like nonsense). *That* something exists cannot be *what* it is. The point which is missed here is, as Edward Feser points out, that the incoherence of such positions would only have merit if one were coming

---

[175] Dolezal, *God without Parts*, 39.

[176] Further, Richards does distinguish between essential and accidental properties in God. This differs, however, in identifying an essence specifically as a bundle of properties, which is not the traditional view.

from the perspective of univocity.[177] Were one speaking of creatures, certainly to say a thing is good and powerful is to identify two (though perhaps overlapping) distinctive truths about that object. The same is true of a thing's essence or its existence. All language about God is analogical. There is not an exact identification between goodness as it inheres in the creature and as it is in God. This is also true with such ideas as God's existence and essence. To say, "God exists" is *analogous* to, though not *identical* with, the statement that "I exist." To be more precise, God is beyond any creaturely understanding of either existence or essence. The idea of divine simplicity transcends all human logical and linguistic constructs. This does not mean that it is inherently unintelligible, but this serves instead as a reminder that all human theology is ectypal.

The final argument addressed here from Craig and Moreland is the most challenging one. The argument is as follows. If God's attributes are all identical with his essence, this means that God's will and knowledge are his essence. As God's essence is immutable, that means that all of God's acts, and consequently the actions of creatures (which he knows with his unchangeable knowledge) cannot be other than they are. This is a difficult contention to make in light of the consistent biblical testimony regarding God's freedom to act. It appears, from this view, that creation then becomes necessary for God, as it cannot be otherwise.

This challenge, often called the "modal collapse argument," does admittedly pose a real problem for the proponent of divine simplicity in its classical formulation. However, that does not mean that there are no counterarguments to such ideas, as several have been proposed. One suggested solution to this dilemma has been a shifting of the doctrine of simplicity itself to accommodate divine freedom. Eleanor Stump and Norman Kretzmann make this argument, as they contend that God is not the same in all possible worlds, and thus there is no need to tie absolute necessity to the created world as it is, as God himself could be other than he is.[178] As both Ross and

---

[177] Feser, "Craig on Simplicity."

[178] Stump and Kretzmann, "Absolute Simplicity."

Dolezal argue, however, this solution does not really work for one desiring to retain simplicity in its fullest form.[179] Another solution is to say that God's creation *is* necessary, but *conditionally* necessary.[180] In other words, creation itself must exist, because it is an act of God's necessary and immutable will that is identical with his essence; however, this does not mean that God himself is in need of creation for any kind of self-actualization. This argument also maintains the distinction between creation as contingent and God as non-contingent. In order for this proposal to be accepted, one must frame God's freedom not as a choice between several options, but instead as the freedom to act upon his desires. Neither of these proposals, in my view, is entirely consistent with the scriptural witness regarding God's nature and freedom.

Steven Duby offers some helpful points with regard to this conversation. Citing Mastricht, Duby notes three distinct aspects of God's decree: 1) the act of decreeing (i.e., God himself); 2) the decree's tendency toward an object; and 3) the decree as produced in time as distinct from God himself.[181] It is only with regard to the first of these that there is necessity, as the decree is to be identified with the divine essence. With regard to the second, however, or the decree as it actually corresponds to contingent objects, there *is* freedom. As Duby states: "God is *actus purus* and yet also entirely free to create or not to create, or to create one world rather than another."[182] The termination of God's decree within the universe is not to be understood as a movement within God himself from potency to act, but instead as a movement within creation. Somehow, God's freedom must coexist with his being pure act. While Duby does not completely solve the issue here, what he does is provide some helpful guidelines through which this doctrine can be explicated in a manner that is consistent with both divine freedom and divine simplicity.

---

[179] Ross, "Comments on 'Absolute Simplicity,'" Dolezal, *God without Parts*, 197–201.

[180] A good overview of these arguments can be found in Greeley, "Philosophical Objections," in Minich, *The Lord Is One*, 236–42.

[181] Duby, *Divine Simplicity*, 197.

[182] Ibid., 198.

Each of the three challenges posed here by Craig and Moreland (and echoed by Richards) has sufficient answers which negate their challenges as compelling reasons to abandon the classical doctrine. The first two addressed here have two central problems. First, they depend upon the value of the categories of analytic philosophy, which simply are not the best categories to use when addressing this doctrine. Second, they neglect an exposition of the doctrine of analogy, which solves the problem of incoherence. The final issue addressed here is a more complicated one which does not have quite so simple an answer. What is clear, however, is that there *are* solutions to the problem. Ultimately, when addressing the doctrine of God, the theologian must come to a point of mystery, wherein it is to be acknowledged that human theological and philosophical systems simply cannot peer into the mysteries of the divine nature and decree. The distinctions Duby gives here have the benefit of giving important qualifications in this discussion, but without erasing the mystery. Such mysteries should not be shunned for their supposed lack of coherence, but embraced as opportunities for divine worship. This leads us to the final argument addressed in this chapter.

Alvin Plantinga's Argument

One of the most often cited arguments against classical theism in general, and divine simplicity in particular, is Alvin Plantinga's lecture "Does God Have a Nature?" The argument presented, in brief, is that if God's attributes are identical with one another, this means that God has only one property. Furthermore, if God's essence is identical with his attributes, then God himself must simply *be* a property. The problems with this are obvious, as this means that God is no longer a person, but a mere attribute. For Plantinga, then, this conception of God must be disregarded for one more connected to the biblical conception of divine personhood.

It must be granted that in normal parlance, a property is not a person and a person is not a property. Were the proponents of divine simplicity using the term "property" in a univocal manner in relation to God, Plantinga's argument would work. However, when speaking of God's attributes, it is not accurate to refer to them as "properties" in the same manner in which these are attributed to creatures. Properties are not things that inhere in themselves, but things which one partakes in. If God were a property, this would, of course, lead to the absurd conclusion that God does not inhere in himself. If the term "property" is used to refer to God's attributes by a proponent of divine simplicity (which, to be clear, it usually is not), it is done in an analogical manner. If a human has, for example, the property of goodness, this would indicate her participation in something that is other than herself. God, however, does not *have* goodness at all. He *is* goodness, not as a mere property, but as his self-subsistent being. Creaturely properties (good ones, at least) share partially in God's infinite perfection. Thus, the conflation of properties as a category which God and creatures share in common, which is a necessary part of Plantinga's argument, simply does not work.

Along with the above argument, Plantinga contends that properties are abstractions. God, as personal, is not an abstraction. Therefore, God is not a property, and is thus not simple. This second aspect of Plantinga's argument has the same fundamental error as the first: a pre-commitment to unicity. Plantinga approaches the doctrine of divine simplicity from a univocal perspective, and from that assumption he is correct that the doctrine *doesn't* make sense. If such language is, however, analogical, then these problems are simply not problems. It is, then, more than anything else, a disagreement about analogical language which is at the root of such theological divergences, rather than simplicity as such.

Conclusion

This chapter has demonstrated that the doctrine of divine simplicity has historic precedent within the theology of the Reformation, a foundation in Scripture, and robust philosophical reasoning behind it. While it is to be granted that there is a degree of flexibility as to how such a concept is expressed, and that one should not assume that Thomas's doctrine is the sole orthodox expression of God's unity and aseity, there is no sufficient reason to doubt the doctrine itself. Aquinas's basic line of reasoning still stands, despite the many objections raised against his approach. One simply cannot express that God is composite without positing something more ontologically basic than God himself. Johann Gerhard recognized the strength of such arguments, and that simplicity is the only way to properly express God's unity and aseity, as Scripture consistently teaches. Following Gerhard, Pieper then argues that divine infinity *also* necessitates simplicity.

As has been shown here, there are plenty of authors who contend for an altered doctrine of simplicity or a rejection of the teaching altogether. Some of these proposals argue that simplicity is a foreign philosophical construct that has been imposed on the biblical text, whereas others make the argument that simplicity itself is philosophically untenable. While some arguments do point to genuine difficulties (such as the modal collapse argument), they are often based upon assumptions regarding analogical predication and classical (mostly Aristotelian) categories. When all the alternatives are considered, the doctrine of divine simplicity as explained in the medieval and immediate post-Reformation sources continues to make the best sense of the relevant scriptural and philosophical data.

4

Divine Immutability

Closely connected with divine simplicity, God's immutability has similarly been challenged by a variety of theistic personalist perspectives. This second of our four characteristics of classical theism is criticized as inconsistent with the biblical portrayal of Yahweh, who seems to be anything but unchangeable. He interacts with his creatures, responds to prayer, portrays emotions, and even changes his mind. Yet Christians in the patristic, medieval, and Reformation eras all retained a strong belief that God is without change, despite the prevalence of his real interaction with creatures in history according to the biblical witness.

For the purposes of this chapter, divine immutability is defined as God's inability to experience change. This does not merely refer to the consistency of his character (though that is an implication of the doctrine), but to a lack of potentiality within the divine being himself. Unlike creatures, God is not a mixture of act and potency whose potentiality is enacted throughout time; he is instead pure act. This doctrine does *not* mean that God is simply static and immovable, impersonal, or uninvolved with his creation, as it is sometimes portrayed to teach. As mentioned in the previous chapter, though God does not have passive potency, he does have *active* potency; he can and does move objects outside of himself.

The structure of this chapter is similar to the previous. First, the doctrine of God's immutability is defined according to classical sources —medieval scholastics and then classical Protestants. After the doctrine is displayed as received by the church catholic, the biblical text is examined, with particular attention to analogical language. Finally, some challenges to the doctrine are discussed, beginning with Dorner's foundational work *Divine Immutability*.

Divine Immutability in the Medieval Period

The question of change and constancy drove the early Greek philosophers perhaps more than any other.[183] Thus, it is inevitable that those Christian theologians who are steeped in classical thought would consider such questions in relation to the God of Scripture. Though mentions of God's unchangeable nature extend back to the second-century apologists, it is Augustine who provides the most robust explanation of the doctrine throughout his *City of God*. This Augustinian concern retained its importance in the West throughout the medieval period and formed a significant portion of the scholastic treatment of the divine nature. Here, an overview is given of the doctrine as it appears in Peter Lombard and then Thomas Aquinas.

Peter Lombard

Though not so widely read today, Peter Lombard's *Sentences* was the most influential theological work of the medieval period. Nearly every following figure wrote and/or lectured on the work, and it thus was a standard backdrop for nearly all theological conversation in the scholastic era. In Book I, Lombard summarizes the developed patristic doctrine of God's essence, attributes, and works. With regard to God's unchangeable nature, Lombard outlines the definition and reason for the doctrine with several arguments from St. Augustine.

The first argument that Lombard lays out is as follows: Non-divine objects are composed of both their essence and accidental qualities. God,

---

[183] See Copleston, *From Greece and Rome* on classical Greek and Roman thought.

of whom "being most fittingly and truly pertains," has no non-essential parts or qualities. For one to change is to have a change in being. If one's being can, in any way, be changed, then it cannot be pure being.[184] This stems from the Augustinian conception of God as pure being, which arises from his own Neoplatonic background. That which is changeable is able to change by more or less participation in being, or its form. God does not have anything which he himself participates in to be who or what he is (as then he could not be being itself), and thus cannot change. It is important to note the connection here in Augustine's argument between God's immutability and his lack of composition. Divine simplicity and divine immutability are interrelated doctrines.

The second point made by Lombard—again taken from Augustine—is that God alone has immortality.[185] Immortality cannot refer *only* to an infinite duration of life, as this then would include the human soul. Augustine argues that God's immortality differs from that of the soul precisely in its unchangeable nature. Lombard identifies three ways in which humans experience change that God does not: in places, in time, and in affection. Here, the tenets of classical theism are all tied together as aspects of immutability. For Augustine, and consequently Lombard, immutability entails both atemporality and impassibility. All of these incommunicable attributes are what distinguish God from creatures.

The third argument here is that changeability entails death, which is improper to the divine nature.[186] What Lombard and Augustine mean here is not only literal physical death, but loss more generally. If a being changes, that means that part of its being no longer *is*; it has died. The example cited here is of the human soul. A fallen human soul is immortal in a sense, as in faith one is granted eternal existence. However, the believing Christian does still experience death, such as one's death to sin, and the complete loss of the fallen nature at the resurrection. God's immortality differs from that

---

[184] Lombard, *Sentences*, Book I Dist. VIII. Ch.2.1.

[185] Ibid., Ch.2.2.

[186] Ibid., Ch.2.3.

of creatures in that no part of him can cease to be. He does not experience *any* kind of death (apart from the hypostatic union, of course). He, therefore, must be unchangeable.

The fourth point made here from Augustine is not an argument in favor of God's immutability, but instead a clarifying statement.[187] Augustine contends that though God is unchangeable, he is the source and Creator of all changeable things. Similarly, though God is atemporal, he has created all temporal things. The point here is that God differs from creation in his immutability, but that this does not mean that God is not himself actively involved within his mutable creation. The Christian must affirm both God's real interaction with creatures and his lack of ontological mutability.

The reasoning put forth in Lombard's arguments here may not be compelling for many today, as they largely are dependent upon a Neoplatonic idea of God as being as mediated through Augustine. Further, Lombard's statements here are brief summaries of arguments, rather than an extended defense of each proposition, and must be treated as such. There are some important points made here, however, which are to be kept in mind throughout the present discussion. First, Lombard views immutability as a necessary corollary to simplicity and atemporality. These doctrines imply one another. Second, immutability is necessary in order to distinguish God from creatures. Third, perfection in being requires a lack of change. Finally, God's immutability does not negate true relationship with creatures. These themes are developed in Thomas.

St. Thomas Aquinas

Aquinas addresses the topic of immutability in question 9 of the first part of his *Summa Theologiae*, under the heading "Whether God Is Altogether Immutable?" As is his usual practice, he presents various objections to the claim that God is not mutable, and then responds to each. Following this,

---

[187] Ibid., Ch.2.4.

Aquinas then asks the related question: "Whether to Be Immutable Belongs to God Alone?" The argument Thomas presents is summarized here.[188]

Thomas's treatment of immutability begins with a presentation of three arguments in favor of the doctrine. First, Aquinas argues from the nature of divine simplicity, depending, of course, upon the conviction that simplicity is a correct notion. Simplicity necessitates that God is not a composite being, including a composition of act and potency. If God were changeable, then he would, by definition, have a mixture of act and potency. Since God is simple, this cannot be true, and God is therefore immutable. Like Lombard, Thomas affirms the intimate connection between these two doctrines. Immutability and simplicity necessitate one another.

The second argument proposed by Aquinas is essentially the same as Lombard's third point above. When something moves, it loses something of itself. If an object moves, for example, it loses its prior location. A change in human emotion means that one's prior emotional state no longer exists. If God were to change, then he would have the ability to lose part of himself. This cannot be the case if God is 1) the fullness of being, and 2) not composite.

The third point Aquinas makes is the logical corollary to the second. If God had motion, then his actions would lead not only to some kind of loss of being, but also to the gaining of something. If God, for example, had emotional change, he would then gain an emotional state which was not his previously. The problem here is that God is the fullness of infinite perfection. If this is the case, how can God be said to gain something? If that were true, then he would have ontological lack prior to this, and thus not be infinite. Further, if his perfection were dependent upon gained attributes in response to creatures, this would mean that God needed creation in order to attain perfection. Neither of these solutions makes sense.

Throughout this discussion, Aquinas is well aware of the consistent biblical language which attributes motion to God in various ways. In response to those who would claim that this negates divine immutability, Thomas brings up two points. First, Aquinas notes that it is correct in some sense to speak

---

[188] White, *Trinity*, 292–307.

of movement in God so long as one understands that this is not a move from potency to act. He specifies here the fact that God both understands and loves himself, which may be described as some kind of *ad intra* movement. This movement, however, is eternal and unchanging.[189] Second, Aquinas appeals to the consistency of metaphorical language. For example, an individual may say that the sun has entered into their kitchen window. In reality, the sun has not moved, but the earth is in such a position (as are the clouds) at that time that the light of the sun hits the window in a way that makes the room brighter. Language about God's movement must be understood in a similar manner.

A final point to be addressed in Aquinas's exposition is the relationship between God's immutability and creaturely existence. Here, Aquinas distinguishes two kinds of immutability. A thing can be immutable by the power of another, or by a power in itself. No created thing has existence through its own power, as God himself brings all things into existence. Thus, Aquinas's distinction between essence and existence secures that whatever can be attributed to creatures is derivative, and therefore distinct from God's self-existent being. As to immutability in things themselves (granting that such may be divinely derived), this is also not true of any created objects, whether physical or not. Physical objects move from potency to act in a number of ways throughout their existence. Angelic beings also move from potency to act, such as the move from potentiality to sin to a state of perfection after the demonic rebellion. Similarly, even without physical bodies, spirits choose to exercise their power in certain places, whereas God is omnipresent in a repletive manner.[190] As do Lombard and Augustine, Aquinas contends that immutability distinguishes Creator from creature.

Depending on some of the earlier arguments from Augustine, Aquinas develops divine immutability further than Lombard. He anticipates some

---

[189] A simple read of this section shows rather clearly the flaws in some treatments of Thomas, such as that of Jeffrey Johnson in *Failure of Natural Theology*.

[190] The term "repletive presence" is used to distinguish God's being completely present in all places according to his whole being from an ordinary physical presence. Weidner, *System of Dogmatics*, 1:263.

important objections to the doctrine, and answers in a way that is an attempt at being philosophically and biblically consistent. These same basic premises are retained within the major figures of the Protestant Reformation—both Lutheran and Reformed.

Immutability in Protestant Confessions

As with divine simplicity, there is no singular article in the early Protestant confessions of faith that exposits immutability, as this was not a point of contention at the time. Nonetheless, the affirmation of this central tenet of Christian theism is apparent in a number of places where it is assumed or mentioned in brief. Such an affirmation extends from the Lutheran Confessions, various strands of the Reformed tradition, and classical Anglicanism.[191] The magisterial Reformation traditions made no shift in this teaching from what had been received.

The Lutheran Confessions

The Augsburg Confession does not explicitly discuss immutability in its definition of God as one might expect. One can certainly infer such a teaching from the affirmations of both simplicity (God is *"impartibilis"*) and eternality (the divine nature is *"aeternus"*) in the first article, but one must look at other places in the Lutheran Confessions for a clearer affirmation. Keep in mind that Article I of the Augsburg Confession is not meant to be an extensive listing of all received divine attributes, but is instead a brief affirmation that the reformers accepted the patristic and medieval expositions of the divine nature (which certainly included immutability). It is the Formula of Concord which is more explicit.

The Formula of Concord, like the Augsburg Confession, has no doctrinal

---

[191] There is no statement affirming immutability in the Thirty-nine Articles themselves, but Anglican divines defended the doctrine thoroughly.

article specifically addressing the immutable nature of God. However, there are mentions of this teaching in the midst of three articles that deal with related controversies: the nature of predestination, and the definition of God's law as it relates to the gospel.

Predestination is the topic of Article XI of the Formula of Concord. Unlike the other issues addressed throughout this document, there was no heated debate among Lutherans on this subject in the immediate post-Reformation era.[192] However, with the growth of the Calvinistic Reformation through strong double-predestinarian theologians like Theodore Beza, it became a necessity for Lutherans to produce some statement surrounding the doctrine. There are basically two questions addressed here: Is grace universal? and, Is there something within us that is a cause of God's election? The former question is answered with an unambiguous yes, as the redemptive exclusivism in the Calvinistic system is rejected. With regard to the second question, the Formula strongly opposes synergism, which posits some cause of election within the human person's disposition or actions.[193] At issue with regard to both questions is the identification of the elect. If grace is universal—as is the Lutheran contention—then does this mean that all are elect? If that is the case, can someone who is elect become unelect by their own actions?

According to the Formula of Concord, the act of election is immutable.[194] Though grace extends to all people through the word and sacraments, the term "elect" in its most proper sense is used in reference only to those who will finally be saved. For the Formula (and later Lutheran expositors), the immutability of both God's love and election is ontologically grounded in his own being. The text states that "our election unto eternal life is founded not upon our godliness or virtue, but alone upon the merit of Christ and the gracious will of His Father, who cannot deny Himself, because He is

---

[192] There would, however, be a lengthy debate on the topic in the nineteenth century over the use of the phrase *"intuitu fidei,"* or election "in view of faith." This debate continues today.

[193] Arand, Kolb, and Nestingen, *Lutheran Confessions*, 211–15.

[194] Hoenecke, *Lutheran Dogmatics*, 3:52.

unchangeable (*immutabilis*) in will and essence" (FC SD XI.75). The text takes it as a given that God himself is immutable, so that the immutability of election is proven by means of such a generally accepted truth regarding the divine nature. If God is unchangeable, then so is his will. If election is an expression of the divine will, then this also must be regarded as immutable. Along with its treatment of election, the Formula of Concord also invokes the teaching of divine immutability in its definition of God's law.

The fifth and sixth articles of the Formula of Concord speak directly to the topic of God's law. Article V addresses a debate surrounding how to properly define the law and the gospel. Some theologians included the doctrine of repentance under the rubric of gospel, whereas others (including the authors of the Formula) argued that repentance is brought about by the law. The text outlines the scriptural linguistic variance wherein language of "law" can be used in either a broad or narrow sense, and "gospel" similarly has various uses. In their most proper senses, the law and the gospel are to be strongly distinguished from each other. The gospel is to be identified with God's promise of redemption, and the law with God's demands.

With regard to this proper definition of the law, the Formula describes law as the "immutable will of God" (FC SD V.17). Contrary to some later Lutheran formulations, the second-generation reformers were explicit in their rejection of voluntarism.[195] The law is not an arbitrary set of demands which God established for a time; it is a reflection of the divine essence. As God is eternal, so is the law. As God himself is immutable, so is his will—as expressed in the law—immutable. This is also the reasoning behind the defense of the law in its third use for the Christian in Article VI. If the law is unchangeable, then it is the duty of the human creature at all times to obey it. To do the law is to walk "in accordance with the eternal and immutable will of God" (FC SD VI.3). The doctrine of divine immutability stands firmly as the ground upon which the distinction between law and gospel is built.

There are then these three references to immutability in the Formula of Concord. They do not explain the doctrine of immutability, but assume it. As

---

[195] For a critique of the voluntarist approach, see Cooper, *Lex Aeterna*.

later authors explained theology in a more systematic way, this affirmation of God's immutable nature would be given the in-depth treatment that the topic received from earlier medieval theologians.

The Reformed Confessions

Unlike the Lutheran tradition, the Reformed church as a whole does not simply have one set of confessions of faith. Because of that, we can examine a broader range of documents testifying to accepted ideas regarding the divine nature. Importantly, the immutability of God appears throughout these confessions from different times and places. As did the Lutheran Reformers, Reformed theologians retained the classical Christian teaching regarding God's unchangeable nature.

The Westminster Standards explicitly affirm immutability in a number of places. In its comprehensive listing of divine attributes, God's being "immutable" is included (WCF 2.1). Further, the same article also speaks of the divine will as immutable. Like Article XI of the Formula of Concord, the Westminster Confession applies immutability to both God's essence and his will. This is also apparent in the following section which, like the Formula, ties God's immutable will to the nature of predestination. For the Westminster divines, God has ordained all things "unchangeably" (WCF 3.1). Further, the number of both the elect and the damned according to the decree is "unchangeably designed" (WCF 3.4). This is part of God's "immutable purpose" (WCF 3.5). These statements are also reiterated in the Westminster Larger Catechism (WLC 7, 13).

Along with the Westminster Confession, the Dutch Three Forms of Unity also contain affirmations of God's immutable nature. Though the Heidelberg Catechism's discussion of the divine nature is brief and not explicit about immutability (Q. 26–28), the Belgic Confession refers to God as "unchangeable" in its first article.[196] Divine immutability is further seen through the unchangeable nature of God's decree of election (Article 16). The Canons of Dort, written as a response to the Remonstrant movement, contend similarly that election is due to "God's unchangeable purpose" (Article 7).[197] Thus, two of the three central Dutch Reformed documents affirm immutability.

It should be pointed out that the practical use of the doctrine of immutability differs significantly in the Lutheran and Reformed traditions, as is apparent in these confessional statements. As with other doctrines, the Lutheran church generally applies the teaching of immutability within the context of law and gospel. Discussions of the law tend to invoke this doctrine, as God's demands upon us are not something that shift which we can escape from, or somehow diminish through acts of works-righteousness. Rather, God's righteous law hands over all of us at all times. Further, immutability is used in its gospel application as affirmation that God's saving will cannot change, thereby providing assurance to the sinner that God has, does, and will always desire redemption. Reformed discussions of immutability often arise within the context of the general nature of God's decree over both good and evil, with a particular emphasis on predestination and reprobation.

Conclusion: Protestant Consensus

Though the two great branches of the Reformation differ on several significant points, the Lutheran and Reformed confessions are united in their affirmation of God's immutability. For both traditions, this differentiates the divine essence from God's ever-changing creation. Further, God's will is unchangeable. The extent of God's saving will was (and remains) a point of divergence. However, the relationship of God's will to his nature—along

---

[196] This language is taken from the English translation used by the United Reformed Churches in North America: https://threeforms.org/the-belgic-confession/.

[197] See https://threeforms.org/canons-of-dort/.

with the necessary immutability of both—was not. This is further clarified in the development of this doctrine in later Protestant theological texts.

Gerhard on God's Immutability

As with each of the divine attributes discussed in this volume, Johann Gerhard serves as the representative figure of the post-Reformation Lutheran tradition on the subject. Following his treatment of God's eternity, Gerhard formulates a strong doctrine of God's immutable essence and will through an exposition of Scripture and citations from various patristic sources. As with simplicity, Gerhard also contends that God's immutability can be discovered by way of natural revelation, as is evident in philosophical proofs for the doctrine.

Gerhard contends that if God is *actus purus* (which was central to his earlier exposition of simplicity), he is devoid of potentiality and thus cannot be changed.[198] He further explains this lack of change by defining types of change which rational creatures experience. First, a thing can change with regard to its existence. It can come into being from nothing, or it can cease to be. Such cannot be true of God, in whom there is an identity between essence and existence. Second, a thing can experience a change in place. This cannot occur in God, as the divine nature is omnipresent. Further, the divine presence is a repletive presence rather than a local one. This means that wherever the divine essence is, there is not only a part of but the entirety of the divine essence. Third, the quality or quantity of particular accidents can change in creatures. Because of God's simplicity, he has no accidental qualities and thus cannot experience this kind of change. Fourth, rational creatures can have changes in their intellectual apprehension. Someone might gain knowledge or come to correct a previous understanding of a subject. As the divine nature is omniscient, God cannot experience such intellectual shifts. Fifth, a rational creature can experience a change of will.

---

[198] Gerhard, *God and Trinity*, 148.

One might have an idea of what to do and then change that decision based on the gaining of new knowledge or a changing of circumstances. God, however, is always consistent with his own immutable will. In short, each of the five ways in which rational creatures experience change is contradictory to God's nature.

After citing figures such as Hilary, Augustine, and John of Damascus to demonstrate the patristic consensus on immutability, Gerhard responds to some arguments held out against the doctrine.[199] In a reading of Gerhard's opponents, it is rather remarkable how consistent the arguments against immutability have been in the last four hundred years. The three groups that Gerhard opposes here are Manicheans, some Remonstrants, and the Socinians. He also poses a challenge to Calvinists, who Gerhard claims are inconsistent in their affirmation of divine immutability.

Conrad Vorstius, the opponent whom Gerhard devotes the most time to, was a successor to Jacob Arminius at Leyden University.[200] Though initially praised by other Protestants for his thorough responses to the Roman Catholic theologian Robert Bellarmine, he soon came under suspicion for a number of his heterodox theological views. Among such heterodox views was his approach to the nature of God that Gerhard critiques here. As a Remonstrant, Vorstius opposed the Calvinist insistence upon the immutability of an eternal decree. In his formulation of God's decree, Vorstius contended that God's actions in time often are done in opposition to his eternal will. For example, God's decree included the destruction of the Israelites after their worshiping of the golden calf. However, through Moses's intercession, Yahweh relents from this decision and spares the people. God, for Vorstius, is absolutely free, even to contradict his own will. This freedom is exercised in God's mutualistic dealings with his creatures.

Gerhard identifies the fundamental problem with Vorstius's view in his separation of the divine will from the divine essence. As Gerhard summarizes, the classical orthodox approach contends that "God's will is

---

[199] Ibid., 148–49.

[200] Shriver, "Orthodoxy and Diplomacy," 449–74.

nothing else but God who wills, that is, the very essence of God."[201] For Vorstius, God's will is accidental, rather than essential. This allows him to posit a divine essence which is simple and unchangeable with a free and changeable will as a separable aspect of God.

In response to this separation of God's essence from God's will, Gerhard uses the same threefold distinction in the divine decree promoted by Mastricht as mentioned in the previous chapter.[202] The first way in which the decree is to be understood is in the act of decreeing (identical with the divine essence). Second, this decree is to be understood actively, as a statement or decree is issued from the divine essence just as a king's decree would come out of his mouth or pen. This, for Gerhard, is not something which exists within God actually as distinct from his essence. It is to be understood metaphorically. Third is the decree with respect to its object that is outside of God. Because God's will interacts with mutable and complex creatures, the divine will has multiple effects. Though God's will is singular in his essence, it is experienced through a multiplicity of acts. What appears to be mutability in the exercise of the divine will is not related to God, but to the creature. For example, God's relenting over punishing a particular group of people is due to a change in those people: a repentant heart, the intercession of a mediatorial figure, or the like, rather than a mutability in the divine essence itself.

There are three important challenges to immutability which Gerhard addresses here: God's act of creation, the incarnation, and the biblical testimony to God's repentance. Each of these merits some interaction, as they continue to be the primary points of challenge to the traditional doctrine today.

According to the doctrine of creation *ex nihilo*, creation moved from a state of non-existence to existence. This seems to imply that God himself transitioned in some way from not-Creator to Creator. How could God be the Creator before such an act ever occurred in the first place? I will

---

[201] Gerhard, *God and Trinity*, 150.

[202] Ibid.

put aside the question of time for now, as to whether there really was a time before creation, or a "when" in which one could even identify God as something other than Creator in the first place. Such will be addressed in the chapter on atemporality. Assuming that it is valid to even speak in such a way, one could say that prior to creation, God did not have the property of "being a Creator," and then he did gain the property of "being a Creator." This certainly sounds like a clear instance of change with regard to the divine nature.

This would be the case if the doctrine of immutability were making a claim about the lack of any changing relations between God and creation. It is not, and this again shows the inadequacy of simply speaking in categories of property. Gerhard explains this connection between God and creatures by citing the scholastic distinction between the active and passive aspects of creation.[203] Actively, creation is "the divine action itself," meaning that it consists in God's active potency in actualizing the existence of things outside of himself.[204] Passively, creation refers to that which the creature has received from God—namely, its being. In short, the act of creation makes changes *outside of the divine essence*, not to God's own nature.

The incarnation is perhaps more of a difficulty because of the nature of a personal and hypostatic union between God and the human nature. Socinus leveled this criticism of immutability, and contemporary thinkers continue to promote such an idea as inconsistent with classical theism.[205] The response to this charge remains essentially the same as the previous point. When it is confessed that God became man in the person of Jesus, this does not mean that the divine nature became something other than itself. The divine essence retained its own nature even while hypostatically united to the impersonal humanity of Christ. The details of this are reserved for a future volume in this series, on Christology.

The final point, which is the most common objection (and is dealt with

---

[203] Ibid., 152–53.

[204] Ibid., 153.

[205] Ogonowski, "Faustus Socinus," 195–210.

more thoroughly below), is that God appears to change his mind at various times in the biblical narrative. Gerhard admits that Scripture does speak about divine repentance, but he questions what such a statement actually means. There are essentially two options: either repentance is used properly, or it is intended metaphorically.[206] If it is used properly, then God is not immutable. If it is used metaphorically, then this is an instance of God's communication via analogy. For Gerhard, there are sufficient reasons to adopt the latter view.

If repentance is used univocally in reference to God, then one can extrapolate from human examples of repentance what the biblical authors mean when attributing such a thing to God. In defining repentance in its normal human usage, Gerhard refers to it as "grief that comes from one's own actions done by mistake of the mind or by a weakness or inconstancy of the will or a changeability of emotions."[207] He then further defines these causes of repentance. First, people are ill informed about the results of their actions, and then due to such intellectual weakness, are sorry for a decision made. Second, the human will sometimes makes decisions that are inconsistent with goodness or truth and then later regrets those actions. Third, humans, in their weakness, make bad choices which they feel grief over later. Fourth, human emotions constantly shift, and things are sometimes done out of an impulse of emotion rather than a reasoned consideration of outcomes. Since repentance necessarily arises out of these areas of weakness, and God has no such weaknesses, this language therefore *must* be used metaphorically rather than literally.

The treatment in Gerhard is representative of later authors such as Calov, Quenstedt, and Hollaz, who all vigorously affirm God's immutable essence against the Socinians and some Remonstrants.[208] It would later be challenged from within the Lutheran tradition of the nineteenth century and in an even more robust manner within the so-called theology of hope of the

---

[206] Gerhard, *God and Trinity*, 153.

[207] Ibid.

[208] Preus, *Post-Reformation Lutheranism*, 2:100–103.

twentieth century. Prior to examining the biblical evidence and challenges to this teaching, we examine a prominent thinker in the later Reformed tradition who defended divine immutability against its detractors: Herman Bavinck.

Herman Bavinck on Immutability

In recent years, the Dutch Reformed theologian Herman Bavinck (1854–1921) has grown considerably in influence.[209] A contemporary of Abraham Kuyper, Bavinck developed a rigorous theological system which was based upon classical Reformed thought, while engaging with the rising theological liberalism of his day. With regard to our current study, Bavinck stands out as an example of a theologian who remained committed to defending classical theism in an age when those theological propositions were increasingly challenged.

Like Gerhard, Bavinck recognizes that there are statements in Scripture which seem, at first glance, to imply movement in God.[210] He creates, his presence moves from place to place, and he changes his attitude toward various peoples. Bavinck also mentions the fact of the incarnation, which appears to be a rather significant change to the divine nature. Alongside of this, however, Scripture also confesses God's unchangeability in a number of places (Mal. 3:6, James 1:17). Thus, also like Gerhard, Bavinck contends that these instances of change in God are not to be read literally, but as anthropomorphisms. These statements do refer to actual change, but not within the divine essence. Instead, change occurs "around, about, and outside of" God.[211] God enters into relations with creatures, and can even do so to an infinite extent, but in such a way that it does not hamper his own unchangeable nature.

---

[209] Eglinton, *Bavinck*.

[210] Bavinck, *Reformed Dogmatics*, 2:153.

[211] Ibid., 158.

In a literal sense, then, God's essence is purely immutable. In fact, Bavinck states rather boldly that "if God were not immutable, he would not be God."[212] This is no minor doctrinal point. For the Dutch thinker, the very distinction between God and creation "hinges on the contrast between being and becoming."[213] Immutability is definitional to the Christian conception of God. Bavinck stands firmly within the Platonic tradition in his affirmation of the supremacy of being over becoming. He praises the Greek philosophical tradition as having supremacy over mythology in its understanding of God's immutable nature and will. Bavinck argues that Aristotle was correct to posit God as the unmoved mover.[214] Further, he uses the popular Thomistic phrase that God is *actus purus*. God is not a mixture of actuality and potentiality as creatures are, but is instead pure act. Bavinck further argues that God's immutability is implied in the Christian conception of God as the absolute. One who is absolute need not (indeed cannot) grow or change.[215]

This consistency of being that Bavinck defends refers not only to God's essence, but also to his will and knowledge. Bavinck echoes Gerhard's criticisms of Vorstius, as he contends that there can be no divorce between essence and will, so that immutability only has reference to the former. God's will is one with his essence.

As this broad overview of the doctrine of immutability has shown the foundational principles of the classical theistic notion, we now move on to examining the biblical data regarding God's relationship to change.

---

[212] Ibid., 154.

[213] Ibid., 156.

[214] Ibid., 154.

[215] Ibid., 157–58.

The Biblical Witness

Interpreters have generally explained immutability in its biblical context in a twofold manner: the immutability of God's essence, and the immutability of God's will and purpose. Here, we examine first the divine essence, and second, the revealed will that flows from this essence. Some of the key texts used by theologians to defend the classical view are addressed here.

Psalm 102:25–27

> *Of old You laid the foundation of the earth,*
>   *And the heavens are the work of Your hands.*
> *They will perish, but You will endure;*
> *Yes, they will all grow old like a garment;*
> *Like a cloak You will change them,*
> *And they will be changed.*
> *But You are the same,*
> *And Your years will have no end.*

This text is one of the complaint psalms, in which the psalmist is in the midst of a time of great trial.[216] He likens his life to smoke and his heart to withering grass (Ps. 102:3–4). Human life, as part of creation, is changing and temporary. This is contrasted with God, whose essence remains the same unto eternity. It is precisely in the difference between change and constancy that creation differs from the Creator. Note also that this contrast identifies God as one who is the agent of change ("You will change them"), though he himself remains without mutability ("You are the same"). One might even say that the psalmist identifies God as an unmoved mover.

---

[216] Kurtz, *No Shadow of Turning*, 126–27.

Malachi 3:6

For I am the Lord, I do not change.

This statement from the prophet Malachi seems to be a rather straightforward affirmation of divine immutability. In its most concise definition, immutability means that God does not change, and that is precisely what the text says. Nonetheless, in order to avoid the charge of mere proof-texting, it is worthwhile to examine the context of the prophet's statement.

This third chapter in the last of the prophetic books of the Old Testament has generally been understood in Christian interpretation to be a prophecy of the ministry of John the Baptist. God would send a messenger to prepare the way for his own coming via the incarnation (Mal. 3:1). Along with the coming of John and then subsequently the Messiah is judgment likened to a refiner's fire (Mal. 3:2). This includes God's condemnation of wickedness as outlined by Malachi, but also God's ultimate deliverance for Israel. The condemnation of the law leads to redemption through the gospel. It is in the midst of this gospel application that the phrase "I do not change" appears. It is immediately followed by, "Therefore you are not consumed, O sons of Jacob" (Mal. 3:6). It is because of God's unchanging nature that his promise to redeem Israel remains sure.

The way in which this statement (among others) is dealt with by those who do not affirm God's ontological immutability is to point out that because the context is God's faithfulness to Israel, the statement simply refers to the unchangeable nature of divine faithfulness.[217] It is certainly to be granted that Malachi is not presenting a systematic theological treatise on the divine nature here, and that it is indeed God's faithfulness to his promises that is primarily in view. Nonetheless, the text simply does not say, "my promises do not change," but "*I* do not change" (emphasis mine). It is ontological immutability which serves as the groundwork for the immutability of divine faithfulness. It is precisely *because* God cannot change in essence that we

---

[217] Ibid., 176–83.

therefore trust that he cannot take back his promises. Mutabilists claim to affirm God's faithful consistency but simultaneously remove the foundation upon which such a conviction stands.

James 1:17

Every good gift and every perfect gift is from above, and comes down from the Father of lights, with whom there is no variation or shadow of turning.

As with the previous passage, James uses the doctrine of God's immutability in order to encourage his readers with the consistency of divine promises. Anything good that is received in this life is a gift of God, who is referred to as the "Father of lights." This phrase is not used elsewhere in the New Testament, but seems to be a reference to the stars. A traveler can always rely on the stability and consistency of stars to remain in their places.[218] Regardless of the change or decay that happens on earth, these sources of light continue to perform their role in the same manner. God is the Father of lights, meaning that he is the ultimate source of light. This is possibly an allusion to the creation week of Genesis 1, in which God serves as the light of creation even prior to the making of the sun and moon.

As this source of light, God is without any shadow or change. A lesser light may dim, but the ultimate light cannot. This further serves as a powerful illustration of how something can remain unchanged yet have a profound impact upon things outside of it. The light of the sun, for instance, is not in any way affected by the rotation of the earth. However, the earth itself is impacted by its own relationship to the light and heat of the sun through its own motion. God does not receive anything from us, as he has the fullness of being in himself. Rather, he is the giver of all things.

---

[218] See the discussion in Scaer, *James*, 59–60.

We see, again, that ontological immutability is the foundation for the unchangeable nature of God's faithfulness. It is because God is the Father of lights, the unchanging source that gives but does not receive, that humans can and should rely upon his blessings.

Passages on God's Unchanging Purposes

Along with the passages above that speak to the divine nature are a number of texts that deal with the changeless nature of God's will and purpose. Some examples are included here. Psalm 33 speaks of the everlasting nature of God's counsels (Ps. 33:11). This stands in stark contrast to the will of earthly rulers, whose plans are often thwarted (Ps. 33:10). This same contrast is made in Proverbs 19, where it is said that human plans falter, but God's counsels always remain (Prov. 19:21). When God declares Christ's priestly role in the order of Melchizedek, this—as part of that unchanging counsel—is a sure promise (Ps. 110:4). This is reiterated in the Book of Hebrews (Heb. 7:20–21). Further, other places in Scripture speak about God's attributes as unchanging, attributes such as his kindness (Is. 54:10) and his wrath (John 3:36).

Craig Carter has convincingly demonstrated that the prophecies of Isaiah are a foundational component to the biblical testament of the immutability of God and his purposes. Even more broadly, these texts are a core element to the conception of classical theism as a whole in the Old Testament.[219] Regarding the immutability of God's promises and will, the prophet Isaiah portrays the then-coming exile not as a random happenstance, but as a divinely orchestrated punishment upon the nation of Israel (Is. 6:11–12). God's plans for Israel cannot be thwarted, regardless of what other false prophets might claim. If Yahweh has determined it, it will come to pass.

As Carter notes, the often discussed naming of King Cyrus in Isaiah 44:28

---

[219] Carter, *Contemplating God*, 147–74.

is a key part of Isaiah's argument.[220] After Isaiah's prophecies regarding Israel's coming exile from the land, the prophet promises God's eventual act of redemption by which God would use the Persian king Cyrus to allow the Jewish people to return to the land of Israel. Unlike many other prophetic texts, Isaiah gets so specific as to name the individual whom God would use to fulfill his promise. The text is so clear that scholars have argued that the name Cyrus must have been added after the fact to the text. This is what is often referred to as *vaticinum ex eventu* (a prophecy written after the fact). As a supernaturalist, I have no reason to doubt the validity of the prophecy as original to Isaiah, especially as no manuscript or textual evidence has demonstrated otherwise. With this being the case, then, assuming that this text is actually from Isaiah, the specific naming of this king is a defining element of Isaiah's claims that God really is the sovereign Lord of all history. God does not merely direct the broad scope of world events, or prophesy by means of an educated guess; he has an unchangeable plan which is so secure and specific that even the specific individuals involved can be named one hundred years prior to the events themselves.

The naming of Cyrus does not stand alone, but is part of a poem that extends from Isaiah 44:24 to 44:28. The poem begins with God's self-identification as universal Creator. He is not just a tribal deity alongside of others, but he is the Lord of all the earth. God stretches out the heavens "alone," and has made the earth "by Myself" (Is. 44:24). It is this sovereign power expressed through God's identification as sole Creator that sets the precedent for the validity of God's words spoken through his prophets. God will always perform the works which he sends his messengers to proclaim (Is. 44:26). This Creator's will for Israel is certain and unchanging, as he is sole Sovereign over the events of history. The naming of Cyrus then appears at the end as a testimony to God's infallible plans and knowledge.

This is merely a section of the prophet which demonstrates immutability, but these convictions are clear throughout the text. Though I reject the idea that Jewish monotheism was a mere development of the later prophetic

---

[220] Ibid., 157.

tradition without precedent in earlier Old Testament sources, critical scholars are right that the Book of Isaiah is more explicitly monotheistic than most other texts in the Old Testament canon.[221] As Isaiah largely has a polemical purpose (though not exclusively that), he consistently distinguishes Yahweh from ancient Near Eastern pantheons of deities. He does this in both excluding any other being from claims of deity, and by exalting the power, unity, and unchangeable nature of God and his purposes. Thus, the text above is far clearer within the context of the entirety of the Book of Isaiah, and the text from the prophet as a whole is perhaps the clearest biblical portrait of the immutability of God.

God Does Not Repent

The final texts to be dealt with here are those which speak against God's identification with human repentance. Proponents of divine mutability consistently point to the various instances of God changing his mind or shifting his actions in response to something that humans do or say. It is often stated that it is they who are simply taking the texts at face value, and that classical theists impose Greek ideas of being upon the text. I contend, however, that the hermeneutical method used to argue for immutability is the same as that which Christians use to affirm accepted truths like God's immateriality. Scripture often attributes physical attributes to God, such as arms (Jer. 21:5), nostrils (Ex. 15:8), and wings (Ps. 91:4). Yet none but the strictest biblical literalist believes that God the Father actually has such physical properties. Because of other clear testimonies to immateriality (John 4:24), interpreters acknowledge that such physical attributes are simply anthropomorphisms. In the same manner, if clear texts affirm that God does *not* change, this should cause us to read texts which speak otherwise in

---

[221] I attribute this to the reality of progressive revelation, rather than a naturalistic development of human religion. There are, however, still points in which monotheism is clear in the *Tanak*, such as in the creation account and the Shema.

a similarly metaphorical manner.

Numbers 23:19

> *God is not a man, that He should lie,*
> *Nor a son of man, that He should repent.*
> *Has He said, and will He not do?*
> *Or has He spoken, and will He not make it good?*

This section of the Book of Numbers tells the story of Balaam and Balak. Toward the end of the Israelites' forty years of wandering, they had completed successful military engagements with some of the rival kings in the surrounding area. After hearing about these victories, Balak, the king of Moab, calls upon the diviner Balaam to curse Israel and thus protect himself against the Jewish people. God then enters into this engagement by delivering words of prophecy through the mouth of the wicked Balaam. In the first of Balaam's utterances from God, he offers an extensive blessing upon Israel (Num. 23:7–10). Being disappointed in Balaam's actions, Balak once again asks the diviner to curse Israel. It is here that the second utterance from Balaam occurs, which has the text presently under discussion.

In this second of his four prophecies, Balaam proclaims that he cannot take back his blessing toward Israel. The reasoning for this is that God, unlike humans, is unable to relent from his promises. God must always do exactly what he says he will do, as his will cannot change. God will not then allow Balaam to curse his people. Here, the distinction between God and man lies precisely in God's immutable nature. Men repent from their decisions; God does not. Such texts must be read in concert with those often seen as teaching that the divine will can and does change in response to human actions, such as God's seeming relenting over his desire to destroy the children of Israel following the intercession of Moses (Ex. 32:14). The Numbers text proclaims simply that God *cannot* relent from his decisions, and the Exodus text states that God *does* relent from a particular decision. One is forced to either posit a contradiction between the two texts or recognize that the Exodus narrative was an instance of anthropomorphic accommodation. In the narrative, Moses typologically prefigures Christ in his mediatorial role that saves the people of Israel from destruction. God did not actually intend the annihilation of his people only to have his mind changed by Moses's plea.[222]

1 Samuel 15:29

> *And also the Strength of Israel will not lie nor relent. For He is not a man, that He should relent.*

This statement arises after the failure of King Saul to kill King Agag. God expresses his disappointment in Saul's disobedience regarding this matter, and claims that "I greatly regret that I have set up Saul as king" (1 Sam. 15:11). He then calls the prophet Samuel to speak as his mouthpiece to the king. Through Samuel, God proclaims to Saul that he has taken away his right as king over the nation of Israel. Though Saul asked for forgiveness for his disobedience, Samuel told Saul that it was impossible for God now to reinstate Saul into this position since God cannot relent from his promises. God must always do what he says. Further, the text then comments again that "the Lord regretted that he had made Saul king over Israel" (1 Sam. 15:35).

If all of the phrases used throughout this text that refer to God's actions are understood literalistically, one is forced into a contradiction. It begins with a statement about God's regret in putting Saul in the position of king, and then ends with the reiteration of this same thought. In the middle of these two statements we are informed that God cannot relent from his decisions, because to relent is definitional to humans rather than God. If such is the case, how can it be that the text states twice that God relented from his

---

[222] Kurtz, *No Shadow of Turning*, 123.

decision of making Saul king of Israel? One might posit that the author contradicts himself in just a few verses, or that the text which denies God's ability to repent was some kind of later theological interpolation made to correct the implications of the text (not that there is any evidence of such a thing). If one isn't willing to go such a route, it simply must be admitted that one of these statements must not be taken in its most literal sense.

As much as the proponents of mutability in God claim that they read the text in a far more straightforward manner than the supposedly Greek philosophy-infused defenders of immutability, they too reject the clear meaning of a series of texts. The mutabilist is forced to say that God actually *does* relent, and that the Lord *does* change, in opposition to verses which blatantly state the opposite. This is of course is qualified heavily, so that it is stated that some things about God don't change (i.e., his faithfulness) but that change remains nonetheless. The fact is that *everyone* has one set of texts which they read in a manner that is less than straightforward. One can either claim that "I do not change" and "I do not relent" really mean "My faithfulness does not change," or one can acknowledge that statements of divine repentance are to be understood analogically as anthropomorphic accommodation.

Contrary to my thesis, many thinkers have opted for the former approach in recent years, arguing for a less than clear understanding of the above proof texts for immutability. They have presented a variety of reasons for their rejection of strong immutability—both scriptural and philosophical. Some of these challenges are now addressed, beginning with the work of Isaak A. Dorner.

Challenges to Immutability

As with the other classical attributes, challenges to immutability have arisen from a variety of areas in the church. Open theists reject the thesis that God operates even with an infallible knowledge of the future, with himself being captive to the passing of time (though by divine choice rather than by necessity). Process theologians found their system upon God's changeability and his continual progression. Wolfhart Pannenberg, Robert Jenson, and Bruce McCormick all posit that in some way, God's acts in the divine economy are determinative of his own being. Evangelical theologians like John Frame, Bruce Ware, and Scott Oliphint reject strong immutability in order to defend God's real interaction with creatures. To be clear, nearly everyone affirms that there is *something* about God which does not change (and do this to varying degrees), but this immutable something has increasingly been identified with God's faithfulness or character rather than his being.

Though many of these challenges have already been in view throughout this chapter, here I address some objections which have not yet been directly addressed. I have chosen to interact primarily with the writings of Isaak August Dorner.

Isaak August Dorner is, without any question, the most influential figure in recent challenges to divine immutability. Though now a century and a half old, his writing on divine immutability laid the groundwork for many later developments in theology—perhaps most notably that of Karl Barth, who cited Dorner as a significant influence on his theology proper.[223] These themes were then developed through the theology of hope, which expanded upon Barth's actualistic ontology (though with a stronger focus on eschatology).[224] Nearly every contemporary critique of the classical doctrine has its roots here. In most respects, the arguments put forth today have not significantly deviated from those set forth by Dorner, and—in my view—his treatment remains the most robust defense of divine mutability. It is for these reasons that I have chosen this work over the many more modern texts which make essentially the same points.[225] Throughout, I reference more contemporary authors who reiterate these arguments.

---

[223] As cited by Robert R. Williams in his intro to Dorner, *Divine Immutability*, 4–5.

[224] On Barth's actualism, see Cassidy, *God's Time for Us*.

[225] For more modern treatments, see Peckham, *Divine Attributes*; Sanders, *God Who Risks*.

Dorner's Ideological Context

Before exploring the arguments of the text itself, some things must be said about the historical circumstances in which Dorner wrote. There are two ideological movements which dominated debate in the German academy at this time—one theological, and one philosophical. The former was the question of Christological kenoticism, in which it was posited that the divine nature of Christ underwent some kind of change in the hypostatic union.[226] The second is the popularization of Hegel's idealism as truth began to be sought as the result of a progressive historical development rather than in the unchanging being of classical philosophy.[227] Both of these play a role in Dorner's thought.

Nineteenth-century theologians had to grapple with the development of naturalistic critiques of religion along with the beginnings of Protestant liberalism with Friedrich Schleiermacher. The existence of the supernatural was no longer taken for granted by historians and scientists, and this meant that it was imperative for theologians to either defend classical orthodox supernaturalism against the consensus of the academy, or to find new theological systems that fit within these ideological developments in Europe. One of these developments was the publication of lives of Jesus, beginning with Richard Strauss's *The Life of Jesus: Critically Examined*.[228] This work, and those following it, sought to give a sort of biography of Jesus without the supernatural elements explained in the Gospels. These historians contended that the Gospel narratives were to be treated mythologically, as texts with a basis in a historical figure, but with layers of early mythological development that explains the miraculous in the life of Christ. The character who emerges in these biographies is a human Jesus who has no conception of his own divinity. Ideas of Christ's two natures and the hypostatic union were the

---

[226] Evans, *Exploring Kenotic Christology*.

[227] Hegel, *Phenomenology of Spirit*.

[228] For an overview of the first phase of this movement, see Schweitzer's classic work *The Quest of the Historical Jesus*.

product of the development of dogma in the later Christian church.

It was out of this emphasis upon Jesus's humanity, and particularly his lack of knowledge of certain events and the supposed failed prophecy of the eschaton (Matt. 24), that theologians began to reconsider the relationship between the two natures in Christ's state of humiliation. The idea known as kenoticism posited that Strauss was correct in his portrayal of a very human Christ, but that this did not contradict orthodox belief in the full divinity of the eternal Logos. A variety of theories began to emerge wherein it was proposed that at the incarnation, Christ divested himself of his divine attributes of omnipotence, omniscience, and the like. More moderate views, like those of Gottfried Thomasius, grounded their theology on the Lutheran view of the communication of attributes in Christ. They argued that along with the divinity operating through Christ's humanity, so does Christ's humanity change the attributes of the divinity of the Son in some way during the humiliation. Other more extreme views, like that of Wolfgang Friedrich Gess, rejected classical Chalcedonian Christology altogether, speaking of the Son as only human at the incarnation.[229] Dorner's work relies heavily on these debates. While he himself is not a kenotic theologian, Dorner argues that those theologians are correct in their affirmation of change in God. For Dorner, however, this is not merely tied to the incarnation, but to the divine nature itself.

The second prominent ideological shift in Germany that impacted Dorner's perspective was the publication of Hegel's *Phenomenology of Spirit* in 1807. Though a thorough exposition of Hegel's thought is beyond the scope of this chapter, there are some basic points which are relevant to the move away from divine immutability. In classical Platonic idealism, that which is the most real is the realm of ideas. These ideas are both eternal and without change. Hegel retained Plato's emphasis on the reality of ideas, but rejected the ontological superiority of being over becoming. Like his Greek precursor Heraclitus, Hegel posited becoming as the ultimate reality.

---

[229] These are simplified summaries. The volume on Christology in this series will expand upon this debate in more detail.

History, for Hegel, is a process of change often summarized as the steps of thesis, antithesis, and synthesis.[230] In his earlier theological writings, Hegel posits a doctrine of the Trinity which accords with such an idea.[231] These ideas impacted nearly every discipline in one way or another. Marx and Engels developed their political philosophy as a materialist version of Hegel's system, and the rise of Darwinian thought brought about a scientific basis for such a focus on reality as a process of becoming.

Theology, similarly, began to speak more explicitly about change and process; this led to a view of God who is capable of change in his own being, sometimes as part of the broader historical process of growth. In its most extreme form, this developed into the process theism of Alfred North Whitehead. Out of Whitehead's work came the movements of both process philosophy and process theology.[232] While Dorner is not strictly Hegelian to the extreme of some of these later authors, it is undoubted that German idealism lay behind some of his critiques of classical theism.

Dorner's Argument

Though Dorner treats patristic and medieval doctrine in his text, this overview here begins with his discussion of the Reformation and post-Reformation contexts. In Dorner's telling, the Reformation principle of justification by faith contained within it "the seed of a new doctrine of God," but that these principles were not consistently developed.[233] In the Protestant scholastic view of history, a classical patristic and medieval theology proper was rightly inherited by the reformers, and areas of divergence were in the realms of soteriology and the nature of church authority. For Dorner, there

---

[230] To be clear, Hegel himself does not use this schema explicitly, and there has been some debate regarding its usefulness as a summary of the German idealist.

[231] Hegel, *Early Theological Writings*.

[232] Whitehead, *Process and Reality*.

[233] Dorner, *Divine Immutability*, 99.

was a broader shift with the rise of Protestantism from the area of ontology to an ethical conception of Christianity. The reformers, in contrast to the medievals, viewed God through the lens of personhood rather than pure being. Nonetheless, Dorner acknowledged that the post-Reformation era did retain the basic elements of the medieval doctrine. However, he viewed the doctrine of immutability and other classical attributes as strictures that stop a full-blown ethical-personal doctrine of God from expanding into its fully developed form. It was only in the nineteenth century that this uniquely Protestant doctrine of God would develop.

Dorner cites Gerhard and Quenstedt as representative of the Protestant scholastic adoption of Thomistic concepts in their formulation of divine immutability (along with other classical attributes).[234] As is a common critique, Dorner challenges whether the doctrines of the incarnation and creation *ex nihilo* can coherently coexist with strong immutability. He finds Gerhard's and Quenstedt's responses unconvincing, and presses this supposed inconsistency between immutability and these central doctrines of the Christian faith. Further, in order to promote his conception of mutability in opposition to these scholastics, Dorner also challenges the doctrines of simplicity and atemporality. Regarding atemporality, Dorner defines the view of Quenstedt of God's eternity as his "opposition to all succession."[235] This view, for Dorner, means that God's relationship to the temporal world is one of pure contrast. Rather than being immanent in time, God lives in a present in which is the opposite of creaturely experiences of succession. Any view of God in which he acts in mutuality with creatures must, in some way, revise this classical view. For Dorner, a mutable God necessitates a being who exists within historical process.

Dorner's critique of the scholastic approach can be most clearly summarized with his argument that the classical doctrine is guilty of both acosmism (the idea that the physical cosmos does not have any real being in itself)

---

[234] Ibid., 100.

[235] Ibid., 103.

and deism.[236] Dorner's argument begins with a negative evaluation of the scholastic identification between God and his will. Divine simplicity necessitates that God decrees all things, not as separate events in response to creaturely actions, but in one single unified act of will. If this is the case, for Dorner, God can no longer be described via personal acts. This leads to the denial of any real freedom in creatures at all, as they exist only contingently as the result of God's singular eternal act. Scholasticism thus promotes a view of the material external world which relegates it to the realm of shadows, with the only true reality being that which exists in the divine mind. If true reality is found only within the intellect of God (the realm of the forms), then true being is immovable and timeless. Any relational aspect of creatures (and God) is downplayed as secondary, or as shadowy. For Dorner, this is fundamentally incompatible with the reformers' ethical conception of God and also of evil as "contradictory to God," rather than simple non-existence in eternal being.[237] Further, this denial of real being in creatures (as they are mere shadows) conflates all true reality with God, thus leading to the acosmic conclusion.[238]

While I strongly contest the assertion that classic immutability attributes some kind of non-real existence to material reality, some of Dorner's concerns here are not *completely* without warrant. Regarding Dorner's concerns about metaphysical abstraction, there is no question that Scripture defines God as a relational being, and creatures as really encountering him through judgment, redemption, and prayer. Any conception of God which delegates him *merely* to the realm of the metaphysical, and thus does not center itself on the redemptive triune economy as foundational for the creature's knowledge of God, is an unbiblical one. Aristotle, for example, was forced into a deistic position through his reasoning regarding the mind

---

[236] Ibid., 105.

[237] Ibid., 106.

[238] Dorner argues that this acosmism was the reason for Calvinism's strict predestinarianism, as well as a divorce between the realm of the religious and that of the ethical within Protestant lands. Ibid., 133–34.

of the unmoved mover, concluding that God was unconcerned with the world, spending eternity in an act of self-contemplation. A mere uncritical adoption of Aristotle (or other Greeks) into a Christian framework would be a disastrous move. The question here is whether the Protestant scholastics are actually guilty of such a thing, or if they were able to consistently retain both the ethical and personal nature of God and the classical commitment to immutability.

Much of the discussion here (and not just in Dorner) centers around Aquinas's denial of God's real relations with creatures. This has often been cited as a definitive point at which Thomas's commitment to Aristotle overrides the clear biblical data. If the biblical God is clearly anything, he is relational. The theologian is left with a choice: is God relational (as in Scripture), or does he have no real relations with creatures (as Aquinas claims)? In order to address this supposed dilemma, it is important to define exactly what Thomas means by his statement that God has no real relation with creatures.

The topic of relations appears in Question 13 of the *Summa Theologiae*, which addresses the use of the divine names. Under the heading "Whether names which imply relation to creatures are predicated of God temporally," Aquinas responds to objections with the following:

> Since therefore God is outside the whole order of creation, and all creatures are ordered to Him, and not conversely, it is manifest that creatures are really related to God Himself; whereas in God there is no real relation to creatures, but a relation only in idea, inasmuch as creatures are referred to Him. Thus there is nothing to prevent these names which import relation to the creature from being predicated of God temporally, not by reason of any change in Him, but by reason of the change of the creature; as a column is on the right of an animal, without change in itself, but by change in the animal.[239]

One can certainly see how this statement would appear to be at odds with Yahweh as portrayed interacting with his people. However, the initial objections one may have fade rather quickly when some important points regarding Aquinas's thought are clarified.

First, the topic under discussion is immutability rather than a general treatment of God's interaction with people. Aquinas is asking whether using a name such as "Creator" is proper, since such a thing speaks about something which is partially dependent upon something apart from himself: the existence of creation. Does calling God "Creator" imply that God himself is something different prior to or apart from creation? Aquinas argues that it is proper to use such names (Scripture certainly does), but that this does not imply change in God. With creation *ex nihilo*, the change occurs not in God, but in creation, which goes from non-existence to existence. Second, then, and most importantly, Aquinas is using "real relations" here as a synonym for *a relation by which one is changed*. In other words, this is simply a rejection of mutualism. Nothing in God is actualized by the creature. Third, it is important to note that Aquinas speaks of "real" relations as those which occur among multiple things within the same order of being. As God and man are ontologically distinct, God, as a higher order of being, cannot have such relations with humanity. This absolutely does not mean that God does not interact with creatures, hear prayers, or love. He simply does not do so in a way that effects ontological change in him.

A second problem which is to be addressed is the relationship between God's consequent and antecedent wills in Lutheran theology (which is at least as ancient as John Chrysostom) and how this relates to the identification of God's will as being unchanged by creatures. One can certainly imagine a situation in which the affirmation of the absoluteness of the divine will leads to a strict fatalism, wherein there is no creaturely freedom or responsibility whatsoever. However, none but the most extreme supralapsarian Calvinist would affirm such a conclusion.

---

[239] *Summa*, Part 1, Q. 13.7.

Adolph Hoenecke provides a helpful definition of the classic antecedent/consequent will distinction. He refers to the antecedent will of God as "God's universal loving will that precedes all conduct of people."[240] God wills that all people be saved (2 Pet. 3:9). Not being an absolute universalist, Hoenecke acknowledges that this will is not fulfilled. One must grapple with the question of how it is that an all-powerful God can have a will that is thwarted. While Calvinists argue that God's will is *not* that all would be saved, Lutheran theologians are convinced that this idea is incommensurate with Scripture. In order to explain the reality that only some are saved, the consequent will is posited as "the will that refers to the conduct of people."[241] This consequent will is God's will in accord with human actions. Since God has made his antecedent will resistible according to the creature, he has willed punishment for those who reject his offer of grace.

What Dorner challenges here is not the distinction between the consequent and antecedent wills, but the compatibility between this distinction and classical theistic convictions surrounding simplicity and immutability. For Dorner, if God has to look at any human conduct in order to make a decree, this then makes God's will synthetic. He makes his decree based at least in part upon the actions of free creatures. This means, then, that the divine will is mutable, and therefore either it must be distinct from the divine essence, or the essence is mutable. Thus, in Dorner's estimation, consistency would mandate either some absolute fatalism or a denial of immutability. Dorner opts for the latter.[242]

It must be affirmed again, in response to Dorner, that these distinctions in the divine will are all analogical rather than univocal. In his treatment of the subject, Gerhard reminds his readers that "prescience is attributed to God anthropopathically and according to condescension."[243] God does not literally have one will to save, and then in time see the rejection of sinners,

---

[240] Hoenecke, *Lutheran Dogmatics*, 3:8.

[241] Ibid.

[242] Dorner, *Divine Immutability*, 106.

[243] Gerhard, *Creation and Predestination*, 52.

and then consequently add some secondary will on top of the primary. These distinctions are merely human means by which one is able to grasp, in some way, the inexpressible. In reality, the divine will is singular, as it is with the divine essence. Yet God condescends to speak in sequential language because that is the only means by which human comprehension is possible.

Now we must address Dorner's second accusation regarding the classical teaching of immutability—that it leads to deism. This accusation of deism arises from Dorner's affirmation of succession in God. Throughout history, God begins all sorts of new acts within creation. This is especially true with the act of incarnation, but it is evident throughout the entirety of redemptive history.[244] Dorner rejects the idea that such a reality can be explained only as a change in human receptivity rather than a real change in God and his will. Seemingly, Dorner proposes that if God truly willed creation, redemption, and consummation all within a singular act, then such would all occur simultaneously. Further, he expresses his confusion about the idea that creation itself took six days and was not instead an instantaneous act simultaneous with God's own eternal present.

As his solution to this proposed dilemma, Dorner argues that immutabilists are forced into either one of two positions. First, it might be posited that God's eternal act was not all fulfilled at once because of some hostile force that opposed such a will (that of sinful humans and evil angels). Yet, as Dorner writes, this leads to an essentially Manichean conclusion and also posits human freedom as something in competition with God's own liberty that stops God from fulfilling his eternal will. The other solution is to propose that God *did* finalize his will in one single creative act, yet that this was done through the making of objects with potentialities only to be actualized on their own through natural potentialities. This is deism.

It is unclear why one would be forced into either of these positions as Dorner contends. The singularity of the act of divine willing does not somehow limit God's interaction with the world to one singular *ad extra* act. It is almost as if Dorner portrays God's eternal now as a singular time at

---

[244] Dorner, *Divine Immutability*, 108.

the beginning of creation, whereby if all God's acts are without succession, they must be limited to the historical past. However, this is precisely the opposite of what divine atemporality actually means. God is always acting, because that singular will and act is an eternal one. Though the acts of God are singular in the divine essence itself, they are divided as experienced by God's creation. There is no incongruity between God's one act of willing and his many operations in time throughout history. One need not reject the former proposition to adopt the latter.

This leads to the further critique which has been repeated in recent years that immutability is some kind of "immobility."[245] It is argued that the God of classical theism is some kind of rock-like object with no vitality. Dorner refers to the classical approach to God as a "simple, unmoving, rigid essence."[246] This is contrasted by Dorner and other critics with the living and active God of Holy Scripture. Such a critique would have validity if it were indeed the claim that immutability means inactivity. It does not. Aquinas's definition of God as pure act identifies him as one who is indeed the *most* active of all existences. Creatures only actualize some potentialities at any given time and are thus limited in the amount of activity in which they can be engaged. In contrast to this, as pure act, God's activity is unlimited. In other words, his activity is infinite and eternal. One cannot speak of this always acting, infinite, living God as "rigid" in any meaningful sense whatsoever if the classical definition of immutability is properly understood.

Conclusion

Nearly every argument against a classical understanding of immutability follows one of two lines of argument. First, it is argued that immutability and a relational understanding of God are fundamentally incompatible. Second,

---

[245] Johnson, *Failure of Natural Theology* is a recent example of this argument, though certainly in a less compelling form than Dorner's work.

[246] Dorner, *Divine Immutability*, 141.

critics contend that a biblical realism necessitates a non-anthropomorphic reading about texts that speak of God changing his mind and actions. This latter point usually includes a strong opposition between Greek and Hebrew conceptions of deity. Neither of these arguments provides significant enough reasons to reject the traditional approach. Further, they create a number of additional problems which are not present in the older view.

As has been discussed throughout this chapter, there is a proper caution that one must have in explaining immutability, as such a doctrine is prone to misunderstandings. God is pure actuality, not a totally immovable and unloving rock. He is actively engaged with his creation at each moment, sustaining its existence and providentially guiding all that happens. The Thomistic phrase, echoed by Gerhard, that God has no real relations is perhaps best uttered only within a context wherein the definitions of Aquinas here are carefully set forth, lest one make the assumption that God is not relational in any sense. It is certainly not my proposal that every utterance of Scripture which speaks in mutual language needs to be immediately clarified by a lengthy exposition of immutability. Scripture does not itself do that. However, it is important to lay this groundwork underneath such speech so that it can be understood properly as analogical.

Along with these affirmations that God is unchanging, we must also center our own Christian theological knowledge upon the incarnate Christ, who in some way *does* interact in mutuality according to his human nature. Lest one merely contemplate the divine attributes apart from Christ, the proper Christian attitude is that of the theologian of the cross, who *does* encounter God through his taking upon himself a mutable human nature that faces the common infirmities of humanity—centrally, his taking upon himself the reality of death. However, these truths must be understood incarnationally, rather than read back into the divine nature itself. In Christ, the immutable has become mutable; and yet in doing so, the Son remains immutable according to his divinity.

5

Divine Atemporality

The changing theological landscape regarding God's immutability in the post-Enlightenment period had a strong impact on, among other things, how one understands God's relationship to time. In a classical approach, God exists outside of any temporal dimensions in what is sometimes referred to as an eternal now. As there is no succession in his being, he does not place himself under the confines of past, present, and future. This does not mean that God has no relation to time to any degree, as he does act in and through the temporal world. Yet he stands above it and is unaffected in his own being by temporal happenings.

The modern commitment to the supposed biblical realism of God acting in tandem with his creatures through changing his mind and actions (as found in Dorner and other mutabilists) has led thinkers to reject God's atemporal existence. It is simply an impossibility for God to change his mind through his creaturely relations if he is not temporal in any sense, as this necessitates changing states in God, or a before and after. Like the other divine attributes described in this volume, a significant number of alternative proposals have been offered as to how God relates to time. One is the idea that though God does essentially exist outside of time, he has condescended to his creation in such a way that he has placed himself *within* time (this is the view of open theism). Another view, espoused by some such as Pannenberg and Jenson, posits time as part of God's own essence, and then consequently argues that

God's temporal interactions with creation constitute his own self-identity.

This chapter begins with an overview of the relationship between time and eternity as expressed in Augustine, followed by an overview of how God's eternity is expressed in Protestant scholastic sources. Following this, the biblical texts are examined with relation to this question, and then contemporary challenges and proposals are addressed.

Augustine on Time

The first extensive exposition of God's relationship to time within the early church is in Book XI of Augustine's *Confessions*. This is often cited as the foundational theological text for God's atemporal existence, and it remains influential in contemporary debates on the subject. This part of Augustine's book is a significant departure from the prior sections of this work, which are largely autobiographical in nature. Following the story of his conversion to Christianity, Augustine uses this section to explain some of his most contemplated philosophical questions, which include the manner of creation, God's knowledge, and the nature of time.

The view of time which Augustine proposes is often given the label "presentism," as in his view it is only the present which has real existence. The past has already occurred and therefore no longer is, and the future is not yet. Creatures, therefore, only live within a momentary temporal existence in which the present is the only reality. This momentary nature of human existence leads to a restlessness in the human soul, as one constantly wavers in thought between present, past, and future. Think, for example, of the common human phenomenon of nostalgia, wherein one looks back to the past both with fondness for what was and sadness over what no longer is. The passing of time is a phenomenon of continual loss. Augustine explains that eternity is the converse of this, for all things are simultaneous as there is no passing of time. There is therefore no loss in eternity as there is in time, as there is no change. For the human soul, it is eternity that is longed for, which is why temporal momentary pleasures never truly fulfill.[247]

God exists only in this eternal moment. Augustine refers to God as the "Creator of all times," as he is prior to, and the source of, time.[248] Augustine notes a question that people often ask about how God occupied himself before the creation of the world. For the bishop of Hippo, there is no such thing as "before creation," since the creation of the material world coincides with the making of time itself. There is no before or after to God, and thus there is no time at which God is not Creator. This distinction between time and eternity is, for Augustine, a key component of the distinction between the Creator and the creature. God's eternity is what distinguishes him from created reality, which is always to some degree bound by temporality.

Eternity, in its Augustinian conception, is also explicitly Trinitarian. The North African theologian mentions the *ad intra* reality of the generation of the Son as an eternal act. He cites Psalm 2:7, in which God states, regarding the Son, "today I have begotten you," as proof of this. While the Arians used this text to argue for the Son having a beginning to his existence,[249] Augustine uses his conception of God's eternity to view this text as the description of an eternal act. God's "today" is his eternal present. Therefore, if the begetting of the Son can be explained as occurring in a day, this is not a reference to a human day at all, but to God's eternity. The Father and Son then are co-eternal, but existing outside of the bounds of time.

Augustine further explains that this difference between God and man in connection with time accounts further for the difference between creaturely and divine knowledge. Humans are bound by our temporality in our comprehension of reality. We know the present by a direct apprehension, but the past and future are far more uncertain. Memories are often distorted or forgotten, and the future is only known by way of probable guessing rather than certainty. In contradistinction to this, God has a complete comprehensive knowledge of all things that are. Augustine refers

---

[247] Augustine, *Confessions*, XI.12 (*NPNF*[2] 1).

[248] Ibid., XI.15.

[249] Williams, *Arius*.

to both God's knowledge and foreknowledge here. It is to be noted that "foreknowledge" does not imply that God knows that which is future to him, as there is no future to God. Rather, this is an anthropomorphic use of language which identifies the fact that what is future to us is known already to God, not by prescience, but by the fact that it is already present to him.[250]

These basic affirmations found in Augustine here are reiterated throughout the later Christian tradition in nearly every discussion of God's eternal nature. God does not exist within the confines of time, nor does time exist as part of God's being. Rather, all things are present to him; time is as much a creation of God as is the material world. While Augustine is philosophically oriented in his discussion here, it should also be made clear that there is a consistent citing of Scripture throughout this section of Augustine's work. The bishop wrestles here not just with intellectual quandaries, but with the teaching of the texts of both the Old and New Testaments. The passages cited by Augustine are explored later in this chapter.

Boethius's Definition of Eternity

The early medieval philosopher Boethius follows Augustine's concept of eternity throughout his classic book *The Consolation of Philosophy*. In terms of its impact, this treatment of the subject is at least as important as Augustine's, as Boethius is cited throughout the medieval and modern periods on this point. Aquinas and Anselm (along with many others) rely heavily on this work as foundational for a proper understanding of God's relationship to time, and these treatments inform the explanations present in the Protestant scholastics.

This topic shows up at the end of the work as Boethius discusses the difficulty of reconciling God's foreknowledge and human freedom. Boethius asks: If God infallibly knows all events, can true freedom exist in any real way in creatures? If God has a determinate knowledge of what is going to

---

[250] Augustine, *Confessions*, XI.41.

pass, that implies that the creature cannot make any decision other than that singular one which is known to God. This means that there is no actual free decision-making to the contrary. As important as this question is, we are not focusing here on the entirety of Boethius's answer here. Rather, this present chapter focuses on his explanation of eternity in view of these concerns.

In a concise definition, Boethius explains that eternity is "the possession of endless life whole and perfect at a single moment."[251] Created things exist in transitory moments which quickly pass from one to the next. Like Augustine, Boethius speaks of temporal existence as one of continual loss, as the past is fleeting. Further, one constantly makes decisions in view of the future, but the realities of the future are not actually known, thus leaving us in a place of uncertainty. Temporality, then, is not defined so much by having a beginning or end of existence, but of the partial nature of one's experience and knowledge. Boethius explains that if Plato's view of an always-existing cosmos were correct, this still would not make matter eternal, since matter is still subject to the strictures of the passing of time. God, in opposition to this, is without succession or a passing from present to future.

God's atemporality, for Boethius, is tied to his infinite knowledge. As God's present transcends the divisions of past and future, he knows all things by a direct cognition in a single present act of comprehension. If such a perfect knowledge of all future events exists, how then can one account for creaturely freedom? Boethius uses an analogy from human cognition to explain how perfect divine knowledge and freedom in creatures can coexist. One could, in a single act of viewing, spot both a man walking and the sun rising. These two events differ significantly, as the walking of the man is a self-chosen free act, whereas the rising of the sun is a necessary movement of nature rather than will. Similarly, God's knowledge includes both those events which happen by necessity and those that are the free decisions of creatures. Thus, while it is true that things cannot happen other than how God knows that they will, this does not mean that God directly causes all events without human freedom.

---

[251] Boethius, *Consolation of Philosophy*, Book VI.

Though Boethius's treatment of this subject here is rather brief, it is highly influential. His definition of eternity as the lack of succession in God and the perfection of knowledge in a singular moment is echoed repeatedly by the medieval scholastics and is reiterated in the fathers of Protestant scholasticism.

Thomas Aquinas on Eternity

In his treatment of the subject of divine eternity, Aquinas depends largely upon the two previous figures. However, there are some distinct nuances to his approach, especially in light of Thomas's commitment to Aristotle's view of motion. This section first provides a summary of Thomas's explanation of the eternity of God from the *Summa Contra Gentiles*, and this is then followed with an examination of his responses to various objections in the *Summa Theologia*.

Aquinas grounds God's eternity upon his immutability. If a thing is not eternal, its beginning or ending must be due to some change from potency to act. God, as the unmoved mover, cannot experience change from potency to act. Thus, he must be eternal.[252] Time itself is motion from one thing to another. With such a definition, God cannot be temporal. Further, Thomas explains that any non-eternal thing must pass from non-being to being (or vice versa). If God were not eternal, he would have to pass from non-being to being. This could not occur without a cause, and thus God himself would have a cause outside of himself. In this case, he would not be God. There must, for Aquinas, be one single necessary being who exists eternally who is the first cause of all change in the universe, though himself remaining unchanged. This being is God.

In the *Summa Theologia*, Aquinas counters a variety of objections to his contention that God exists in an eternal moment without succession. A few of the most relevant objections are overviewed here. First, Scripture

---

[252] *Summa* 15.2.

itself seems to attribute past, present, and future to God. Thomas's view of non-succession thus appears to be at odds with the biblical text.[253] This basic contention is at the heart of many critiques of atemporality today. In response, Aquinas points to the fact that God's eternity is not in contradiction with time, but encapsulates all time within itself. Therefore, God *does* in fact exist in past, present, and future, though his own eternal state transcends such limitations. When a text speaks about God doing some kind of act in the past, this does not mean that God is confined to the past, but that the past (as creatures experience it) is encapsulated within God's eternal now.

A second set of objections to Aquinas's proposal are related to the difference between time and eternity. One might argue, against Thomas, that eternity and time are not substantially different from one another. If each refers to some measure of duration, one must be part of the other. As an hour is part of a day, so is time part of eternity which encapsulates all time. In response, Thomas contends that time and eternity *are* substantially different from one another. He rejects the assertion that the difference between time and eternity is simply that time has a beginning and end whereas eternity extends infinitely in both directions. This is important, as here Aquinas speaks against the basic contention of contemporary proposals by mutualists, who often accept a definition of eternity as infinite duration.[254] For Aquinas, this definition would make the difference between time and eternity an accidental, rather than substantial, one—thus blurring the distinction between creature and Creator.

Citing Boethius, Thomas argues that the difference between time and eternity would remain even if the material universe had always existed, as was taught by the Greeks. This means that time and eternity are ontologically distinct, just as creation and Creator are distinct. Thomas defines eternity as "the measure of permanent being" and time as "a measure of movement." If time necessitates movement, and God is unmoved, he cannot be measured by

---

[253] *Summa*, Q. 10, 2. Obj. 4.

[254] Keller, *On the Mystery*.

such means. Eternity, in contrast to time, is a "simultaneous whole," existing at once. Further, to speak of eternity as a measure at all is not really accurate, as God himself cannot be measured due to his infinitude. Due to Thomas's commitment to divine simplicity, it is accurate to say that God's eternity is identical with his essence.

The final point addressed here relates to the difference between eternity and aeviternity. The latter term refers to the state of the angels and saints in heaven, which is neither identical neither to time in its experience of creatures on earth nor with God's own eternity. Thomas counters objections to the category of aeviternity which argue that it is not distinct from time. As noted above, Thomas's conception of eternity is simultaneous with permanent and changeless being, and time is synonymous with change. Between permanence and change are gradations. Beings subject to corruption are the most changeable and are temporal. Spiritual beings, like the angels, are unchangeable in one sense but changeable in another. Angels are unchangeable in their being and in the duration of their existence; they are changeable with regard to choice, place, and intelligence. This kind of intermediate state between time and eternity also belongs to the glorified saints in the church triumphant. This state is aeviternity.

In terms of the basic structure of thought on eternity, Aquinas does not depart significantly from the earlier Augustinian/Boethian tradition. He does, however, through his adoption of Aristotle's distinction between act and potency, give some more precision in terms of the connection between changeability and temporality. Further, Aquinas adds the category of aeviternity, which helpfully clarifies how angels and glorified saints are both free from the corruptions of time while still being distinct from God's own eternal existence.

Johann Gerhard on Eternity

As with the other divine attributes, Gerhard expands upon God's relationship to time in a manner that is consistent with the Augustinian tradition as mediated by the medieval scholastics such as Thomas Aquinas. Along with his philosophical explanations, Gerhard also provides an extensive scriptural background to support divine atemporality as not only a construct of logic, but a teaching derived from a consistent exegesis of Scripture.

As he begins his discussion, Gerhard cites the definition of eternity as articulated by Boethius above. He then further defines eternity as consisting in three affirmations. First, eternity is interminable, meaning that it does not begin or end at any moment. Second, God's eternity is indivisible, as he does not experience time by way of temporal succession. Third, God's eternity is independent, meaning that his eternal existence is in no way affected by anything outside of himself.[255] These three elements are definitional to what Gerhard refers to as a "proper" use of the word "eternity." As evidenced by various texts in the Old Testament (Ex. 21:6, Gen. 17:13), there is an "improper" use of the language of eternity which denotes either an extensive period of time, or the existence of beings which have a beginning but no end (i.e., human souls and angels). It is important to distinguish these usages of the terms, as it is only the first and proper definition that is under consideration here, as this is singularly applied to God.

Biblical Support

The scriptural defense offered by Gerhard of such a definition of divine eternity is fourfold.[256] First, a variety of texts state in a straightforward manner that God is eternal (Gen. 21:33, Isa. 40:28, Rom. 16:26). These texts do not conclude what *kind* of eternity is applied to God, of course, but he is

---

[255] Gerhard, *God and Trinity*, 139.

[256] Ibid., 139–40.

defined as eternal nonetheless. The second set of texts distinguish between the successive nature of time with regard to creatures and God's eternity (Job 36:26, Isa. 43:10, 2 Pet. 3:8). Third, God's operations and attributes are described as eternal (Ps. 33:11, Dan. 6:26, 1 Pet. 5:10). Fourth, Scripture at times makes it clear that days in a human sense can only be applied to God in a metaphorical manner (Dan. 7:9, Ps. 102:27, Job 10:5).

Of all the texts offered here as evidence by Gerhard, the most significant are those which speak of contrast between God's relationship to time and that of creatures. As has been discussed, classical theism posits eternity in God not as endless duration, but as a lack of any temporal succession whatsoever. The question at issue here then is whether the latter point can be demonstrated in the scriptural data. Evidence for this is found in texts like 2 Peter 3:8 which go beyond the affirmation of infinite duration. The apostle writes: "But, beloved, do not forget this one thing, that with the Lord one day is as a thousand years, and a thousand years as one day."[257] This text arises in a discussion about the timing of Christ's return, which is unknown to both Peter and the readers of his epistle. Some in the church had expected that the *parousia* would have already occurred and are now fearful that this event would not happen. Peter assures his readers that God's timing is not perceptible to us in the present moment, and that this event would be a surprise like "a thief in the night" (2 Pet. 3:10). It is as an answer to this worry that the statement under discussion occurs, through which Peter argues that God does not experience time as we do. While this event appears far off to us, it is not far off to God. Note that Peter does not *only* say that one thousand years is as a day. If this were the case, one might contend that Peter is simply saying that one thousand years passes quickly to God in that he has a longer duration than humans have. Peter adds to this also that one day is as a thousand years. In other words, God's experience of one day and of one thousand years is the same. It is only if God stands completely outside of the confines of time (atemporality) that such a statement can be

---

[257] "With the Lord time is evidently not what it is to us who live in time. He is above time." Lenski, *Peter, John, Jude*, 344.

affirmed as fully truthful.

Similar contrasts between God's experience of time and that of humans can be found in other texts, such as Job 10, in which Job asks: "Are Your days like the days of a mortal man? Are Your years like the days of a mighty man?" (Job 10:5). This arises in the midst of a series of contrasts between God and creation, as Job also speaks to God's sight as differing from that of human eyes (Job 10:4). The point is that just as God sees all things without the limited physical eyes humans have, so does he know all time, unlike temporal and limited creatures. There are also texts like Isaiah 43:13 and John 8:58, which contrast God's present eternal existence with the past events of history. It is because of God's atemporality that Jesus can utter the seemingly paradoxical statement, "before Abraham was, I AM" (John 8:58). As Gerhard argues, these texts present God's eternity as an encapsulation of all time within his own present, rather than a mere infinite duration of temporal moments.

Philosophical and Historical Support

Though Gerhard's primary foundation on this point, as well as with regard to his other theological convictions, is the text of Scripture, he also gives defenses of the doctrine from philosophy and history. The view promoted by Gerhard of eternity as non-succession has precedent in both pagan pre-Christian sources and in the most important divines in the history of the church up until his day.

As far as pagan thinkers are concerned, Gerhard mentions two: Thales and Plato.[258] Thales is often known as the father of Western philosophy, as Aristotle viewed the earlier thinker as the first of the Greek philosophers.[259] Though his own writings have not survived, records of his life and thought are found in Aristotle and Laertius, along with a number of later authors.

---

[258] Gerhard, *God and Trinity*, 141.

[259] See my overview of Thales in Cooper, *True, Good, and Beautiful*, 8–9.

Due to the lack of contemporaneous sources, there is some doubt as to the validity of many of the descriptions of the philosopher. At least according to Laertius's account, Thales viewed God primarily as mind. He differs from creatures in his eternity, as God had no beginning and has no ending. This early Greek thought is far clearer in Plato, who argues that neither past nor future is to be attributed to God, as he is beyond the bounds of temporality. Many other instances could be mentioned here of such Greek acknowledgments of God's eternity, which Gerhard contends are due to their use of natural revelation as mentioned in Romans 1:20.

With reference to Christian consensus, Gerhard points to both Irenaeus and Justin Martyr as early testaments to God's eternal existence. The quote from Justin is especially telling, as he writes that "Nothing in God is temporal."[260] Such an affirmation negates the modern contention made by some that though God's essence is eternal, he takes some kinds of temporal properties upon himself in order to interact with his creation. Gerhard then further cites Hilary, John of Damascus, and Augustine as sources which affirm God's non-temporal existence. As might be expected, it is Augustine who gets the most interaction, as Gerhard stands largely upon the North African bishop's doctrine of God.

Gerhard also contends that God's atemporality is known by way of reason. If he is truly Creator of all things, he must then be the Creator of time and exist prior to and apart from time. Atemporality, for Gerhard, is also necessitated by other truths regarding the divine nature, such as simplicity and immutability. Were God to exist within the confines of time, there would be a past and future in him, and he thus could not be a purely simple being. Further, this would threaten his unchangeable nature. Gerhard proves the rational nature of this conclusion with a citation from Aristotle (or "the Philosopher," as he calls him, taking a cue from Aquinas). For Aristotle, eternity has two facets: non-succession and the lack of any beginning or end of existence. God, if he is truly eternal, must conform to both of these things.

---

[260] Gerhard, *God and Trinity*, 140.

Gerhard Confronts Vorstius

As in the other sections of this work, Gerhard includes his antithesis section, in which he counters arguments to the contrary. He interacts here with those who argue for the eternity of the angels or of physical creation. For Gerhard, there is no such thing as a "participated eternity" in which some created objects share in divine eternity. These considerations do not, however, quite touch the topic at hand in this chapter regarding God's own relationship to time. Most relevant to the present discussion is Gerhard's critique of Vorstius, and his discussion of non-temporal succession in God.

As discussed in the last chapter, Conrad Vorstius was a controversial Arminian theologian who posited a unique approach to God's interactions with creation. His denial of God's immutability led as well to a reframing of God's relation to time. For Vorstius, God experiences past, present, and future; he is not outside of the confines of temporality.[261] Gerhard points out the inconsistency of Vorstius's own position here, because elsewhere the Arminian theologian affirms divine simplicity through the identification of God's properties with his essence. If God is not infinite temporally, this would mean that his essence itself is finite—a conclusion which Vorstius himself would reject. As Gerhard rightly sees here, all of the classical attributes identified with classical theism stand or fall together. The rejection of one necessitates a reframing of all the others.

As evidence for his claim, Vorstius cites a number of scriptural passages in which God is said to exist within the past, present, and future. God is often said to remember the past and promises that he will act in the future. For Vorstius, the most straightforward reading of such statements leads to a denial of atemporality. These arguments are essentially the same ones made by theistic personalists today who argue against the Augustinian view. It is said that the classical theist does not take the texts as seriously as the mutualist, as they impose a foreign philosophical framework upon the text.

Gerhard responds to this challenge by defending analogical predication.

---

[261] Ibid., 143.

As Gerhard notes, Vorstius himself acknowledges that texts which speak about corporeality in God, for example, are not to be taken in the strictest literal sense. God the Father does not have the nostrils, wings, and arms which are poetically attributed to God throughout the Old Testament. God accommodates human intellectual limitations through using language that is identified with ordinary human experience. This is why God speaks of his own past and future.

The question one must ask here is, How does one know which texts are to be taken in a strictly literal sense, and which are analogical? Are classical theists merely forcing non-literal interpretations conveniently upon any texts which oppose their foreign metaphysical conclusions? Gerhard's answer is not simply a statement of a pre-commitment to the ideas of the Greek philosophers, but he instead points to texts of Scripture which themselves describe God's relationship to time as one which is non-linear. Scripture is explicit in repeated statements that God does not change—and that would include a change in his temporal existence from past to future (Ps. 102:27, James 1:17). Further, as mentioned above, there are a number of texts which explicitly contrast God's relationship to men with that of temporal beings (Dan. 7:9, Ps. 102:27, Job 10:5, John 8:58). Thus, it is simply a matter of affirming the entirety of the biblical data. One must either interpret the texts that attribute temporality to God as analogical, *or* one must interpret the latter texts in a temporal or non-literal sense. The former approach is far more consistent with both the entirety of biblical revelation and with the *analogia fidei*.[262]

Gerhard: Conclusions

Just as each of the previous figures here draws upon and develops that of the others, so does Gerhard reiterate and expand the ideas of Augustine, Boethius, and Aquinas. This again demonstrates the concern for the

---

[262] Johnson, "Analogia Fidei as Hermeneutical Principle."

Protestant scholastics to build upon, rather than reject, the Western theological tradition in its patristic and medieval forms—especially with regard to the doctrine of God. What differentiates Gerhard from Aquinas is not the nature of the doctrine itself, but the central place of the exegetical task in forming theology. While Thomas focuses more explicitly on philosophical argumentation in his defense of eternity, Gerhard's treatment is more scripturally saturated, though without negating the importance of rational argumentation.

Western Catholic Consensus

The exposition of the thought of these four figures presents the broader Western consensus on divine eternity from its patristic, medieval, and post-Reformation formulations. There are basic commitments shared by each of these thinkers which define this classical approach. First, eternity is not merely an endless duration of life, but is instead freedom from the limits of time altogether. Second, God's eternal nature means that there is a lack of succession in God. Third, temporality implies corruption and loss as are common to fallen creation. These cannot be attributable to God. Fourth, though God exists in an eternal present moment, he still interacts with creation in time, though without himself being bound by it. In the following section, we engage some critiques of these four theological commitments.

Challenges

Divergences from the classical understanding of God's non-temporal existences are a rather new phenomenon that begins—at least on a significant scale—with G. W. F. Hegel. Classical Greek thinkers, from Parmenides to Aristotle, argue that the transcendent order is one that is unchanging and non-temporal. Particulars that decay are, for Plato, a mere shadow of the atemporal forms. This equating of the atemporal with the transcendent was adopted nearly universally among the church fathers and was then transmitted throughout the medieval period and Reformation as described above. With the later Enlightenment philosophers, though metaphysical realism was rejected, the privileging of universal unchanging truths over historical and changing ones was retained. The truths of logic were to be preferred over the events of history. With Hegel, this shifts.

Hegel is an idealist, meaning that like Plato, he argues that the realm of ideas is the most-real. Yet the idealism of Hegel differs significantly from Platonism in holding that underlying reality is a singular Geist that develops in a historical process. This world-spirit unites all things in itself, and is in a process of growing rationality, freedom, and self-actualization.[263] With some theological training, Hegel used Christian, and particularly Trinitarian, terminology to explain this process. Those who were considered the conservative Hegelians began to interpret his thought in a metaphysically realist manner and applied these ideas to Christian theology. The affirmation that God existed totally outside of temporality could now no longer be taken for granted.

Though many critics of Augustinian eternity, such as Robert W. Jenson, have rejected the Hegelian label,[264] I have a difficult time believing that the theology of hope and process theologies could exist apart from the German idealist. This move from the transcendent into the realm of history which occurs in Hegel has an impact upon nearly every intellectual field in the Western world. There is a change from a transcendent God who, though he remains outside of time, acts within time, to a divine being who is in some way internally changed by world history.

---

[263] Westphal, *Hegel's Phenomenology*.

[264] Jenson, "Ipse Pater Non Est Impassibilis," in Keating and White, *Divine Impassibility*, 117.

Robert W. Jenson

As an outline of Jenson's theology has already been presented in an earlier chapter, the basics of his underlying thought are not discussed here. What are addressed in particular are his statements surrounding God's relationship to temporality and the critique of the Augustinian perspective.

Jenson's approach arises from his context of the theology of hope. Like Moltmann, Jenson contends that eschatology should be understood not merely as the end to a series of doctrines, but instead as the means by which all theology is to be understood. In his view, Christian theologians, for most of history, have not viewed the eschatological end as anything truly new. Rather, there is a narrative of a perfect creation which then is corrupted by the fall only to be restored to its former perfection. This makes redemption a mere "repair job."[265] If the ultimate reality (i.e., the transcendent Good) is non-temporal and unchanging, this means that there can be no significant differentiation from beginning to end. God retains his unchanging essence, and history plays out in a way that it recaptures what it was in the first place. This, for Jenson, is a misunderstanding of God's eternity, and particularly his relationship to eschatology.

Before moving on in Jenson's argument, this contention merits a response. The connection between the Garden of Eden and the new heavens and earth is clearly a biblical one. There is no question that Edenic imagery is used both by the Old Testament prophets and in John's Apocalypse to describe the last days. Thus there is some sense in which the end is a "going back" to the beginning.[266] However, this does not imply that redemption is purely restoration to Eden. Adam and Eve were created in a temporary state of probation, in which all things are "good," but evil still exists (via the serpent) and sin is still a possibility; in Augustinian terms, humanity had the *"posse peccare"* (the capability of sinning). The state of *"non posse non peccare"* (the

---

[265] Jenson, *Revisionary Metaphysics*, 43.

[266] See G. K. Beale, *The Temple and the Church's Mission*.

inability to commit sin) was yet to be received.[267] The first humans were as children, asked to cultivate the creation and spread their dominion over the earth. There is no indication of some kind of static state of timelessness on Adam and Eve's part here. The *telos* of humanity has always been to live in harmony with God and creation, and to participate in the divine life. Thus humanity, if it fulfilled its original calling, would grow and mature, eventually cultivating the earth and bearing many children as the divine glory expanded throughout all of creation.

Reformed theologian Gerhardus Vos summarizes this well with his phrase that "eschatology precedes soteriology."[268] In other words, humanity was created with a destination to be reached, not as a present possession. Thus the need for an eschaton is not merely the result of sin. Even if there were no need for salvation, there would be an eschatological end. With this being the case, there is no reason to deny God's non-temporal existence in order to affirm the fact that creation is eschatologically oriented. Jenson's argument is dependent upon a reading of the classical approach to the fall that is not consistent with classical Protestant sources. Redemption is not a "repair job," but the glorification of man and woman, along with the rest of creation, in a manner that far surpasses Edenic innocence.

For Jenson the root of this problem that he identifies is with the ancient Greeks. Parmenides's contention that reality is unchanging has "confused Christian theology" from the first centuries of the church.[269] Jenson defines this central error as "the posit of eternity as the sheer negation of time."[270] This eternity is immunity to the corruption, change, and suffering which time brings. This view of the eternal assured the Greeks that there was some kind of stability in world history, and that they too could perhaps participate in this eternal existence. This view of eternity as timelessness is described by Jenson as tied together with a belief in God's impassibility and immutability.

---

[267] Boston, *Fourfold State*.

[268] This is a popular summarization of what he says in *Biblical Theology*, 140.

[269] Jenson, *Revisionary Metaphysics*, 43.

[270] Ibid.

Atemporality is posited because it is only if God is outside of time that he is immune to the effects of time upon his being and actions.[271] It is only if God is in some sense temporal, as Jenson argues, that he can really interact with creation.

In Jenson's estimation, Hegel is correct in some important ways. He concurs that God is to be identified as historical process. However, for Jenson, Hegel is wrong in his Trinitarian theology—in particular in his lack of a strong pneumatology.[272] This misunderstanding of the Spirit, on Hegel's part, leads to a lifeless God that is hardly different from the deity of classical theism that Jenson is so highly critical of. The Spirit is needed as the bond of love that frees the Father and Son for one another as God's future. Yet, despite disagreements with Hegel, Jenson admits that God "indeed is himself a history," and as the "archetype of thesis, antithesis and synthesis."[273] Jenson portrays his concern here as primarily soteriological. As a defender of the doctrine of theosis, Jenson believes that the end of creation is participation in the divine life (and I happen to agree). This teleological view of human nature necessitates, in Jenson's thought, a God who has a historical life. If there is no history of God, then there is no divine life that the human person can be brought into.

The conclusion here does not follow. It is indeed the case that humans are created to share in the divine life, and that theosis is the *telos* of all creation. Yet, the temporal nature of creatures does not somehow necessitate that God share in such temporality in order for any union to be real. The implication of Jenson's language here is that it is only the God of historical process who "has a life to be taken into," and that the classical Christian God does not. The assumption here which Jenson brings is that there is no active life in a timeless God. This is simply untrue. God's atemporality does not imply that God is static and inactive. It is precisely the opposite. God is in fact *infinitely*

---

[271] Ibid.

[272] "The problem with Hegel is that, despite his grandiloquent talk of *Geist*, he like most Western theology did not make the biblical Spirit's role decisive for his construal of deity" (Ibid., 45).

[273] Jenson, *Revisionary Metaphysics*, 45.

active, such that his actions cannot be limited by temporal boundaries. God is far more active, in a classical schema, than any element of creation. This is why atemporality is necessary. If God is temporal, he can be active, but not *infinitely* so. Therefore temporal creatures sharing in the process of Christification does not in any way imply somehow becoming static and lifeless as they grow in the *imago Dei*. It should at least give Jenson some pause that there has never been some perceived necessity of God's temporality in order for theosis to exist among historic Christian theologians. The Hegelian groundwork is assumed here by Jenson, rather than positively argued for. A radical shifting of Christian theology merits a far more robust argument.[274]

A final discussion point here is the formulation of Trinitarian theology that Jenson proposes as an alternative to both classical theism and Hegelian dialectical thought. As this has been addressed more in an earlier chapter, the overview here is brief. As mentioned, the linchpin of Jenson's eschatological theology proper is in his doctrine of the Spirit. The Spirit, for Jenson, is God's future. This future Spirit constitutes God's own life. This then ties together Jenson's doctrine of God with his view of theosis. The life of God exists in his own future: the Spirit. Therefore, theosis, or sharing in the divine life, must also be a partaking of the future of God. Univocity is assumed here, as that which the believer experiences as theosis is imported into God's own eternal being. Erasing all distinction between ontology and the economy, Jenson goes so far as to claim that God "*is* the life lived" between the triune persons in history.[275] What one is left with here is an abstraction which can hardly be substantiated by any honest exegetical study of the relevant biblical texts.

Jenson's approach to God and time has five major problems that stand out in this summary. First, Jenson assumes univocity, that what is true of creational experiences, such as what "life" is, must also be true of the

---

[274] Certainly this is all from one essay of Jenson's and he has written a bit more in various other essays and books. However, what is articulated in this work is the same basic argument as laid forth in the other texts.

[275] Jenson, *Revisionary Metaphysics*, 47.

divine nature. Second, in Jenson's many writings on the subject, he never provides thorough biblical argumentation to demonstrate the veracity of his claims. Third, Jenson approaches classical theism from the mistaken belief that timelessness means inactivity. This is simply not the case. Fourth, his Trinitarian theology is so far removed from what the church has historically taught concerning the divine nature that it is difficult to even refer to it as genuinely Trinitarian as such a term has been classically understood. Fifth, as denial of classical theism always does, Jenson's proposal makes creatures constitutive of God's own being. For Jenson, God is his history, and his history is his history with humanity. If history with creatures is so essential for God, it is difficult to make the claim that the triune God is truly *a se*.[276] Overall, Jenson's model provides far more difficulties theologically, philosophically, and exegetically than does the classical view, and thus should be rejected.

Carl Braaten

Carl Braaten's views on God's future were summarized in an earlier chapter here, but these themes are now revisited for the purpose of critique. Like Jenson, Braaten approaches the issue of God's relationship to time from the perspective of a theology of hope. He identifies a common inheritance of what he refers to as a "third stage" of twentieth-century theology following upon the neo-orthodoxy of Karl Barth and the death-of-God theology in the 1960s. This third stage is the theology of hope formulated by Moltmann and Pannenberg. Braaten contends that he and Jenson differ in theological influences. While Jenson is Barthian, Braaten relies more heavily on Paul Tillich.[277] Despite their different methodologies, Braaten and Jenson arrive at many of the same conclusions.

---

[276] Jenson does not self-consciously argue this, but it is difficult to see how he could possibly come to any other conclusion based upon his argument.

[277] Braaten, *Future of God*, 13.

A Theology of the Future

Braaten's critique of the classical approach to God and time is rooted in his dismissal of classical Greek thought—particularly Platonic realism. With Jenson, Braaten contends that since the Greeks viewed reality through the unchanging present, rather than the eschaton, they believed that the ultimate good includes the past, present, and future, as the unchanging good encapsulates all three. This is shown in patristic theology, wherein Eden is viewed as a perfect state which is not to be superseded but simply recaptured by Christ for the church. Braaten argues that "the Platonic essences were given an earthly embodiment in the way things were before the fall."[278] In his reading of the fathers, there is an emphasis then of the past, rather than the future, in terms of Christian hope. Rather than the eschaton bringing about something truly new, the end is merely a reversion back to the beginning. This is essentially the same argument made by Jenson when he asserts that redemption is a mere "repair job" for the classical theologian.

The critique that I offer on this point is simply the same one made above regarding Jenson's work. Braaten's reading of both the church fathers and the later Lutheran tradition simply cannot be substantiated from the primary sources. Christians have consistently, throughout the entire history of theology, spoken of the new heavens and new earth not merely as a pure recapturing of Eden, but a realization of that which far supersedes all previous states of humanity. These kinds of broad statements are made rather consistently in this text (and in many of the texts put forth by these eschatologically driven thinkers) without substantiation. Braaten overstates his case rather significantly on this point.

It should also be noted that Braaten's perspective on the fall narrative in Scripture is that it is mere myth, meaning that it has no historical veracity.[279] Braaten is clear here that he is not saying that only certain *elements* of the narrative are mythological or symbolic rather than literal, but that there

---

[278] Ibid., 45.

[279] Ibid., 44–46.

never was a state of innocence at all. Thus, in his estimation, it is the idea of a state of innocence in any sense that is to blame for the lack of a truly eschatological theology. He sets up a strict dichotomy here. Either a historical fall occurred and the eschaton brings about no new state of affairs at all, or the fall is purely mythological and the eschaton is actually new. Despite Braaten's argument, there is no reason why such a false dilemma must exist. There is no need to choose between the reality of the state of innocence and the reality of eschatological newness. Both are simply biblical realities. But for Braaten, humanity is created in an imperfect state and is in need of development. He tries to ground his approach to the early chapters of Genesis in the fathers with mention of Origen and Clement of Alexandria. It is a bit of a strange use of sources here, as these are two of the most devoted Platonists in the history of the church. And, regardless of whether or not their approach to the story of Adam is only allegory (and there are reasons for thinking that Origen does not *only* take this approach to the text), they both clearly affirm a state of innocence.[280] Braaten's conclusions here lead to a number of theological and exegetical problems, but those cannot all be dealt with in this volume. The reason this is so significant here is that it demonstrates the manner in which this modified approach to divine temporality impacts doctrines far beyond itself. It requires a rereading of much of the biblical narrative.

It is clear that rather than pure exegesis, Braaten's argument for God's temporality is primarily based upon his metaphysical conclusions surrounding the nature of things. He is particularly critical of the idea that there is a universal and unchanging human nature. The classical Christian approach is "protological," meaning that the human essence exists in its dignified and good state at the creation of man and woman.[281] It is not in some kind of process of self-development or actualization. Braaten's rejection of realism is clarified in his condemnation of the statement that "essence precedes

---

[280] This is partially why Origen defends the soul's preexistence, such that in Adam, *every* soul literally fell with him.

[281] Braaten, *Future of God*, 46.

existence." Lest one assume that Braaten is some kind of existentialist like Bultmann, Braaten also rejects the Sartrian idea that "existence precedes essence."[282] For Braaten, both classical realism and existentialism are wrong in that they assume that a thing can be defined by what it is in the present. In contrast to this, Braaten argues that the "essence of a thing is neither in its past nor in its present but in its future."[283] And here is the core of Braaten's view of God. If the essence of a thing is in its future, then God's own essence must be in his future. Therefore, God has a future. The importance of metaphysics for one's theological conclusions is hard to overstate. The question then is ultimately one of realism (addressed in volume one of this series).

Braaten does, however, offer some biblical argumentation to support his approach. He founds his argument first and foremost on the divine name as explained in Exodus 3:14. As discussed previously, the Hebrew expression used can be translated either as "I am what I am" or as "I will be who I will be."[284] The former reading is taken by classical theists generally, while many Old Testament scholars have opted for the latter rendering. While Braaten admits that the phrase is ambiguous and could be translated in either manner, he offers a contextual argument as to why the future reading is more likely. This name arises in the midst of the narrative of Moses and the redemption of the people of God from Egypt. In other words, this is a story about hope—moving from slavery to freedom. Thus, in Braaten's view, this futurist rendering of the divine name is grounded in the same hope with which Moses trusted God to follow through with his promises. This is contrasted with the timeless god Apollo who is not such a god of hope. Braaten then summarizes his conclusions from this text by citing Ernst Bloch, who contends that God has "future as his essential nature."[285]

---

[282] Sartre first used this quote explicitly in his lecture "Existentialism Is a Humanism," given in 1945.

[283] Braaten, *Future of God*, 46.

[284] Ibid., 48.

[285] Ibid., 49.

If the biblical narrative is based upon hope in the future, then God must also experience the future.

This argument simply does not hold. Braaten, Jenson, and others are certainly correct in their emphasis upon redemptive history. God can rightly be called a God of hope who acts within the history of his people, continually pointing them toward union with him in the eschatological state. Yet none of this necessitates that God is some kind of temporal being himself. The contention here is that Israel experiences God temporally through acts of redemption, and therefore God himself must experience the same in order for such a relationship between Yahweh and Israel to be genuine. This does not follow. Further, in engaging in the debates surrounding the divine name, Braaten fails to cite Jesus's own interpretation of the name in John 8. When Jesus does so, he claims that "before Abraham was, I am" (John 8:58). Jesus erases both past and present distinctions in using the present tense of "am" here and clearly affirms the classical understanding of Exodus 3:14. While the Hebrew text is ambiguous, the Greek here is not. This is especially important because Braaten does not merely place Exodus 3:14 in his argument as one text among many, but as "[t]he ultimate source of this dynamic futurizing of religion."[286] The rest of his exploration of this theology of hope points to the increased emphasis on the last day in the prophets, who simply say nothing about whether such change is inherent in God himself. Such change, in Braaten's argument, is almost solely grounded in the Exodus text, which, if we are to take Jesus's interpretation, does not affirm what Braaten claims.

The Temporal God

With the basic grounding of Braaten's contention here both philosophically and biblically being laid, we can now move toward an exploration of the doctrine of God that flows out from these convictions. What is evident when

---

[286] Ibid., 48.

one reads Braaten on these points (as with Jenson) is that this temporalizing of God results in a loss of divine aseity along with a radical departure from Nicene Trinitarian theology.

Along with Barth and many of other twentieth-century Protestant theologians, Braaten rejects natural theology. The classical philosophical proofs for God's existence do not, for Braaten, logically demonstrate the necessity of the divine. Rather, natural theology simply demonstrates the human longing for God. Therefore, Braaten does not believe that there is significant overlap between philosophical conclusions of the ancients and a genuinely Christian perspective on God. The Christian approach is centered upon the person of Jesus and on God's identification with him rather than philosophical abstraction about a timeless being. He speaks of the person of Jesus as "the exclusive medium of the divine self-revelation."[287] What this means is that, for Braaten, God is defined not in his eternal essence, but by the economy of redemption through the work of Jesus of Nazareth. Ontology is determined by the economy.[288]

Braaten argues that the patristics functioned with a preconceived notion of God which they then were forced to contextualize in light of the incarnation. It was this inheritance that forced these theologians to somehow find a way to defend the idea of an infinite being becoming finite through the incarnation. This results in "a kind of ontological collapse" of the divine being.[289] All of the difficulties with the classical view, for Braaten, are resolved when one begins with the person of Jesus, rather than with this abstract Greek notion of divinity. For Braaten, Jesus himself never provides such a metaphysical description of God, but instead he presents God as "the power of the future."[290] He further demonstrates this with his contention that "[f]uturity is essential to his very being."[291] When God makes promises to

---

[287] Ibid., 65.

[288] Ibid., 64–65.

[289] Ibid., 67.

[290] Ibid., 69.

[291] Ibid.

his creation, he is *identical* with those promises. Similarly, Braaten argues that God is his kingdom—especially the *coming* kingdom. This again, makes God identical with his *ad extra* operations. It is thus, for Braaten's temporal God, the future of God with his creation that defines his own essence. However one wants to parse this out, it inevitably makes creatures necessary and constitutive for the divine being. Braaten's God cannot then be *a se*. A further point to be made here is that Braaten provides biblical texts which speak of the future, but in none of these texts is there any indication that the future is definitional of God.

Here perhaps is a place to demonstrate how the denial of God's non-temporal existence completely changes classical theological convictions from their historic roots: it affects Christology. Since Braaten does not believe that essences are defined by either past or present, but by their future, there is no longer any need for the belief in a preexistent Christ. He refers to Christ's eternal existence as a "later symbol" that developed to explain the reality of the resurrection.[292] Here is a clear example of Braaten's metaphysical convictions overruling the clear text of the New Testament. Certainly, the apostle John presents a preexistent Logos who is present at creation in both his prologue in John 1 and the high priestly prayer of John 17. Yet Braaten simply dismisses such claims as "symbols" of an eschatological reality. Nothing in the text merits such a conclusion, of course, but Braaten's neo-Hegelianism is not to be challenged by the apostles.

The alternative to classical orthodox Christology that Braaten proposes is a resurrection which has retroactive causality. He states this rather clearly: "The resurrection was thus the pivotal point by which God defined himself retroactively in the life of Jesus."[293] This event in the economy has determinative power for God's past, since God is not defined by the past, but by his own eschatology. The positive of such a move, if there is one, is that Braaten recognizes the centrality of the resurrection in Christian

---

[292] Ibid., 74.
[293] Ibid., 73.

doctrine.[294] However, his temporalizing of God has made it central not only for human salvation, but for God's being. This, in a way, makes the resurrection a saving event for both God and creation. No longer is the life of Christ an act of pure mercy accomplished by an infinite and glorious triune God, but a divine necessity in order to make his own identity.

Braaten is an example here of why atemporality matters. Attempts to reimagine God's relationship to time nearly always end in a denial of divine aseity and a collapsing of the ontological Trinity with the economy of salvation. Further, such attempts consistently claim that the classical view is an imposition of Greek philosophy, but do not themselves present any extensive or compelling argument that the biblical authors have a view that is different than the Augustinian one. Perhaps it is Braaten who is actually forcing late Hegelianism into theology instead of Augustine doing the same with Plato. Braaten, along with Jenson and Pannenberg, also shows that a future-oriented view of the divine nature cannot exist alongside of Nicene Christology. The ground underneath the preexistence of Christ has been removed, and the Logos is temporalized. Once again, Braaten creates far more problems than he solves with his theology of hope.

Conclusion

The classical view of God's relationship to time remains the best explanation of the biblical texts and of the philosophical and theological concerns that arise from them. Jenson and Braaten are only two figures, but the arguments they set forth are representative of a far larger number of theologians. Ultimately, those thinkers who reject God's non-atemporal existence end up in a position where they cannot honestly confess that God is *a se*. The temporal God of the theology of hope is dependent upon creation in order to be who he is. This drastically changes the biblical narrative of redemption.

---

[294] Even here, Braaten is not willing to actually affirm a literal physical resurrection, but argues that subjective theories of the resurrection appearance provide enough theological backing. Braaten, *Future of God*, 75.

In a classical theology, God is completely self-sufficient in himself without time or any relationship to the temporal. However, God freely chooses to create that which cannot in any way increase his being or glory. As God is infinite, the increase of anything in God is an impossibility. It is God's self-sufficiency that makes grace truly grace. It is because he has nothing to gain that God acts out of complete, unconditioned love in both creation and redemption. The theology of hope makes God's redemptive work ultimately self-actualizing. It is no longer pure grace. In this theology, the redemptive activity of the Son is necessary in order to create the Father-Son relationship. The Trinity itself becomes dependent upon creatures for its existence as Trinity.

It is also apparent in these thinkers that there simply is no non-philosophical theology. All theologians have metaphysical convictions that, to some degree, shape their thought and writing. The question is simply whether one is conscious of and honest about what those philosophical systems are. It may be true that Augustine's view of time was shaped by Platonism, but Jenson's is shaped by Hegel. For all of Jenson's claims that he presents a metaphysic that is explained by Scripture rather than pagan philosophers, there is no biblical warrant for many of his central claims, such as the retroactive divinity of the Son. By all appearances, his work is driven by metaphysics as much as (or more than) that of the fathers and medievals. The question then is which of these philosophical systems makes sense of the biblical material. When placed alongside one another, the classical approach has far more explanatory power in analyzing the biblical text than the alternative proposed by Jenson, Braaten, and others.

Along with those theologians discussed in this chapter, there are those like William Lane Craig who opt for a view which sits between the classical perspective and different forms of process theism. In this view, God is atemporal in himself but takes on some kind of time-boundedness in order to interact with his creation. Though this does not have the same extensive theological problems as Jenson or Braaten's approaches, there remain several reasons to reject such ideas. Many of these have already been addressed through an analysis of Gerhard's response to Vorstius regarding immutability, as Vorstius's view reformulated God's relationship to temporal creatures. But along with that, another point must be made. If God takes on some kind of self-limitation in order to have genuine relationship with creation, this creates a kind of incarnation before the incarnation. The Father lessens himself to commune with us. Further, this approach says essentially that God cannot interact with creation in himself. He has to take on something other than he is in order to be truly relational and commune with creation. This is a challenge to divine immanence which is simply not present in the classical view. It is sin which makes such a strong barrier between God and man—not the ontological differences between God and man as such. These modified views create an ontological problem which is not part of the biblical narrative.

6

Divine Impassibility

At the heart of the Christian faith stands the conviction that God died on the cross. This truth which Paul referred to as "foolishness to the Greeks" (1 Cor. 1:23) continues to confound non-Christian thinkers, as in a classical understanding, God *cannot* die. Thus, this paradox stands at the forefront of Christian theological thinking: the impassible God died. A number of proposals have been offered throughout the centuries explaining how such a claim can be both logically and exegetically consistent. The early patripassianists argued that the God died in the most literal sense—thus including the Father in the passion. The Nestorians divided the human and divine natures in such a way that rather than the *person* of the Son, the *human nature* died on the cross. Many modern theologians argue that God suffered in such a way that his very being is constituted by the passion of Christ. Yet, despite the lack of consensus that these various proposals might suggest, there remains a rather consistent classical approach to divine suffering which confesses the reality of the death of God *and* the impassible nature of divinity.

Often bound up with divine immutability, classical impassibility claims that suffering belongs only to creaturely existence, and thus cannot be properly attributed to God. Were God able to experience suffering, then he would be mutable. Thus, impassibility necessitates immutability. However, though classical theists affirm a strong impassibility, they (Christian ones, at least) *do not* deny the reality of the suffering of Christ, nor do they speak merely of a *nature* suffering on the cross. The mystery of Christ's passion involves the conviction that the person of the Son suffered, though this experience occurred by means of the human nature. On the cross, Jesus both suffered and also remained immutable. In this chapter, we explain the classical approach to this final of our four central claims of classical theism through medieval and post-Reformation thinkers. This is then followed by an evaluation of modern proposals in favor of divine passibility.

Thomas Aquinas on God's Passions

As the Westminster Confession defines God's essence (insofar as such a thing can be defined), God is "without body, parts, or passions" (WC II.1). This final word, "passions," denotes God's lack of human emotion and suffering. The claim regarding impassibility then goes beyond the affirmation that God does not experience suffering in a manner that is synonymous with that of humanity, but further, that he does not experience *any* emotional responses corresponding to those of creatures. This strong affirmation as found here in this post-Reformation document expresses the approach to divine passions as found in Aquinas (among other medievals).

Aquinas discusses God's lack of passions in section 89 of his *Summa Contra Gentiles*. In beginning his explanation, Thomas contends that "the passions of the appetites are not in God" (SCG 89.I). He then claims that passions arise not from the intellect, but from sensation. Here, Aquinas is drawing upon Aristotle's threefold category of souls. The Greek thinker posits that, first, there are nutritive souls, which is the aspect of an organism that desires the reception of nutrients and growth. This belongs to all living physical creatures, including animals and plants. The second type of soul is the sensitive soul (which Aquinas is speaking about here), that is, the aspect of a living creature which senses the world around it. It is the sensitive soul which is attracted to things such as food or sex to fulfill natural urges in the organism. This recognition of the external world is in the capacity of animals and humans. The third and highest soul is the intellectual, wherein rational deductions are made.[295] This is, for Aristotle, what distinguishes humans from animals.

These categories are essential for understanding Aquinas's argument here, because for Aquinas, passion arises from the sensitive soul. God does not have a sensitive soul, and thus cannot have passions. This is further explained through the distinction between appetites. Both the sensitive and intellectual souls have appetites, or desires. These desires differ significantly. The sensitive soul is, by necessity, embodied; it is that which desires bodily needs. The hungry person desires food, and thus there arises a passion for food. Aquinas also demonstrates that these passions arise from instances of bodily change. Hunger (for most people) is not a constant state, but comes from the needs of the body after digesting food and converting food to energy. God cannot experience such passions for two reasons. First, he is disembodied, and is thus not subject to bodily desires. Second, God is immutable, and he thus cannot transfer from one state to another, as happens with creaturely passions.

Another reason God cannot be said to have passions is that these arise in creatures based upon some kind of need outside of themselves. Passion for food arises from the need of the body to have more energy. Through the appetites, one is brought out of one's natural condition in order to partake of some action or object to enter into some other state (such as the movement from a state of hunger to that of satiation). This creaturely following of the passions is often negative, as Thomas points out that disordered passions often lead to death (SCG 89.4). These passions also necessitate existence in potency. A passion for some object moves from potency to act when a subject acts upon such desires. God, as pure act, cannot have passions if he has no potency (SCG 89.6). A further characteristic of passions in humans which is unbefitting to God is their need to be regulated by reason. As is common in the Platonic tradition, Aquinas holds to the belief that humans should not base decisions merely upon internal desires. In order to act

---

[295] Copleston, *From Greece and Rome*, 320–31.

ethically, the human person has a duty to use reason to regulate his or her passions. This regulation serves in a twofold capacity: first, when a desire arises that is unethical, the rational mind should recognize such a thing and thus the person can make a choice not to act. Second, reason can distinguish between moderation and excess, and thus helps the person to avoid gluttony. God has no internal need in himself for some kind of self-regulation. God's essence is simple, and he has no need for anything outside of himself which needs to be regulated, as is the case with creatures (SCG 89.5). In summary, Thomas contends that if God had passions, his self-sufficiency, simplicity, and immutability would be in question.

Passions can be spoken of not merely in terms of bodily needs, but they also include higher desires such as joy and hope (SCG 89.10). Such things should ultimately be the highest longings for creatures, as they are fulfilled in God himself. Hope implies something which one does not yet possess. To say that God has hope is to deny that God is the fullness of being, as it implies that God's fullness is found in something which he does not already possess. Because God is the sum of all good, he therefore cannot have hope. As discussed below, Aquinas does acknowledge that God has joy, but not in a univocal sense to humans. Along with these positive passions, emotional responses to evil like fear, sadness, or repentance are also not attributable to God according to Thomas (SCG 89.11–15). These negative emotions, such as sorrow or pain, are by necessity connected to evil, as they arise from the presence of such evil. God, being eternal blessedness, cannot be threatened by any evil that exists, and therefore does not have passions which would arise from evil. Some of these passions, such as fear, also arise from the lack of knowledge of the future. Such can also not be justly attributed to God. Along with its connection to sadness, the emotional response of repentance also challenges divine immutability, as discussed previously. Emotional responses like envy are also in contradiction with God's nature, as they arise from a feeling of lack in one's self and possessions. This is an impossibility for God.

With all of this being said, the modern critic of Thomas is likely to question whether such a picture is really consistent with the biblical portrayal of

Yahweh as a loving, interactive, and empathetic being. Has Aquinas made God into an unfeeling static object who is no more personal than a stone or a mathematical equation? This is not an unfair question, as the faithful Christian does not encounter God primarily as the object of metaphysical inquiry, but as his or her personal Lord in prayer and the reception of the sacraments. Can we really be comfortably sharing our deepest emotional needs to a being who is totally detached from such experiences? A quick read of Aquinas's own devotional material makes it clear that the Angelic Doctor is not attempting to depersonalize God in any way. This is clarified in his discussion of God's delight and joy which follows the previously discussed statements on the passions.

Aquinas contends that God does indeed have joy and delight, though they are not to be categorized properly as "passions" in reference to the divine nature (SCG 90.1). Delight and joy differ from hope in that the latter is always future-oriented, whereas the former are present realities (SCG 90.2). God presently has delight, as it exists in the perfection of his being. In accord with divine simplicity, God's delight and joy differ from ours in that God does not merely *have* joy, but he *is* joy. This reality should put to rest the fears of God's emotionless detachment. God himself is eternal delight, joy, and love. Unlike our average human experiences of constantly shifting emotional states, God is eternal and unchanging bliss. Thomas also points out that joy and delight are not dependent upon the sensitive appetite alone, but also properly belong to the intellect (SCG 90.3). The sensitive soul distinguishes between good and evil with regard to sense experience, but the rational soul understands universals. Thus, the rightly ordered intellect delights in the Good. God therefore rejoices eternally in himself through a continual state of eternal bliss. As Aquinas summarizes: "God, therefore, through His will supremely rejoices in Himself" (SCG 90.4). Thomas here follows Plato, who argues that delight corresponds to one's participation in perfection. If God is the fullness of perfection, so then is he the most delightful of all beings (SCG 90.5). In these ways Aquinas affirms that God is both without passions, and also the most delighted and joyful of all things.

The thorough and philosophically rigorous treatment given by Thomas here is a strong basis upon which to argue for the continued validity of the doctrine of divine impassibility. Through his reception of both Platonic and Aristotelian conceptions of the passions and appetites, Aquinas demonstrates that one cannot attribute passions to the divine nature in the manner in which one speaks of the same with relation to humans and animals. Just as in other areas of theology, Scripture does use emotional language with relation to God, but does so analogically rather than univocally. As Thomas shows, this does not by any means make God a detached and emotionless being; rather, he is eternal joy, delight, and love.

Gerhard on Impassibility and the Cross

Unlike with the prior three aspects of classical theism discussed in this volume, Gerhard does not devote a separate section in his works to the topic of God's impassible nature. The reason for this is likely that this topic had not yet been a significant area of debate. It was not until the kenotic controversy of the nineteenth century that Lutheran theologians began exploring the relationship between suffering and the divine nature in significant depth. Nonetheless, there are still some insights Gerhard gives on the subject in two parts of his *Loci Theologici*. The first is in his treatment of the divine attributes, in which he treats God's blessedness, and the second is in his discussion of Christology and the atonement.

Unlike Aquinas, Gerhard does not begin with the denial of passions in God, but instead with the affirmation of God's blessed state. This blessedness is the eternal, unchanging joy and delight which belong to the triune God. As does Thomas, Gerhard connects blessedness to divine perfection. Blessedness is that which belongs to the perfection of any nature, and it is hindered by the presence of evil. As God is free from all evil, and is the source of all perfection, he is the most blessed. As Gerhard notes, "He is blessed essentially and in His nature and, in fact, is blessedness itself."[296] God's blessedness is unique

---

[296] Gerhard, *God and Trinity*, 260.

in that it arises from his nature and in fact *is* his nature; all other delight is participatory. This blessedness is connected, according to Gerhard, to a perfection in God's intellect, love, and will. God delights in his own perfect understanding, loves his own perfection in his fullness, and wills the good. Because of his aseity, this blessedness belongs to God apart from anything external to him.

It is after this discussion of God's blessed state that Gerhard then counters objections related to divine emotions. How can God actually be truly blessed in a complete sense if his will is often broken? It seems as if the rebellion of his creatures would lead to a lessening of God's happy state. Regarding the divine will, Gerhard argues that while it is true that God's will is broken by creatures in one sense (his moral will), no one truly escapes or acts apart from the divine will, as the creature then falls captive to God's punishing will.[297] This answer does not, however, address the most fundamental problem: the biblical texts. In a number of places in both Testaments, God is said to experience sorrow, regret, or other negative emotions. As a committed *sola Scriptura*–promoting Protestant, how does Gerhard explain these verses? His solution is to posit two senses of attribution of emotions to God. The first is to understand them affectively. This affective approach says that God's emotions are essentially like those of humans, and that as he views the disturbances in the world, he takes those very emotions into himself. The second approach, which Gerhard opts for, is the effective. This effective approach says that when Scripture attributes these emotions to God, it is speaking of God's interactions with creatures and of the reception of divine wrath, anger, and so forth on the part of creation. This does not necessitate a true internal emotional change within the divine being. Gerhard summarizes his approach to these texts thus:

> [These verses] uniquely emphasize the atrocity of the sin that offends God, namely, that so great is the gravity and atrocity of sin that to the extent that it is in Him, through it the utterly blessed

---

[297] Ibid., 262.

> God is affected with grief, sadness, and reproach, and that God detests sin so much that it appears to injure Him, to stir Him to sorrow and bitterness, and to do violence in His honor.[298]

Again, Gerhard affirms that these emotional states are attributed to God analogically. This is especially clear in light of the many verses that speak openly about God's eternal blessedness, which Gerhard cites throughout this section of his work.[299]

The second place in Gerhard's writing where the topic of God's impassible nature arises is in his treatment of the *genus maiestaticum*. This second genus of the *communicatio idiomatum* states that through the hypostatic union, there is a communication of the properties of divinity to the human nature in Christ. This doctrine, which was often the core of inter-Protestant debates in this era, was subject to a number of important qualifications put in place to affirm the integrity of both natures in opposition to the common Reformed critique that the Lutheran view led to monophysitism. Among these qualifications was the contention that the attributes of humanity are *not* transferred to the divine nature; the communication is not reciprocal. Unlike the later kenotic theologians, Gerhard adamantly defends the immutability of the divine nature, even within the incarnation.

In the heading for this section of his work, Gerhard writes that "the divine nature ... remains free of the sufferings of the flesh."[300] The unity of the human and divine natures causes the deification of the humanity of Christ while the human nature retains its essence without absorption into divinity. The human nature is, in virtue of its status as creature, changeable. This is why the humanity can experience such an exaltation, yet remain fully human. The divine nature, on the other hand, is not changeable. Therefore, if the divinity were to take upon itself aspects of a human nature, such as suffering, God would no longer be immutable and thus no longer God. Gerhard points

---

[298] Ibid., 263.

[299] Ibid., 261.

[300] Gerhard, *On Christ*, in *Loci Theologici*, 203.

out that theologians use the language "the Word assumed the flesh," but they do not say that the flesh assumed the Word.[301] The flesh is exalted, but the divinity is not lessened in any way.

In light of this, the question arises: how does this relate to the death of the Son? If Gerhard is correct here, is he then left to conclude that only the human nature, rather than the person, died on the cross? This, as mentioned above, is the Nestorian error. Gerhard clarifies on this point that in the most proper sense, it is correct to say, "Christ suffered *according to the flesh.*"[302] In other words, the person suffered, but did so by means of the human nature rather than the divine. This is what the first genus of the *communicatio idiomatum* affirms: that which occurs through one nature is attributed to the whole person, including the other nature. Scripture freely interchanges divine and human titles of Christ to affirm all aspects of the life and characteristics of the Son, such as when it is said that Jesus was preexistent, even though the human nature was created in time (Heb. 13:8), or that the Lord died (1 Cor. 2:8).[303] As with other truths of the Christian faith, the hypostatic union is a profound mystery whose depths the human intellect does not have access to. Nonetheless, as Gerhard demonstrates, one can consistently both affirm that the atonement was wrought by the whole Christ, and deny that the divine nature, in itself, actually suffered.

Gerhard demonstrates that divine immutability is a doctrine which is proven by both reason and Scripture. If God truly is fully blessed, as Scripture contends, this state cannot be altered by sorrow in suffering as humans experience such realities. Furthermore, God cannot suffer since this would contradict other truths about the divine nature such as simplicity and immutability. This teaching regarding God's inability to suffer does not do any harm to the central theological claim of Christianity that the Son suffered because the hypostatic union allows for the suffering of the Son by means of his created nature.

---

[301] Ibid., 204.

[302] Ibid.

[303] Ibid., 181.

Patristic Foundations

Like other scholastic distinctives regarding the doctrine of God, divine impassibility is no medieval novelty, but has consistent testimony throughout the writings of the early church fathers. Nearly as early as Christians began writing in the post–New Testament era, there were affirmations of God's lack of suffering. Statements affirming such things begin with the apostolic fathers and continue into the Christological debates of the sixth century.[304]

The earliest currently available reference to God's impassibility is in Ignatius's epistle to Polycarp. In this text, he writes:

> Wait for the one who is above time: the Eternal, the Invisible, who for our sake became visible; the Intangible, the Unsuffering, who for our sake suffered, who for our sake endured in every way. (Polycarp 3:2)

This verse contrasts the physical, material world to the immaterial God. These kinds of strong distinctions between heaven and earth are common in the patristics and echo the Platonic approach to the realm of the forms in contradistinction to the corruptible particularities of material reality. Early Christian authors revel in the paradoxes of the incarnation, that the invisible has become visible. This is apparent, for example, in the famous passage regarding the sweet exchange in the anonymous *Epistle to Diognetus* (Diogn. 9:2–5), where the incorruptible God has become corruptible in the incarnation. For Ignatius, this distinction between the two natures in Christ includes the unity of the "Unsuffering" (ἀπαθη) with human suffering. Though the divine nature is impassible, the Son did suffer by means of the incarnation.

Another early testimony to the Christian belief in God's impassibility arises

---

[304] The standard text on this subject is Gavrilyuk's *The Suffering of the Impassible God*. A helpful brief overview of the patristic era on this doctrine can be found in Bray, "Impassibility in the Church Fathers."

in Justin Martyr's *First Apology*. This treatise is one of the earliest works of Christian apologetics in conversation with the pagan beliefs of Rome along with then-contemporary philosophical schools. One of the primary forms of argument here is done by contrasting the heathen gods' flaws with the perfection of the Christian God. In the midst of these contrasts, Justin argues that Christians have "dedicated ourselves to the unbegotten and impassible God."[305] The Greek gods (and their Roman equivalents) were neither unbegotten nor without passions. Even the great god Zeus was born at a point in time as the son of Cronus and Rhea. The Christian God, in contrast, had no beginning. Secondly, the Greek gods were often driven by their passions. Justin mentions some specific examples of passion driving the gods in various myths, such as Theseus's lust for Antiope,[306] Ganymede's capture by Zeus out of homosexual desire,[307] and Thetis's fear regarding her son during the events of the *Iliad*. For Justin, these are human attributes that the true God is not capable of. He is thus without passions.[308]

As the church's theology developed through Christological and Trinitarian debates, the subject of impassibility arose with reference to the divinity of Christ. One such example is in Gregory of Nyssa's refutation of Eunomius. Eunomius of Cyzicus was an influential fourth-century Arian writer.[309] Of the most extreme variety, Eunomius contended that the Son is unlike (ἕτερος) the Father, not sharing in the divine essence. This led to the publication of two important treatises in response from the Cappadocian fathers Basil of Caesarea and Gregory of Nyssa. In his response to Eunomius, Gregory addresses the critique offered that Christ's suffering negates his divinity, as the Arians claimed. According to Gregory, Trinitarians do not deny

---

[305] Justin, *First Apology*, XXV.

[306] In some versions of the myth, Theseus is the son of Poseidon, though in others he is not divine.

[307] There are alternative versions of this story, and some do not include clear lustful intent.

[308] For a further exploration of the early apologists on this topic, see Little, "Emotions and the Divine Nature."

[309] The best treatment of these debates is Anatolios, *Retrieving Nicea*.

the reality of impassibility. He confesses that "as God, the Son is certainly impassible and incapable of corruption."[310] The Arians were not wrong to claim that divinity is impassible, but they were wrong in their assumption that the suffering of the Son must occur according to the divine nature. Gregory is clear that any pain and suffering faced by Christ is "by means of the human nature." However, this does not negate the unity of natures. He writes that "the suffering was of the body, but the operation was of God." In other words, the whole person contributed to the work of the passion, though it is properly only the human nature that suffers.

Some have followed Adolph von Harnack's Hellenization thesis and argued that this early and consistent testimony to impassibility is the product of a gradual capitulation to Greek philosophical claims. If that is the case, this capitulation occurred almost immediately following the death of the apostles to essentially remain unchallenged until the modern era. Others have contended that while the earliest Christian authors do indeed speak about impassibility, they do not clearly articulate the kind of strong formulation as found in Aquinas.[311] This latter point is a fair one, as it is difficult to find a strict definition of impassibility in any of these sources. What is clear is that the ability to suffer or be swayed by shifting emotional states are aspects of creation and cannot be attributed to the divine essence. The more precise definitions discussed above would not be given until the development of scholasticism.

The Biblical Evidence

Unlike immutability or divine eternity, there is no set of clear texts which affirm that God is without passions. It is perhaps for this reason that Moltmann's arguments for divine suffering have been compelling to so many. The fact that there are not such texts, however, does not mean that

---

[310] Gregory, *Against Eunomius* VI.1 (*NPNF*² 5).

[311] As an example, see Lister, *God Is Impassible*.

there is no scriptural reason to affirm impassibility. God's distance from personal suffering can be demonstrated through the consistent application of doctrines which are clearly stated at various points, along with finding implications of other texts.

The first argument in favor of impassibility from the biblical text is from the consistent testimony to immutability. As discussed previously in this book, there are points at which the Bible says that God does not change (Mal. 3:6, James 1:17). If we take a strong immutability stance to these texts (as was argued for previously), then we simply cannot attribute emotions to God in any univocal sense. Humans experience emotions and pain through the changing of one's life circumstances, hormones, or need for bodily requirements like food or sleep. If God were capable of inner emotional turmoil or pain, then he would, by necessity, be mutable. Such emotional states only arise through change. Further, this would mean that God's own internal state would be determined by something outside of himself—thus questioning divine aseity in making God dependent in some manner (say, with regard to his blessedness) upon creatures.

Second, God's impassibility is clear in the same texts addressed previously, wherein God is said to be incapable of repentance (1 Sam. 15:29). Repentance arises as a result of an internal change of emotional state or an intellectual apprehension of some sort of wrongdoing or mistake. Such texts help the reader to interpret those times in which God *is* said to repent, so that it is clear that use of such language is the result of accommodation rather than strict literalism. Therefore, just as the language of "change" is used only in an analogical way with regard to God's nature, so is the emotional content of repentance. This, again, does not mean that these texts (that is, those which attribute suffering and sorrow to God) are not saying something which is true about God, but simply that they are not to be applied in the same manner in which such things are said of creatures.

Third, as Gerhard shows, divine blessedness is inconsistent with divine suffering. Gerhard presents four distinct sets of biblical passages which demonstrate that God is indeed blessed.[312] First, there are verses which state the fact clearly that God is blessed (1 Tim. 1:11, 1 Tim. 6:15). Second, some texts speak about God's inability to be harmed by anything (Job 35:6–7, Ps. 16:2, Ps. 50:12). Third, God is described as light, which is used as a metaphor for perfection and majesty (1 John 1:5). Fourth, God's blessedness is described with regard to the delight that it brings to those who enter into his presence and life (Ps. 16:11, Ps. 27:13, Ps. 36:8). If God truly is the perfection of delight and joy—as is the meaning of blessedness—then he cannot suffer. Any limitation on divine delight would limit his blessed state. Thus, God is impassible.

Fourth, texts related to divine aseity and simplicity also necessitate impassibility. As discussed in our exploration of divine simplicity, the divine name "I AM" implies God's ontological self-sufficiency. Yahweh relies upon no one outside of himself for his existence or essence. God stands alone in that he is determined in no way by anything outside of himself. Regarding divine emotion, the question, then, is whether God, in his relations with creatures, has anything to gain or lose from such interactions. If God has gain or loss from creatures, then he is no longer self-sufficient in the fullest sense. In this view, his being (even if relationally or accidentally) is determined by his mutual interactions with human beings. Any argument for emotional change in God would necessitate such a thing. Some have made attempts to affirm some kind of ontological impassibility while then distinguishing this from God's relations with creatures. This creates a separate relational passibility (discussed below) which is distinct from the divine essence. This is quite a difficult path to follow. As Ronald S. Baines writes, "when God relates to men, he does so as the same eternal, transcendent I AM who is infinite in being and perfection."[313] If divine aseity is true, then God is impassible.

Related to aseity, then, is simplicity. If God is non-composite, then he cannot experience emotional change. If he has emotions, the question is,

---

[312] Gerhard, *God and Trinity*, 261.

[313] Baines et al., *Confessing the Impassible God*, 103.

are they the divine essence itself, or are they added to the divine essence? If emotional states are identified with the divine essence, then God's essence itself is changed relationally. Most do not want to conclude that the divine essence itself is in some way determined by us in our relations to God. If, on the other hand, these emotions are something superadded to the divine essence, then God is no longer non-composite, and is thus a complex being rather than an ontologically simple one. This is hard to defend in light of the biblical statements regarding divine unity and aseity.

Fifth, the apostolic preaching in the Book of Acts strongly distinguishes between God and creation in a manner that is consistent with impassibility. In Paul's famous speech at the Areopogus, the apostle praises some insights of Greek philosophers regarding God's existence while simultaneously condemning pagan idolatry. Unlike the idols, God does not "need" anything; rather he is the one that gives life to all other things (Acts 17:25). Creation is dependent upon God to be what it is, but in no way is God dependent upon creation to be what *he* is. Paul further explains this when he says that God is not "something shaped by art and man's devising" (Acts 17:29). If God has real emotional states that are changed by human actions, then in some way he *is* shaped by man. This is perhaps even clearer in an event which occurs earlier in the Book of Acts.[314] When Paul and Barnabas begin to perform miracles in the city of Lystra during their first missionary journey, the people of the city begin to identify the apostles as gods. In response, Paul tells the people that he and Barnabas are "men with the same nature as you" (Acts 14:15). What is particularly significant about this phrase is that the term translated as "same nature" is the Greek word "ὁμοιοπαθεῖς," which is more literally rendered as "like passions." In other words, Paul and Barnabas are distinct from God precisely in that they have passions that are identical with other men. God does *not* have passion in a human sense.

It is important to remember that each of these arguments speaks strictly to the divine nature in itself and *not* to the reality of the incarnation. According to the human nature of Christ, God does experience suffering, change,

---

[314] Baines et al., *Confessing the Impassible God*, 193–95.

human emotion, and even death. This is the miracle of the incarnation. But this reality is downplayed when one attempts to define these human characteristics as already present within the divine essence itself.

Moltmann and the Denial of Impassibility

Jürgen Moltmann is by no means the first theologian to deny a classical understanding of impassibility. Such moves had been made in Dorner, Whitehead, and even Barth to some extent. Nonetheless, it is Moltmann's treatment of this question in his book *The Crucified God* which has been most often referenced as the primary influence upon current takes regarding this question. Moltmann's view is therefore addressed here first, and then some other critiques which follow Moltmann are addressed.

Following up on his earlier *Theology of Hope*, *The Crucified God* expresses Moltmann's Christocentric theology, in which the cross is not one locus in a dogmatic system, but is instead the doctrine upon which all of Christian theology builds. He introduces his work claiming that "the cross is the test of everything which deserves to be called Christian."[315] From a Lutheran theological approach, this certainly *sounds* appealing, as Luther's *theologia crucis* forms our theology and piety in a cruciform manner. However, Moltmann goes far beyond Luther here in his claims. For Luther, the Christian *knows* God by means of the cross, and is justified via the death of Christ. This is why the cross stands at the center of Christian proclamation. The cross is *not*, however, for Luther, constitutive of God's eternal being. Moltmann, in contrast to Luther, does not merely speak here of the epistemological or soteriological centrality of the cross, but its *metaphysical* necessity. In some real way, God himself is constituted by the cross. God is not an eternal impassible being who takes human frailty upon himself freely via the incarnation for the sake of the justification of sinners; he instead suffers—in his own eternal divine being—along with his creation, and is constituted by such suffering.

---

[315] Moltmann, *Crucified God*, 7.

Moltmann refers to the cross as the "nucleus" of everything that Christian theology claims about God. This, again, is not merely a question of epistemology, but, in Moltmann's view, the cross must be understood as an event that occurs "in God's being."[316] This *"critical theory of God"* is set over against the metaphysically oriented theism of the ancient Greeks and the medieval West.[317] The Greek metaphysical deity is conceived of as the opposite of human creatures. Humanity is finite, divisible, mutable, and passible; God is infinite, indivisible, immutable, and impassible.[318] This, for Moltmann, is a pagan theism which should be radically reformulated in a Christian context. Rather than the *actus purus* of Thomas Aquinas, Moltmann's God has suffering as his potentiality which is actualized in the death of Christ. This is set against what Moltmann refers to as a "philosophical and political monotheism."[319] Moltmann even rejects the language of "theism" as a whole, as he contends that this term generally implies the conceptions of unchangeability which form the creature/Creator divide. Instead, Moltmann views his Trinitarian theology of the cross as an alternative to both theism and atheism.[320]

The primary theological argument that Moltmann makes to defend his radical position is in his conception of divine love. In his view, "the one who cannot suffer cannot love either."[321] His argument can be summarized with three basic propositions:

1. Every being that loves must do so through suffering.

2. God is a being that loves.

3. Therefore, since God is a being that loves, he must do so through suffering.

If the first of these premises is untrue, then his argument is not a valid one.

---

[316] Ibid., 205.

[317] Ibid., 69.

[318] Ibid., 214.

[319] Ibid., 216.

[320] And I am prone to agree with his assessment. Where he ends up is tritheism.

[321] Moltmann, *Crucified God*, 222.

In light of that, we must ask, does love indeed need suffering in order to be love? I contend that such is not the case at all, and Moltmann hardly makes any compelling case why this must be so.

The first problem here is with Moltmann's starting point, that the being of God is constituted by the event of the cross. With a classical Christian perspective, God is self-existent, and creation is a free act. This means that God has a life independent of his creation. Within this Trinitarian life, God is love. The Father, Son, and Spirit live in an eternal bond of love and communion. This love, in the divine nature, is surely not in need of suffering to *be* love. Regardless of whether one contends that there can be some kind of suffering of God in connection with creation, certainly there must be an eternal divine life prior to creation's suffering. To argue otherwise is to make God's very nature as love dependent upon creation, and furthermore upon the *suffering* of creation. If love needs suffering, then suffering, and therefore sin—through which suffering entered creation—is a divine necessity. Moltmann's perspective seems to be a denial of any independent inner-Trinitarian life at all. God, for Moltmann, is not *a se*.

It must be admitted that there are places in Moltmann's work where it appears that his meaning might be that love *can* exist without suffering, though it must at least be *capable* of suffering if such empathy is merited. If this is the case, then love could exist without sin and suffering, at least theoretically. Even if this is the case, there is still no clear reason exactly why love must suffer in order to truly exist as love. Further, any hope that Moltmann holds to a Trinitarian identity apart from creaturely relations is negated by his own statements on the Trinitarian relations, as discussed in the next chapter.

The second problem with Moltmann's argument is that it relies on a caricature of the classical perspective. He refers to this unmoved mover of Aristotle as the "loveless beloved."[322] God demands love from all, but cannot actually give love. He is instead like a "stone," or an impersonal object who has no experience or relations. A God who is merely power can only be feared,

---

[322] Ibid.

not truly loved. Thus the God of classical theism is a distant and impersonal deity. In fact, according to Moltmann, humans are more blessed than this God because they understand the realities of suffering and helplessness. Of course, if Moltmann is correct that the classical view necessitates such a distant and impersonal deity, then classical theism cannot possibly be a Christian option, as the triune God of the Old and New Testaments interacts deeply and personally with creation. But the reality is that classical theism, at least in its Christian formulation, does not necessitate any such thing.

Many portrayals of the classical theistic deity speak as if in this view, God is inactive (like a stone), and that mutualism is the only way in which God can truly be active in the world. This is precisely the opposite of what is the case. God is pure act, which means that he is infinitely *more* active and engaged in the world than any creature, not less. It is in fact the human's actions and affections that appear more stone-like by comparison. Further, to say that God is somehow emotionally distant is again a misunderstanding of the divine nature in its classical explanation. As explained above, Aquinas contends that God can properly be said to have joy and love—or more accurately, God *is* joy and love. What humans experience as emotions cannot be predicated of God in the strictest sense, not because God is somehow *less* than them, but because human emotional states are mere reflections of that which is true in an infinitely fuller sense with reference to God. God exists in an infinite act of love which is so abundant that it overflows from the divine inner-triune life into the acts of creation and redemption. In no way can this deity be said to be unloving or impersonal.

To understand Moltmann's view more fully, we must look at his own definition of love. He contends that "love is the acceptance of the other without regard to one's own well-being."[323] It is not clear how this definition of love cannot coexist with classical theism. If God is truly completely self-sufficient and blessed apart from anything outside of himself, then creation is by definition an act that is unconcerned with his own well-being. God cannot possibly be more blessed or glorified than he already is. This means

---

[323] Ibid., 230.

that creation is a free and unconstrained act. In other words, it is an act of love. Moltmann, on the other hand, has actually diminished divine love in creation by making God's triune nature dependent upon his interaction with creatures. Contrary to his argument, it is actually Moltmann's view which makes God's actions with creation, to some degree, for his "own well-being," since the separation of Son from Father on the cross is a metaphysically necessary act (this is addressed in the following chapter). It is thus only a God who truly is in need of nothing outside of himself who can freely give in pure love to the creature.

Further, if acting "without regard to one's own well-being" necessitates suffering on another's behalf (and I am unsure why this is necessary, as there are plenty of examples of loving acts that do not necessitate suffering on behalf of the one who loves), then that too is perfectly explainable in a classical understanding of impassibility. It *does* cost God to save his beloved people, as he takes human frailty, suffering, and death upon himself through the incarnation of the Son. God gains nothing for himself through the incarnate work of Christ other than his people. In the act of creation itself, God freely chose to create while knowing the suffering and death of the Logos that would be the result (Eph. 1). For Moltmann, however, this is not enough, as he views the two-natures explanation of suffering as inadequate. Even though the tradition, through figures like Cyril and Aquinas, is able to confess that the Son suffers by means of his human nature, this *communicatio idiomatum* does not go far enough.[324]

Moltmann argues that there is a way in which the classical tradition is correct. There is no exact correspondence between human suffering and divine suffering. For example, God is not subject to "illness, pain, and death" as creatures are.[325] Here, Moltmann contends that the early church created a false dichotomy between a suffering imposed from the outside (passive suffering) and an inability to suffer (impassibility). Since God was not capable of the former, he must be the latter. For Moltmann, however,

---

[324] Ibid., 229.

[325] Ibid., 230.

there is a middle ground of "active suffering." This is a suffering which one chooses to face for the sake of another. God, though not bound to suffer, has freely chosen to enter into relationships in which suffering is possible. This solution is similar to what Scott Oliphint has more recently suggested, that though God is immutable and impassible in his eternal being, he freely takes upon himself covenantal properties that are subject to change.[326] There are two problems here. First, this assumes that there is some kind of incarnation before the incarnation. God in his own nature must somehow become something else in order to engage with the world. This leads to the second problem, which is that in this view, God cannot actually interact with the world unless he takes on something additional to himself. God appears to be incapable of interacting with creation unless he assumes these covenantal properties. While Moltmann does not use the same terminology as Oliphint, these problems apply to Moltmann's take on the issue as well.

Despite his protests throughout the book, I see no significant reason why Moltmann's concerns here are not addressed simply through the incarnation. One need not question God's impassibility to contend for a divine love which is truly free and unconditioned, in which the good of creation is valued to such an extent that the eternal Logos gives himself unto suffering in order to save a fallen race. There is no need to reformulate the entire Christian tradition to address a concern which is already answered by the central Christian doctrine of the incarnation.

A final point must be brought up here regarding Moltmann's position that has been stated by Thomas Weinandy, Thomas Joseph White, and others.[327] For Moltmann, God's care for the oppressed necessitates some kind of emotional mutuality with the suffering person. This reality of divine suffering is supposed to give some kind of hope and comfort to the one in difficult situations. While perhaps it sounds nice to say that God understands because he suffers too, is this really any word of hope for the downtrodden? The sufferer does not need to hear about a God who empathizes, but of one

---

[326] Oliphint, *God with Us*.

[327] White, *Trinity*, 306–07.

who is powerful enough to overcome suffering. Gerhard Forde refers to Moltmann's take here as a "misery loves company" theology.[328] Is not the more pastorally helpful stance that the God who cannot by nature suffer became incarnate in order to suffer for us so that all suffering would be defeated? We need a conqueror who can bring forth the world to come. That is the God who is revealed in the person of Christ.

Jenson's Approach

In agreement with Moltmann in some ways, Robert Jenson proposes a doctrine of passibility in which suffering is in some real sense the essence of God, though still avoiding the error of patripassianism (at least, that is his claim). Jenson does this by proposing a doctrine of divine suffering which is strongly Trinitarian, identifying suffering solely with the Son, and then identifying the Son with God, thus resulting in a suffering God.

Jenson is critical of the classical discussions surrounding God's attributes, as he views them as capitulations to Hellenism. He refers to the general listing of attributes as found in the Lutheran Orthodox "radically incomplete."[329] This problem arises from the relative attributes which are aspects of God that correspond to realities in creation, such as mercy, justice, and love. This method of categorizing the divine attributes assumes that only those things which are considered good in our conception of the world are to be identified with God. In contrast to this, for Jenson, God's attributes must include that which is not considered good in the world: mortality. For Jenson, "God is mortal."[330] It is clear here that Jenson is working from an entirely different framework of characterizing divine attributes than are classical theologians. Generally, God's attributes are those things which correspond to the divine essence, and not to God's relationship to the human

---

[328] Forde, *Theologian of the Cross*, 83.

[329] Braaten and Jenson, *Christian Dogmatics* 1:188.

[330] Ibid., 188.

nature of the incarnate Christ. If one must include "mortality" in the listing of divine attributes because of the incarnation, then all other human attributes should be included as well. Jenson is forced into this position for two reasons. First, he denies that there is any *Logos asarkos*. There is only the incarnate Logos, which means that all attributes of the human Christ are necessary attributes of the Logos. Second, Jenson conflates the divine essence with the economy of redemption, so that like Moltmann, he views the incarnate acts of Christ as constitutive of God's being.

The question of divine suffering is at the heart of many of the Christological controversies in the patristic era, according to Jenson. Arius could not possibly attribute death to God, and then he denied the divinity of the crucified one. This question was also raised during the patripassianist controversies, in which the suffering of the Father was under dispute. Here, Jenson affirms that the church was correct in its condemnation of the suffering of the Father, as a truly Trinitarian account of passibility must be careful to identify the Son as the subject of the passion. Here, Jenson is far more careful than Moltmann, who does not hold firmly against the patripassianist position.

At this point, we can then explore how it is that Jenson is able to affirm the suffering of the Son as explicitly divine suffering. This can perhaps best be summarized by the following statement: "Jesus' death is constitutive for his relation to the Father and so for both his deity and the Father's. Jesus is not God despite his death; he is God in that he died."[331] In this radical departure from classical Trinitarian theology, Jenson purports that Jesus's death somehow constitutes the eternal relations of Father and Son. This makes the very nature of God somehow dependent upon creaturely relations, not merely in an accidental sense, as some theistic mutualists argue, but essentially. The Son is divine because of his death. The Father is divine in the Son's death. As suffering now is deemed divinity-constituting for the Son, it is true in the fullest sense that God died. Yet it is hard to see still how Jenson avoids patripassianism, at least in some sense, here. Even if it is the

---

[331] Ibid., 189.

Son who suffers, Jenson argues that the Father's divinity is also constituted by the suffering of the Son. In other words, the Father's own divinity is somehow constituted by suffering. Yes, it is the suffering of another, but it still constitutes his own divinity nonetheless. Suffering becomes the very essence of God.

Despite Jenson's consistent protests to the contrary, this is a clearly Hegelian move. There is a self-negation of the Son-Father relationship which then constitutes the greater synthesis of Father and Son into a relationship of solidarity and mutuality after the resurrection. As with his critique of divine timelessness, Jenson argues that being is not to be understood as persistence. Rather, being is defined by "what it will be and now is open to being."[332] Thus there does not need to be an eternal relationship between three divine persons in the past in order for one to confess that God is triune. The triunity of God is the event of Jesus's resurrection in which he is coequal with the Father and Spirit. God is triune in both his present with us in Jesus and in his future as defined by the Spirit. For Jenson, God is an event, rather than a changeless being who exists in the relations of Father, Son, and Spirit.[333] The inevitable result of this formulation is that God's being is dependent upon the cross, and thus upon creation and sin. God, in this system, actually *needs* the limitations of humanity in order to be himself. Jenson writes: "Participation in our finitude, alienation, and consequent disaster thus belongs to the event that in fact God is."[334] In other places, Jenson backs away from the idea that God is in need of creation in order to be God, but it is hard to see how this could possibly be otherwise given these commitments.

This idea of the cross, and therefore suffering, as constitutive of the Father-Son relation (and the divinity of each) is an attempt to synthesize divine transcendence and divine immanence. Classical theology affirms that God is both transcendent and immanent, and does not need to change in order

---

[332] Ibid.

[333] Ibid., 188–89.

[334] Ibid., 189.

to be immanent with creation. For Jenson, the Father is transcendence, and Jesus the Israelite is immanence. The Spirit is the bringing together of immanence and transcendence in the future of God and the world. One problem with this (among many) is that the incarnation is no longer a *free* act. God must be a man, not *only* for the sake of human redemption but in order to truly interact with his own creation, and indeed to be who he is.

Jenson's proposal is no less radical than Moltmann's. Both authors completely redefine fundamental metaphysics, patristic Trinitarian theology, and a classical understanding of God's independence. Those Christians who affirm the ancient creeds are likely put off by such "Hegeling," but may perhaps be sympathetic to other approaches that do not propose quite so extreme a departure from the classical view. One such proposal is from Jenson's colleague, Colin Gunton.

Colin Gunton's Middle Ground

There are several theologians who have rejected Moltmann's boldness in denying impassibility altogether, while still arguing for a reinterpretation of the classical doctrine. One example of this is Colin Gunton, who attempts throughout his work to synthesize elements of classical doctrine with the insights of Karl Barth and other twentieth-century thinkers. His book *Act and Being: Towards a Theology of the Divine Attributes* is a test case in the act of proposing a middle ground between Aquinas and Moltmann.

Gunton is not merely dismissive of the classical attributes as nothing more than the Christianizing of Greek pagan views of the world. Rather, he argues that the fathers had strong polemical reasons to assert what they did regarding the divine being. In particular, impassibility was used largely in a polemical context, in which Christian apologists differentiated the God of Scripture with the Greek deities, who were constantly swayed by the passions. While the Roman pantheon often appeared to be nothing more than jealous and lustful men and women (just with more power than ordinary humans), the triune God is self-consistent and not controllable by outside forces. He is not swayed by ever-evolving emotional states of being. On the other side of this, Gunton argues, there is a danger that such affirmations of impassibility also fall into the danger of negating things like compassion and love, which may also be identified as passions.[335]

Gunton also points to the fact that several heretical groups used the doctrine of impassibility to ground their ideas. Nestorians, for example, divided the divine from the human nature as strongly as they did in order to preserve the distinction between passibility and divinity. Arians, similarly, used the doctrine of the suffering of the Son to argue against his full divinity, since God cannot suffer.[336] To be clear, Gunton does not argue that the doctrine of impassibility necessitates such heretical views, but he is clear that too strong of a doctrine *can* lead to such errors. It is for this reason that Gunton argues for a modified doctrine of impassibility.

On the one hand, Gunton rejects Moltmann's strong assertions that there is some kind of triune rupture in the death of Christ, so that the Father totally forsakes the Son. On the other hand, however, he wants to affirm that there is *some* sense in which the Father can be said to suffer in the atonement. In order to outline what it means that the Father suffers, Gunton defines exactly what suffering means in this context. Gunton distinguishes between "being swayed by" emotion and being internally affected by the sin and brokenness of creation.[337] In other words, God is not changed from without, but his passion must come from within. If one's theology is purely negative, this leads to a view of God that is "metaphysically abstract" and without a heart.[338] Scripture seems, for Gunton, to present the relationship of Father and Son as one of compassion and pity upon the human race, so that there is a *kind* of suffering in the Father's offering the Son. This is not, as it is in Moltmann, a Father who simply feels pain with creation because

---

[335] Gunton, *Act and Being*, 1183.

[336] Ibid.

[337] Ibid., 1215.

[338] Ibid.

suffering makes love genuine. Gunton rightly says that to "say 'I feel your pain' is not much of a help, unless it is a means of overcoming."[339] Further, he absolutely rejects the idea that the atonement creates some kind of divide within God himself.

There are a couple of points to be made regarding Gunton's proposal. First, he is correct in what he perceives the dangers to be if one does theology purely from a negative context. While the Bible does use apophatic statements, the cataphatic language tends to be more prominent. The biblical authors are rather free in making positive statements regarding God's nature and attributes without giving extensive qualifications. There is, I think, a strain of thought in Pseudo-Dionysius and others that focuses so narrowly upon what God is not that every positive statement must be immediately qualified with reference to God's transcendence above creaturely language. With reference to the view found in Thomas and Gerhard, however, these criticisms do not apply. Both Aquinas and Gerhard are explicit in their affirmations of divine compassion, blessedness, love, and joy as truly applicable to God, though recognizing the analogical use of language. One can rightly speak anthropomorphically about the displeasure, pain, and sorrow God feels over the nature of sin as long as it is recognized that this is analogical predication, and that there is no literal movement from potency to act within the divine being.

The second point to be made with regard to Gunton's formulation is that one need not equalize language of wrath, sadness, and pain with that of joy, pity, and compassion. His inclination here is to say that impassibility seems to fit the Christian narrative with regard to anger, but not with compassion. In other words, Gunton recognizes anthropomorphism in the biblical text in statements about judgment, but not as much in texts surrounding redemption. I do not believe that Gunton is entirely wrong here. At least from a Lutheran perspective, classical theism need not lead to a complete and total flattening out of the divine attributes so that God is just as wrathful as he is gracious. Luther speaks, for example, about salvation

---

[339] Ibid., 1231.

as God's "proper work" and judgment as his "alien work."[340] Scripture is abundant with references that God's compassion is greater than his wrath (Ps. 103:8, James 2:13). This does not mean that these are two parts of the divine being or that these are accidental properties added to the divine essence. Rather, terms like "wrath" or "grace" are understood with reference to God as analogies which correspond in some way to the simple divine essence. Like all analogies, some can be closer to the reality itself than others. In other words, it could be said that the human idea of compassion corresponds more to the divine essence than does the idea of wrath. However, both are attributable to God, and are human understandings of the one simple divine essence.

The radical positions of those who completely reformulate classical Trinitarian categories from the patristic era are clearly rejected by theologians of a more classical bent—particularly for realists. However, these modified views as found in Gunton (along with several others like R. T. Mullins or William Lane Craig) might appear to be a more biblically satisfying theology of suffering than the strictly Thomistic one for some readers.[341] As is clear when reading Gunton's criticisms here, however, the problems are usually based upon a misreading of Thomas's account wherein the God of classical theism is portrayed as stiff, unfeeling, inactive, and apathetic. These types of characterizations of Yahweh do not fit his portrayal in the life of the people of Israel or the church. However, these characterizations are also not portrayed by the classical tradition. One can affirm both God's impassible nature and his overflowing love and compassion toward sufferers. Further, God does understand the depths of suffering on an intimate level through his condescension in the incarnation. There need be no lessening of the divine nature in order to affirm this reality.

---

[340] Wilson, "Doctrine of Mortification."

[341] Mullins, *God and Emotion*; Lamb, *Emotions of God*.

Conclusion

As with the other three components of classical theism discussed in this book, the classical approach to God's impassibility fits better with the biblical data and with historical Christian theology than current alternatives. Contrary to some characterizations in sources critical of the classical view, Aquinas does not portray God as some unfeeling monad who is apathetic toward the pain faced by creatures. Rather, as Thomas confesses quite clearly, God is eternal joy and delight. Further, he is merciful toward fallen creation. As always with Aquinas, these terms are to be understood analogously, so that these statements do not have an exact correspondence to creaturely realities. That does not, however, make such statements any less real.

In Johann Gerhard, these themes in Aquinas are presented again, and God is said to be identical in a state of eternal blessedness. It is through this blessedness that one must confess that God is without passions. Unlike creatures, God does not pass through shifting stages of emotions such that his own blessedness could be interrupted by the tragedies of the world. This does not make God uncaring for our sorrows, as God provides the solution for our woes in the incarnation, life, death, and resurrection of the Son. Further, Gerhard's doctrine is clearly driven not simply by philosophical speculation but by the text of Scripture. Though both thinkers draw from classical sources, neither Thomas nor Gerhard simply repeats the ideas of Plato or Aristotle uncritically on this matter. What they both present is a clearly *Christian* view of impassibility.

It is also clear that each of these four aspects of God's nature as presented in the text is dependent upon the others. If God truly is impassible, then he is simple, immutable, and atemporal. Each of these four ideas is simply another way of confessing that God is without limits. He is not limited by composition, change, time, or suffering. God exists beyond all such things. The interconnections of these ideas are seen even perhaps more clearly in our next subject: the doctrine of the Trinity. With a loss of classical metaphysics comes a loss of Trinitarian theology as defined by Nicea. Instead, opposing models are presented by current thinkers that are simply inadequate both exegetically and philosophically.

7

The Challenge of Social Trinitarianism

Along with the shifts away from a classical understanding of the divine attributes in the nineteenth and twentieth centuries, there were also significant alterations to a Christian understanding of the Trinity. Many Protestant liberals such as Friedrich Schleiermacher and Albrecht Ritschl deemphasized the doctrine of the Trinity, as such a teaching was viewed as too metaphysical and abstract.[342] Christian doctrine, for Schleiermacher, should grow out of Christian experience rather than the philosophical commitments which dominated medieval discussions. Due to this shift, Trinitarian thought was set aside as a subsidiary, rather than primary, commitment of the Christian theologian. In the twentieth century, however, this changed.

The twentieth century saw something of a Trinitarian renaissance in theology. Neo-orthodox thinkers in particular began to once again view the commitment to God's triunity as the foundation of any truly Christian system of thought. Though he is sometimes criticized as a crypto-modalist in his exposition, Karl Barth can be rightly credited as the primary figure in this retrieval of Trinitarian theology as the doctrine is thoroughly embedded throughout his *Church Dogmatics*.[343] The impact of Barth here cannot

---

[342] Ritschl, *Three Essays*, 151.

[343] See Molnar, *Faith, Freedom, and the Spirit*.

be overstated, as nearly all students of the Swiss theologian (which most influential twentieth-century theologians are in one way or another) are self-consciously Trinitarian in their theological systems.

It is important to keep in mind, however, that retrieval of triunity is not a wholesale acceptance of the received patristic and medieval doctrine. Neo-orthodoxy is, after all, a *new* orthodoxy. Though a departure from the earlier rationalistic liberalism, neo-orthodoxy is still essentially a movement *within* Protestant liberalism. The same rejection of classical metaphysics which stands behind the development of liberal theology retains its importance in much recent Trinitarian thought. Thus, much development surrounding the Trinity is done in such a way as to formulate a doctrine which is divorced from ontological realism. From this developed a model often referred to as "social trinitarianism," which relies on the concept of community as definitional to God's own being as both one and three.[344] Whereas classical Trinitarian thought speaks primarily in categories of "essence" and "person," social trinitarianism tends to speak of relations and roles of the distinct persons of the Godhead.

This chapter proceeds with explanations of classical Trinitarian thought, social trinitarianism, and then a critique of the latter approach. It must be stated here at the outset that in some ways it is not even accurate to speak of some kind of singular "social trinitarianism," as there are really several social trinitarianisms. Miraslov Volf, Wayne Grudem, and Robert Jenson can all be identified as social trinitarians but with radically different theological convictions. With this being the case, not all important thinkers can possibly be addressed in their uniqueness in a single chapter. Thus, the treatment is limited to a few important thinkers along with what appear in the movement to be some unifying concepts despite significant areas of divergence.

---

[344] Dukeman, *Mutual Hierarchy*, 1–4.

Defining Classical Trinitarianism

As one considers Trinitarian theology in its classical formulations, the most obvious starting point is with the early creedal formulations in the patristic era. With Nicea in particular, both East and West set forth the theological terminology and categories which would define the nature of Trinitarianism for the following centuries. Here, the background of basic Nicene orthodoxy is explained, and this is then followed by an overview of the Western Augustinian tradition's contributions to Trinitarianism.

The Early Development of Trinitarianism

The question of the Son's identity with the father is one of the primary areas of theological exposition among early Christian writers (if not *the* primary one). As Paul identifies the God of the Shema as both Father and Son (1 Cor. 8:4–6), so does the following generation of Christian theologians attempt to explain the nature of the relationship between the divine persons within the singular identity of God. The apologist Athenagoras speaks of the Father, Son, and Holy Spirit as a "triad" who share in one divine unity.[345] The Son is described as the mind (*nous*) of the Father, and as divine reason (*logikos*). Athenagoras is explicit that the Son did not begin to be at any point in time, but is eternally existent. The Spirit is described as the "effluence" of the Father who is likened to the rays of the sun. There is, at this time, no consistent use of the distinction between "essence" and "persons." Rather, Athenagoras speaks of "oneness," "unity," and "communion"[346] to identify God as singular.

The nature of the relations between persons in Athenagoras as well as in Justin Martyr and Cyril of Alexandria is explored within the categories and questions of the middle Platonism in which these thinkers were trained.

---

[345] Athenagoras, *Plea for the Christians*, Ch. X (*ANF* 2:133–34).

[346] Ibid., Ch. XII (*ANF* 2:134).

Wolfson notes that these early apologists considered the relations between persons as those of cause and effect. The Father is the chief cause, as both the Son's and Spirit's being are granted by the Father. The distinction then relates to "priority in nature," or ontological primacy.[347] It is important to note here that by ontological primacy, I do not mean that only the Father is divine while the Son and Spirit are something less. These apologists are clear that Jesus is the object of Christian worship, while simultaneously rejecting the worship of created things as foolish.[348] The Son is eternal, and not a created being. This does not mean that there is no sense of subordination in any of these thinkers, but the details of such things had not yet been worked out.[349]

How the deity of the Father relates to the divinity of the Son and Spirit is a key component of the further development of Trinitarian orthodoxy. Irenaeus touches on this some as he famously describes the Son and Spirit as the hands of God used in the creation of the world. The identity of God (who is other than creation) includes both the Word and the Spirit. The language of "hands" is of course metaphorical, but what is intended as an affirmation is that the Son and Spirit are somehow ontologically connected to the Father who is their source. Justin Martyr sometimes appears to take the Logos language rather literally in identifying the Son with God's eternal reason.[350] This has led some commentators to conclude that Justin views the Son, though eternal and distinct from the Father, as something less than personal. What is clear in Justin is that the distinction between Father, Son, and Spirit is not merely a conceptual one. Rather, the Father, Son, and Spirit are distinct in number. This conclusion of Justin here, as Wolfson notes,

---

[347] Wolfson, *Philosophy of the Church Fathers*, 309.

[348] For example, Cyril of Alexandria, *Exhortation to the Heathen*, Ch. I (*ANF* 2:171).

[349] Justin Martyr is often said to be a subordinationist in some sense. See the discussion in Barnard, *Justin Martyr*, 85–100.

[350] "In developing the biblical teaching of the Incarnation of the logos in Christ Justin conceived of him as the Father's intelligence or rational thought" (Barnard, *Justin Martyr*, 89).

"constitutes from now on the orthodox view."[351] Though the Father, Son, and Spirit share the divine identity, the three are not to be understood as three ways to view one singular divine person, but as distinct in themselves.

It is Origen who first attempts, in a more rigorous manner, to explain the ontology of the Father-Son relation. Many earlier accounts affirm the unity of rule and divinity between the Father and the Son without further exploration regarding how both ontological unity and personal distinction coexist. Origen finds the answer here in the doctrine of eternal generation.[352] For Origen, it is only the Father who is truly "God of himself" (*autotheos*). He is without generation or procession, unlike the Son and the Spirit. Yet the Father is not, in every sense, the only God. God, who is both immutable and atemporal, engages in an eternal and immutable act of generation, through which the Son exists. Origen refers to the Son as a second God (*deuteros Theos*). It is with Origen that the term "hypostasis" is applied to the three persons. Though there is some ambiguity regarding how exactly Origen uses this term (as it can mean something more like "essence" in some contexts), Kelly notes that Origen "more frequently gives it the sense of individual subsistence, and so individual existent."[353] Thus it is in Origen that the terminological distinction between *hypostasis* and *ousia* has its roots.

This does not mean, however, that Origen is yet Nicene in his understanding, as it has been generally understood that some type of subordinationism remains in his treatment—especially in his anti-Sabellian polemics. One of Origen's students, Dionysius of Alexandria, was reprimanded by the bishop of Rome for his perceived division of Father and Son and denial of their consubstantiality. Whether such a reprimand would have been merited toward Origen himself is up for debate, but it is clear that he has at least been read in a subordinationist manner.

Prior to Nicea, many elements of classical Trinitarianism had already been put into place. Early Christians, with the authors of the New Testament, are

---

[351] Wolfson, *Philosophy of the Church Fathers*, 310.

[352] Kelly, *Early Christian Doctrines*, 128–29.

[353] Ibid., 129.

convinced both that there is one God, and that Jesus the Messiah is divine. Irenaeus laid the foundation that God the Father works through the world through his two hands of the Son and the Spirit. Justin and Athenagoras articulate that the Son and Spirit are not created beings, but eternal. The Father, Son, and Spirit are not different only as means of appearances or modes of being, but actual individualities. Origen adds to this that the relationship between Father and Son is one of eternal generation, and that the Father, Son, and Spirit constitute three distinct *hypostases*, though not three fundamentally different divine beings. With the Arian debates in the fourth and fifth centuries, the lingering questions and terminological difficulties would be clarified.

Nicene Trinitarianism

As is often the case with theology, the doctrinal formulations which would come to be associated with orthodox Trinitarianism arose in the midst of debate. The story of the beginnings of this debate is told by the church historian Socrates.[354] In his account, Bishop Alexander of Alexandria was an ardent follower of Origen, and preached strongly on the eternal generation of Christ. This was objected to by an Egyptian priest by the name of Arius who accused Alexander of Sabellianism. Arius, in contrast to Alexander, believed in the unique divinity of the Father to the exclusion of the Son. In Arius's well-known words, "there was when the Son was not." Rather than an eternally existent divine hypostasis, the Son was a created being (albeit the greatest created being). This assertion led to the convening of multiple councils in Egypt and then eventually the first ecumenical council, the Council of Nicea, to resolve the issue in 325. The decision of Nicea and its creed, along with the exposition of these issues by Athanasius, came to define later orthodoxy in both the East and the West.

While the Nicene Creed as it is known today was not fully developed at the

---

[354] *Ecclesiastical History* Book I:V–IX (*NPNF*² 2).

Council of Nicea itself, the major theological points regarding the relation between the Son and the Father were present in the earliest form of the creed. The Arian party contended that it was proper to refer to Jesus as the Son and as one who was "from God" and distinct from the rest of creation.[355] Many present at the council desired a quick solution by proposing a creed with minimal affirmations of Christ's relationship to the Father as that of Son, which would satisfy both the Arian and Alexandrian parties. It became clear, however, that such a solution would not ease tensions. After some debate, the major terminological point came to the forefront: the *homoousios*. Drawing on the writings of Alexander and his young pupil Athanasius, the orthodox party contended that the phrase "of the essence of the Father" be included within the creed to explain the eternal Father-Son relation. The inclusion of this phrase negated the possibility of an approach to the Son in which he was not affirmed as God in precisely the same sense as the Father.[356]

The significance of the Nicene definition cannot be overstated in its securing of the foundational affirmations of Trinitarian orthodoxy. With the *homoousios*, the extreme Arian *heteroousios* (of a different substance), and the semi-Arian *homoiousios* (the Son is like the Father) are both rejected. With now the clear distinction between ousia and hypostasis, it became possible to speak clearly about in what sense God is one, and in what sense he is three. The Father, the Son, and the Holy Spirit are united in ousia but distinct in hypostases. This formulation, though accepted as common orthodoxy today, was not without its naysayers in the post-Nicene age. The *homoiousios* party argued that the Nicene formulation led to modalism. This is largely due to the fact that the Latin and Greek terms used in this controversy did not always translate clearly. The Latin term *substantia*, translated in English usually as "substance" or "essence," was understood by many in the East as

---

[355] Pelikan, *Catholic Tradition*, 193.

[356] Arians, both ancient and modern, note that Scripture does at times use the term "god" in a lesser sense (Ps. 82:6, John 10:34). Therefore it was necessary to affirm that he is divine by sharing of the essence of the Father.

a synonym for hypostasis rather than ousia. Therefore, Greek-speaking Christians feared that the West, in speaking of one *substantia*, promoted a unipersonal view of the Godhead. Nonetheless, the history of the continuing debates between the orthodox, Arian, and semi-Arian parties cannot be explored here. The important point is that it is the Nicene party which was accepted in global Christendom, securing the Trinitarianism of East and West, Roman and classical Protestant, dyophysite and monophysite traditions alike.

In light of contemporary social trinitarian proposals, it is important to point out some aspects of Nicene orthodoxy that are at issue in our further discussions below. The first is that Nicea approaches Trinitarian relations in a clearly metaphysical perspective, concerned not only with redemptive history but foundationally with the immanent Trinity. The Nicenes reject any notion that the status of Christ was in any way constituted by his incarnate state. He is divine by virtue of his eternal relations. The creed presents a Christology "from above," in which the eternal relation between the Father and the Son precedes, and is in no way dependent upon, the divine economy. In fact, within the condemnations (likely not familiar to the average churchgoer), the creed condemns those who confess that the Son is "subject to any change or conversion." Not only is the Son divine, but he is immutably so. In this explanation, the Nicene party uses the terminology and concepts of the Hellenized world. This is not a mere uncritical absorption of Greek thought, as Trinitarian theology led to the distinction between hypostases and ousia, which was not a classical distinction. There is both continuity and development of the Greek philosophical terms and concepts.

Nicea also provides some important clarifications with regard to exactly how the Trinitarian persons relate to one another. The foundation here is Origen's doctrine of eternal generation, which influenced Alexander and consequently Athanasius.[357] This is reflected in the affirmation that the Son is "begotten, not made." The Son is in some sense derivative of the Father, but not in such a way that he had a beginning in time. Instead, this generation is

---

[357] See Giles, *Eternal Generation*.

an eternal act. Nicea goes beyond Origen, however, in the affirmation that Christ is *homoousios* with the Father, thereby denying that the difference between begetting and being begotten necessitates ontological superiority/inferiority. If the divine essence is truly infinite, one who partakes of such an essence cannot be ontologically less than anything else. This generation of the Son from the Father is not merely present in the word "begotten" used in the creed, but it saturates the entire statement on Christ's nature. He is "God from God," "light from light," and "very God from very God." The Father does not receive his essence from the Son; the Son receives his essence from the Father.[358] In some real sense, then, the Father is the fount of divinity. This same reality is then applied to the Spirit in the further development of the creed, which confesses that the Spirit proceeds from the Father (and for a Western Christian like myself, from the Son).

Many social trinitarians have argued that it is at this point that the East and West diverge into their own unique views of the Godhead. One tradition, which emphasizes divine unity, has its roots in Augustine and consequently becomes the standard Western approach. The other, which emphasizes the plurality of persons, begins with the Cappadocian fathers and is then passed on through the Eastern tradition. Social trinitarians claim to be followers of this Eastern route rather than the more commonly accepted Augustinian one. To be clear here, there is no Eastern father who would recognize Jenson's articulation of the triune formulation within the economy as orthodox Trinitarianism. Nonetheless, because it is the Western view that tends to get the most criticism, that is what is addressed here. In the next section, we explain the Augustinian Trinitarian tradition through Western medieval and post-Reformation thinkers. After this groundwork is laid, the contemporary arguments in favor of the social trinitarian models are critiqued.

---

[358] Barrett, *Simply Trinity*, 155–78.

The Western Tradition

While many recent books on classical Trinitarian theology focus on the thought of St. Thomas Aquinas,[359] I discuss two other important theologians in Western Trinitarianism. We begin with the great scholastic author Peter Lombard, and then turn to Johann Gerhard. The exposition here provides the points at which social trinitarian proposals move away from a classical model as discussed in the following section.

Peter Lombard

Our point of departure for medieval Western Trinitarian orthodoxy is in the *Sentences* of Peter Lombard. As discussed previously, Lombard's text is mostly a simple reiteration and systematization of the ideas set forth in St. Augustine's writings. This text serves as the most significant early scholastic writing, which is then followed by Roman and Protestant authors alike. Neither tradition seeks to expand far beyond what is found in the writing of Lombard here.

In writing this work, the medieval theologian begins with an affirmation of two points. First, there is a singular divine essence. Second, there are three divine persons. It is these two basic points which unite all Trinitarian theology.[360] As in the early fathers, Lombard is left then to explain the sense in which the divine essence is singular, and that in which the *hypostases* are three. In answering these questions, Lombard outlines classical Trinitarian categories used in explaining the holy mystery.

As was thoroughly debated during the Arian controversy, Peter Lombard asks whether it is proper in any sense to refer to God as generated. The Arians contended that God, by definition, is ungenerate. If the Son is eternally generated, then, according to the Arians, he cannot, by definition, be divine. Lombard presents here the dilemma with the question: did God

---

[359] Such as White, *Trinity*.

[360] Lombard, *Sentences*, Bk. I Dist. II. Ch. 2.

generate God? It would seem, logically, that if God generated God, this would create two Gods. If this is not the case, it would seem that that God would be self-generative, which is illogical. In response, Lombard contends that God does generate another from himself—not a separate *God*, but a person. In other words, the essence is shared and the *person* generated. Therefore, God is not somehow creating his own essence.[361] God is identical with his essence, and therefore cannot cause that which is identical to himself. The essence of the Father is shared by the Son, while the person of the Son is eternally generated by the Father's begetting.

It is important that Lombard, in his approach to generation, does not attribute the Son's generation to an act of will by the Father. In other words, in contrast to Eunomius and other Arians, Lombard confesses that the generation of the Son is an ontological necessity. There is no possible world in which the Father simply chose not to generate the Son. His existence is as necessary as the Father's. The same is true of the Spirit. The proper terminology, then, is to say that the generation of the Son and the procession of the Spirit are acts of nature rather than will.[362] This then leads to the question of God's divine powers. If the Father has the power of begetting, and the Son has the power of being begotten, does this mean that the Father has some power that the Son does not have and vice versa? If so, this would seem to limit the power of the persons, thereby making them less than omnipotent (and therefore, not equal or fully divine). As a response, Lombard contends that it is by one singular power shared by the Father and the Son by which the Father begets and the Son is begotten.[363]

Along with the begetting of the Son, as a Western theologian, Lombard confesses that the Spirit proceeds from both Father and Son. This procession is equally that of Father and the Son, and it is improper to speak of the Spirit's procession as principally from the Father. He does, however, acknowledge that there is a valid manner of speaking in which it is confessed that the

---

[361] Ibid., Bk. I. Dist. IV. Ch. 2.4.

[362] Ibid., Bk. I. Dist. VI. Ch. 1.

[363] Ibid., Bk. I. Dist. VII.2.

Spirit proceeds from the Father *through* the Son.[364] This procession differs from generation so that it is not correct to say that the Spirit is begotten. The Spirit is not simply a second Son. Occasionally, however, the language is used that the Son proceeds. When such a statement is made, however, it must be clear that such a procession differs from that of the Spirit. Ultimately, Lombard concludes that we do not know the exact difference between the two processions, but are biblically bound to affirm that the difference exists.[365]

Having explained Lombard's treatment of the differences between persons through the eternal acts of generation and procession, it now remains to explain the nature of the unity of the Godhead. Drawing from Augustine, Lombard states that the equality of the Godhead consists in the equality of eternity, greatness, and might. This is further clarified in relation to the doctrine of divine simplicity. All three of these attributes are identical to the divine essence itself; to state that there is a mutual partaking of the divine essence is to say that the persons are therefore equal in all attributes, as the two are identical.[366] In sharing the divine essence, the persons do not make up "parts" of God, but the full divine essence completely and perfectly inheres within each person. This partaking of the divine essence of the persons is not analogous to three humans who all have a human essence. Human people have distinct individualities that strongly differentiate them from one another, unlike God's triune unity. Divinity is not a species of which the Father, Son, and Spirit are a part. Lombard clearly distinguishes between individual people and "persons" as used to refer to the Trinity.[367] Along with sharing in this identical essence, the persons also indwell one another—what is usually labeled perichoresis. Where one person is, there also are the other two.[368]

---

[364] Ibid., Bk. I. Dist. XII. Ch. 2.

[365] Ibid., Bk. I. Dist. XIII., Ch. 3.

[366] Ibid., Bk. I. Dist. XIX. Ch. 1.

[367] Ibid., Bk. I. Dist. XIX. Ch. 7.

[368] Ibid., Bk. I. Dist. XIX.4.

In summary, Lombard provides a comprehensive explanation of the Augustinian tradition's Trinitarian theology. Regarding the distinction between persons, Lombard provides only one way in which they are to be distinguished: the *ad intra* operations of begetting and procession. There is no idea whatsoever that the persons can all take on unique aspects of redemption apart from the other two, or that it is even possible for one to act without the others. Perichoresis necessitates a continual presence and act of each person within the others. Lombard clearly contends that the persons are not separate people with their own wills. Further, the oneness of the Godhead is explained by Lombard as a complete sharing of essence between the persons. It is not a mere unity of will or community analogous to a human team or family. The very essence of the Father is shared, by nature, with the Son, who is eternally begotten, and the Spirit, who eternally proceeds. These categories, solidified in theologians like Lombard, continue to define the Trinitarian theology of the Protestant scholastics.

Gerhard on the Trinity

In the post-Reformation era, the Socinian movement pushed thinkers across the theological spectrum to produce robust defenses of Trinitarian doctrine.[369] According to the Socinians, the Lutheran and Reformed traditions relied on philosophical and historical formulations of the doctrine of the Trinity rather than on Scripture. In Socinian belief, only the Father is divine, and Jesus did not have a preexistent life as the eternal Logos. The presence of this heretical movement, known today through its offshoot, unitarianism, led to the writing of some of the most comprehensive defenses and expositions of Trinitarian doctrine in Christian history by Protestant scholastics. While demonstrating continuity with the early church and the creeds, the foundational arguments for the defense of God's triunity was found within the text of Scripture, as these authors were committed to the

---

[369] On the Socinian movement, see Mortimer, *Reason and Religion*.

sola Scriptura principle of the Reformation.

Gerhard's treatment of Trinitarian theology begins with a discussion of the sources of theology.[370] Against Socinus, he contends that the clear text of Scripture teaches the doctrine of the Trinity in both the Old and New Testaments. The consistent testimony of the church on these matters serves only as a secondary authority attesting to the validity of the doctrine as found in the biblical text. This biblical defense is twofold. First, Scripture uses divine names, speaks of divine works, and attributes worship to the Father, the Son, and the Holy Spirit. Second, Scripture repeatedly confesses that there is one God. If both of these premises are true, then the Father, Son, and Holy Spirit must be one God. A further clarification is made against the error of Sabellianism, that the Father, Son, and Holy Spirit are described as being distinct from one another, rather than as one person who appears in three forms. This is shown especially in Jesus's baptism and the Trinitarian baptismal formula given to the church.

While the theology of Trinitarianism arises from Scripture, Gerhard recognizes the necessity of using terms which are not explicitly used by the New Testament authors. In the Arian controversy, both the Athanasian and Arian parties could confess the words of Scripture without hesitation. However, the parties disagreed as to exactly what the meaning of those debated texts was. To simply reiterate biblical words would be to avoid actually addressing the controverted questions. Because of that, the phrase *"homoousios"* was introduced into Trinitarian theology in order to clarify how one interprets the biblical data and draw clear lines between the divergent approaches. Gerhard recognizes the wisdom of the fathers in using such language as well as the providential work of God in leading the church toward resolution of these Christological debates. Gerhard then explains the terms used in classical Trinitarian thought.

In defining the common Trinitarian language used by the church catholic, Gerhard speaks of ousia and hypostasis. Citing John of Damascus and Athanasius as authorities, Gerhard defines the essence as that which is shared

---

[370] Gerhard, *God and Trinity*, 274–76.

by the Father, Son, and Holy Spirit. This is shared in its completeness so that it cannot be said that the persons constitute parts of God, but the fullness of divinity inheres in each.[371] He further defines this essence as distinct from the use of language of essence in relation to creatures in five ways. First, divinity is not a species in which the persons share as three individual humans have a common human nature. Second, in distinguishing between the persons by number (three), this is analogous, but not identical to, the way in which numbers are applied to the difference between humans. Third, essence is not used in a plural manner in such a way as to say that there are three gods as three people are three humans. Fourth, the divine essence necessarily exists in the three persons, while the essence of an animal species remains the same regardless of how many individual animals exist. Fifth, God's essence is identical with his attributes and his existence, which cannot be said of creatures.[372]

Within this differentiation between human communities and the triune Godhead are the primary distinctions between a social trinitarian perspective and a classical approach. In defining the unity shared by the persons here, Gerhard helpfully describes a list of attributes which are divided between humans that remain undivided between the divine persons. According to Gerhard, the persons share "one essence, and power, and will, and operation."[373] Gerhard's confession of a singular operation among the triune persons is an affirmation of the doctrine of inseparable operations. There are not three separate workings of God in any of his acts (for example, to say that creation is solely the work of the Father or redemption solely the work of the Son), but one *singular* work which is triune in its operation. Further, these operations occur together as the three persons are also not *locally* distinct, as they remain always within one another. There is no sense in which the Father has to leave the Son or Spirit in order to do some particular work by himself. This is an impossibility. Gerhard's affirmation of a unity of will is

---

[371] Ibid., 302.

[372] Ibid., 304–06.

[373] Ibid., 305.

also an essential component to his Trinitarian thought, in contradistinction to some current approaches. If there is one singular divine will, there cannot be relationships of authority and submission in the ontological Trinity as is sometimes claimed.

If there is one will, operation, and work, then what exactly is meant by the distinction between persons in Gerhard? He defines a hypostasis as "a subsisting individual, intelligent, incommunicable, not sustained by another."[374] While an essence can be shared by more than one person, a hypostasis is that which exists only within itself. The divine essence is communicable, but the persons are not. The Father cannot give his Fatherhood to the Son or Spirit, nor can the Son grant his Sonship to the Spirit or Father. These three hypostases must therefore remain distinct in themselves. In existing in these three hypostases, the divine being itself is not divided or granted any extra actuality. The persons are modes of being.[375] Gerhard distinguishes here between the hypostases and the manner of subsisting. Each person is a hypostasis, but the manner in which they subsist differs. The manner in which the Son subsists is through generation, and the manner in which the Spirit subsists is through procession. It is these *ad intra* operations alone which distinguish the persons.

Gerhard, as consistent with the scholastic Protestant authors in general, does not depart from classical orthodoxy as taught by the patristics and in the medieval scholastics. He reiterates the unity of the persons in explicitly metaphysical language, noting that there is one unified, simple, unchanging essence which inheres in its fullness within the three persons. The persons are not described as having distinct wills, powers, or centers of consciousness. Any connection between God's tripersonal existence and human communities is analogical rather than univocal. Further, the distinction between persons is due to the *ad intra* acts of generation and procession, rather than distinct sets of attributes given to each person. A final point to note is that Gerhard, along with the previous authors discussed

---

[374] Ibid., 314.

[375] Gerhard uses this phrase, but it is not to be understood in the modalist sense.

here, never speaks of the divine economy having any constitutive power over the nature of the Godhead. God's triunity is an eternal reality defined by his own self-existence, and is not in any way determined by his economic relations.

Defining Social Trinitarianism

Nearly all of the most influential theologians in the twentieth century were, to some degree, social trinitarians. It is only now in the twenty-first century that these ideas have faced significant challenges from more classically oriented theologians. The roots of this trend are found in the most important Protestant theologian and Catholic theologian, respectively, of the last century: Karl Barth and Karl Rahner. With Barth, Trinitarianism was once again brought into the center of dogmatic formulation. Though traditional in some ways, Barth's Trinitarianism was focused more on the revelation of God than on metaphysics. This set forth a different set of concerns and questions in Trinitarian discourse than in previous centuries. Barth also questioned the classical Western use of *persona* to define the threefold distinction within the Godhead. Rahner introduced into systematic theology the famous "Rahner's rule," whereby it is stated that "the economic Trinity is the ontological Trinity." There is some debate that remains surrounding both Barth's and Rahner's Trinitarian thought. Nonetheless, however one approaches these thinkers themselves, it is clear that the following generation of theologians took their insights into more radical directions, thus departing further from a classical form of Trinitarianism.

Moltmann on the Crucified God

Along with rejecting divine impassibility, Moltmann is also one of the leading proponents of social trinitarian thought. These shifts in his understanding of the Godhead are apparent in his highly influential work *The Crucified God* and are then explored in more detail in *The Trinity and the Kingdom*. The discussion here is mostly from *The Crucified God*, as that text was formative for a number of theology students upon its release. Before the discussion begins, I must note that the criticism of divine impassibility leveled by Moltmann in his book (as explored in the previous chapter) is not reiterated here. It is important, however, to note that Moltmann's Trinitarian theology flows out of his approach to the divine attributes as discussed earlier. It is suffering, in particular, which defines God's nature.

In light of God's relationship to suffering, Moltmann proposes what he refers to as a "Trinitarian theology of the cross."[376] This is necessary for Moltmann, because he rejects all previous Western Trinitarian formulations. As an example of this rejection, in a rather bold statement, he proclaims, "The doctrine of the Trinity enjoys no special significance in the history of Western theology."[377] Such a claim is difficult to take seriously if one has spent any time exploring the broader Augustinian tradition, both Protestant and Catholic—which I contend has a far more robust Trinitarianism than Moltmann and the other students of Hegel are able to offer. Nonetheless, to understand the claim Moltmann is making, one must first grasp exactly what it is that is necessary for Moltmann to have "significance" in Christian theology. He does not deny that the Trinity as a doctrine was taught in the medieval and post-Reformation church. At least until Schleiermarcher,[378] it appears as an early locus in dogmatics textbooks. However, it is taught as "no more than theoretical speculation with no relevance for life."[379] Like many theologians, Moltmann is skeptical of classical metaphysics and the impact of Greek thought upon the development of dogma. A proper Trinitarian theology, for Moltmann, is not defined by metaphysics, but by the cross.

Here, Moltmann makes an argument which has been continually repeated

---

[376] Moltmann, *Crucified God*, 236.

[377] Ibid.

[378] Schleiermacher famously discussed the Trinity last in his *Christian Faith* due to its non-practical nature.

[379] Moltmann, *Crucified God*, 237.

(in Jenson, Gunton, Braaten, Pannenberg, and others) that Aquinas introduced a dubious distinction in theology between *De Deo uno* (on the one God) and *De Deo triunio* (on the triune God).[380] Replacing the earlier Trinitarian orientation of Peter Lombard in the *Sentences*, Aquinas does not begin his description of God with an exposition of the Trinity, but with the singularity of God in the abstract. This includes the famous five proofs of God's existence along with the aspects of classical theism discussed throughout the present work: simplicity, immutability, atemporality, and impassibility. Moltmann faults Protestants here along with Roman Catholics, as they to have traditionally followed the same schema, assuming that one can somehow speak of a divine nature in the abstract without reference to the Trinity. He argues that this trend has only recently been reversed through Karl Barth, who begins his *Church Dogmatics* with a Trinitarian orientation. In making this shift, Moltmann argues that the church should move away from the Thomistic view, and instead build upon the Cappadocians, who place the tripersonality of God in the center of their theology. This narrative of a strict division between the Eastern and Western Trinitarian theologies (often between the Cappadocians and Augustine) is a core part of the polemics against the scholastic doctrine. It is by this means that these social trinitarian theologies purport to remain consistent with the teachings of the early church.

However, Moltmann here goes far beyond the Cappadocians, who clearly distinguish between the economic Trinity and the ontological Trinity. Acknowledging the differences in thought in a post-Kantian context from a classical one, Moltmann proposes a doctrine of the Trinity that is framed without the supposed metaphysical abstraction of classical thought. His solution is the contention that the "material principle of the doctrine of the Trinity is the cross of Christ."[381] In conjunction with this, he argues that the cross is then the formal principle of the doctrine of the Trinity. Here in Moltmann we find a total conflation of God's ontology with his

---

[380] Ibid., 239–40.

[381] Ibid., 241.

economic activity. The cross of Christ is not only the central event in human redemption, but it is definitive of God's own self-definition. Rather than the triune God *revealing* himself at the cross, God's triunity is *defined* by the cross. As with Jenson and Pannenberg, Moltmann's God cannot truly be said to be *a se*. If his own being is in any way dependent upon his interaction with the world, he cannot truly be independent.

In explaining exactly *how* the cross is the material principle of Trinitarian doctrine, Moltmann incorporates a dialectical approach which echoes Hegel and other German idealists. He cites Hegel explicitly on this front, and argues that "one should think of the Trinity as a dialectical event."[382] In this dialectic, Moltmann views the cross as an event of divine negation. Holding onto the citation of Psalm 22 by Jesus (Matt. 27:46), Moltmann contends that the Father has literally forsaken the Son (as something beyond a mere economic reality), thus creating a division between the persons. There is reciprocity here as well, as with the Son's forsakenness "the Father also forsakes himself."[383] Further, the surrendering of the Son on the cross also correlates to a surrendering of the Father. In this event, Moltmann speaks of the Father as "sonless," and the Son as "fatherless."[384] This surrender and forsaking is done out of love. In fact, it is this Father-Son dynamic as played out on the cross which *constitutes* God as love.[385] This event of separation through love then leads the Father and Son into a future of life in and for creation. This love is the Spirit. Moltmann contends that the love God has for fallen humanity is an outgrowth of the love created in the passion narrative.

Just as Hegel defines reality as historical process through the growth of Geist, so does Moltmann identify God with history. In Hegel, the Geist (often translated as world-spirit) develops through a dialectical process of

---

[382] Ibid., 255.

[383] Ibid., 243.

[384] Ibid.

[385] "He constitutes his existence in the event of his love. He exists as love in the event of the cross" (Ibid., 244).

self-negation and then resolution toward unity. This is often referenced as the process of a thesis, an antithesis, and then resolution with a synthesis. This formulation never occurs in Hegel, but it does provide a somewhat helpful (though highly simplistic) summary of this general process. For Moltmann, the Father experiences this kind of self-negation by means of the forsakenness of the Son, which then is brought to resolution through the Spirit, who opens up the future for the triune God and for creation. The Trinity is, as Hegel says, "the history of God."[386] The doctrine of the Trinity is then not an explanation of God's eternal being, but is instead identical with the passion narrative itself. This leads to Moltmann's identifying God not as a person, but as an "event."[387] The Trinity is not a self-existent divinity who is outside of and apart from time and space in three unchanging hypostases. Rather, the Trinity is "an eschatological process" which is grounded in the event of the cross.[388]

A final point to be made regarding Moltmann's trinitarianism is his contention that this is a resolution to the Christian conviction that God is both transcendent and immanent. In his understanding of Christian history, Roman Christians gradually began to import ideas of Roman emperors onto the identity of God, thus creating a being who stands over and above humanity as ruler and judge. Along with this, there was a conflation of Greek philosophy and Christianity whereby God began to be associated with a principle of being, like in Aquinas's unmoved mover. These approaches to God are, for Moltmann, "tantamount to idolatry."[389] The trinitarian theology of the cross proposed here is claimed to be a reconciliation of polarities. The passion narrative unites the transcendence and immanence of God, authority with liberation, law with love, and death with life.

---

[386] Ibid., 246.

[387] Ibid., 247.

[388] Ibid., 249.

[389] Ibid., 250.

A Critique of Moltmann's Approach

The first major problem that appears in Moltmann's approach, as with all mutualistic views, is that God cannot truly be *a se* (of himself). With the conflation of the divine economy with the ontological Trinity, Moltmann has made God's own being dependent upon his historical acts with creatures. This does not align with texts like Acts 17:25, which states: "Nor is He worshiped with men's hands, as though He needed anything, since He gives to all life, breath, and all things." The difference between God and creation is that he is self-sufficient, in no way dependent upon anything other than himself to be who he is. Creation, on the other hand, is that which receives its being from God. Moltmann goes beyond many mutualists, who contend that God experiences *accidental* changes,[390] by instead arguing blatantly that God's own identity as triune is dependent upon a particular historical event. As stated above, God *is* event for Moltmann. This is a conflation of epistemic and metaphysical realities. While cross-centric theologians like Luther contend that the triune God is *known* through the cross, Moltmann contends that God's essence is *constituted* by the cross. The revelation of God's nature must be separated from that nature itself. The triunity of God stands over and apart from any historical event in which his nature is revealed.

This is simply the ordering of Scripture itself. It is surprising how little the biblical text is used in Moltmann's reformulation of nearly all approaches to the Trinity prior to Hegel. Perhaps this is due to the fact that the contention that God's tripersonal existence is constituted by a self-negation of Father and Son on the cross is simply absent from the New Testament. John's Gospel, in particular, is especially clear about the Father-Son relation being one which exists entirely independent of Jesus's own historical life on earth. For John, the relationship between the Father and the *Logos* precedes the event of creation, let alone redemption (John 1:1–3). If this were not clear enough, Jesus references this pre-incarnate reality in the high priestly

---

[390] Such as the proposal from Richards, *Untamed God*, as discussed earlier.

prayer of John 17 (John 17:5). The same can be said regarding Moltmann's understanding of divine love. While he repeatedly states that the love God has for the world *arises* through the passion, there are repeated biblical statements that God's love is the *cause* of the passion (John 3:16, 1 John 4:10).

One might respond to this argument with the idea of retroactive causality as found in Pannenberg.[391] For some who follow Moltmann in the ontological priority of the future, though Trinitarian relations may in some way be constituted by the economy, this retroactively means that God has *always* been triune due to this future event. In other words, there was never a time when the Son was not. Regardless, this still does not solve the issue. Surely, the beauty of a text like John 3:16 is in the freedom of divine love in sending the Son. God did not need to deliver his beloved Son unto death, but did so purely out of grace as a free, unnecessitated decision. Moltmann's and Pannenberg's views make it instead necessary for God to deliver the Son, because it is in the self-giving of Christ at the cross that God is who he is. Salvation is no longer a free overflow of divine love, but becomes a necessity for God himself. None of this is even to mention the fact that the idea of some kind of retroactively causal relationship between Christ's death and/or resurrection and his divinity is simply absent from the biblical text.

There is, however, one verse cited by Moltmann as foundational to his conclusions. That is Psalm 22:1, as cited by Jesus on the cross. The speaking of this verse by Jesus is recorded in both Mark's and Matthew's accounts of the passion as the Messiah's last utterance (Mark 15:34, Matt. 27:46) before his death.[392] In Moltmann's view, this is the moment at which the Son and the Father both experience forsakenness such that the Son is fatherless and the Father sonless. It is this negative of the dialectic that results in the overflow of love by the Spirit, which then unites Father and Son and saves humanity. For such a central text in Moltmann's theology of the cross, there

---

[391] Pannenberg, *Jesus*, 39–114.

[392] Schaeffer writes, "[T]he very term here employed: My God, forbids us to believe that the Lord lamented that He was cast off by His Father in that awful moment; he who proves by such an earnest prayer that he has not forsaken God is surely not himself forsaken" (*Lutheran Commentary*, 2:400).

is not a lot of biblical data to work with here. This phrase is mentioned in two of the four passion narratives without any further theological exposition either in the gospels themselves or the epistolary literature of the New Testament.

Essential to grasping the meaning of Jesus's words here is the Old Testament text that Jesus cites. "My God, my God, why have you forsaken me?" is the first line of Psalm 22. This messianic psalm was written by David during a period of intense persecution and was thereby a prophetic confession of the suffering that Jesus would face on the cross. It includes statements about public mockery (Ps. 22:7), the casting of lots for his garments (Ps. 22:18), and the piercing of his hands and feet (Ps. 22:16). In citing the beginning of this psalm, Jesus evokes the entirety of the text, and in doing so proclaims himself to be the fulfillment of David's words. The notion of Christ's being forsaken cannot be isolated from the rest of the psalm, which is a prophetic testimony to the physical and emotional agony Jesus suffered on the cross. There is nothing in the context of the psalm or the gospels to indicate that this is a literal rupture in the divine being. Rather, it is more plausible that such a text is an expression of Jesus's humanity in the Logos's state of humiliation in which the Son expresses the height of his turmoil in taking human sin upon himself.

A final problem with Moltmann's proposal is his departure from all previous tradition. He is most critical of the Western church's formulation of the Trinity. At one point he blames Aquinas for the abstraction of triunity from a divine essence in general, but it is clear that his critique does not only encapsulate the thought of the Angelic Doctor. In the generalizing statement above, he criticizes the entirety of the Western Trinitarian tradition. There is some indication here that he views the Cappadocians as better expositors of the Godhead than Augustine in his famous *De Trinitate*. Putting aside the question of whether he rightly interprets the Cappadocians, Moltmann's so-called trinitarianism of the cross is foreign to any patristic author, East or West. This is defended by Moltmann in his citation of Alfred North Whitehead, by whom post-Constantinian Christianity is said to have gone wrong due to politicization, moralization, and philosophization.

Moltmann's claims here are radical, and they are bold. According to Moltmann, the tradition has unanimously misunderstood the Trinity, and the right Christian doctrine could only be recovered with the birth of post-Enlightenment German idealism. That much is necessitated by Moltmann's claims. And the argumentation offered is not sufficient to prove anything of the sort.

A Contemporary Example: Jeffrey A. Dukeman

The choice to use Dukeman's text here as a point of interaction might seem a bit odd. Dukeman's work is not a highly cited one, and there are plenty more influential modern social trinitarians whose work could just as easily be discussed. There are two reasons why this work is addressed here. First, as a pastor in the LCMS, Dukeman arises from within my own confessional Lutheran tradition. It is a worthwhile endeavor to explore how this strain of thought impacts theology from a strongly Lutheran perspective (though many of the prominent social trinitarians are self-identifying Lutherans in one way or another). Second, this text demonstrates the often bizarre directions in which social trinitarianism turns. Working within this framework, Dukeman is forced into positions which show the inadequacies of social trinitarian models to solve basic theological problems.

The primary thesis of Dukeman's work is that inter-Trinitarian relations are to be understood as mutually hierarchical. This is placed in opposition to two dominant strains of social trinitarianism. First is the hierarchical trinitarian thought of Roman Catholic theologian Hans Urs von Balthasar which holds to a strong view of hierarchical relations within the interpersonal interactions within the Godhead.[393] Second is Miroslav Volf's[394] egalitarian trinitarianism, in which there is a mutuality of operations between triune persons such that there can be no dominance or leadership

---

[393] McInerny, *Trinitarian Theology*.
[394] Volf, *God's Life*.

of one person over the other two. Both proposals further serve particular practical ends in assuming that the structure of the persons of the Godhead is the basis for human organizations and social institutions. For Balthasar, this hierarchical relationship serves as foundational for a defense of the hierarchy of the Roman Catholic Church as centered in the magisterium. A similar application is made by complementarian evangelicals who posit the submissive relationship of the Son to the Father as paradigmatic for the wife-and-husband relationship. Volf's egalitarian social trinitarianism is used as an argument *against* a strongly hierarchical church structure. Dukeman rejects both paradigms in favor of one which includes both hierarchy and mutuality as a solution to these positions.

This mutual hierarchical approach which Dukeman formulates begins with the foundational conviction that the social trinitarian models are correct. Yet in affirming social trinitarianism, Dukeman rejects both the hierarchical and egalitarian models. Both, in his view, are not social enough. He contends: "both Balthasar and Volf do not adequately account for the sociality of the divine persons, for a maximally social understanding of the Trinity, by not adequately accounting for the uniqueness and dignity of the divine persons necessary for this sociality."[395] In a hierarchical approach, the relationship between the Father and Son is oppressive, and it thereby does not adequately affirm the dignity of the Son. The egalitarian approach does, on the other hand, affirm the dignity of the Son along with the Father and Spirit, but does not adequately distinguish between the persons.

Dukeman formulates his approach first by distinguishing between the vocations of the Father, Son, and Spirit. By "vocation," Dukeman means the *ad extra* works of the Godhead, beginning with creation. In explaining the Christological model of creation according St. John, Dukeman contends that the Father "does not work directly in the world" and that the Son and the Spirit work instead "on his behalf."[396] This contention aligns Dukeman with common Hellenistic Logos philosophies in which the transcendent

---

[395] Dukeman, *Mutual Hierarchy*, 69.

[396] Ibid., 73.

source of being cannot act in direct contact with the world, and thus works through intermediaries in order to preserve his own transcendence. On this point, Dukeman echoes the approach to transcendence as taught by the Arians, rather than the orthodox party of Athanasius. According to Pelikan, Arius believed that "God in his transcendent being had to be kept aloof from any involvement with the world of being." God's transcendence is such that "there was not, and ontologically could not be, a direct point of contact between [God and the world]."[397] As God's transcendence separated God from the world, some kind of intermediary figure was needed for him to work. Thus, the Logos took this intermediate role as serving as a representative of God who could directly interact with creatures, since such is impossible for the Father. In response to this, Athanasius and other Nicenes contended that the Father could and did act directly within creation. No intermediary is needed.[398] God's transcendence must also recognize his immanence within creation. For the orthodox view, in no way does the Father's direct contact with creatures negate his supremacy or ontological distinctness. At least on this point, Dukeman sides with the Arian view over that of Athanasius.

In relation to the Son and Spirit, according to Dukeman, the Father provides "stability" and is "able to empower" the work of the Son and Spirit. Dukeman argues that this means that the Father's transcendence is "not in danger in any way."[399] The seeming implication of this is that if the Father were to work in the world directly, his transcendence *would* be in danger. If this is the case, does that not mean that the Son's and Spirit's transcendence is "in danger" with their direct interaction in the world? The only logical solution here would be the Arian conclusion, that the Father is transcendent in a way the Son and Spirit are not.

In order to defend against a subordinationist view of the Son, Dukeman contends that while the Father exercises authority over the Son, so does

---

[397] Pelikan, *Catholic Tradition*, 195.

[398] Ibid., 197.

[399] Dukeman, *Mutual Hierarchy*, 73.

the Son exercise hierarchy over the Father. In short, Dukeman defines the Son's hierarchy as the Father's dependence upon the Son for the work of redemption.[400] The Father must rely upon the Son in order for redemption to be accomplished, thus in some way making himself dependent upon the Son. His argument regarding the hierarchy of the Spirit is essentially the same. The Father relies upon the Spirit to bring people to faith, and thus the Spirit exercises hierarchical authority over the Father. There are two problems with this argument. First, Dukeman posits nothing here that would be rejected by an Arian. Certainly Arius believed that the work of the Son was necessary for human redemption, but this in no way secures the Son's divinity. Second, and centrally, Dukeman simply reworks the definition of hierarchy to include reliance upon a subordinate. This essentially inverts the nature of the term itself. If I exercise hierarchy by having someone dependent upon my work, then I exercise hierarchical authority over nearly every authority in my life. This is incoherent. Ultimately, Dukeman is left with a reformulated Arianism where the Father is transcendent and divorced from the world in a way that the Son and Spirit are not.

Along with these Arian tendencies, Dukeman's work demonstrates some of the dangers in rejecting the Augustinian principle *"omnia opera Trinitatis ad extra indivisa sunt"* (all of the external works of the Trinity are undivided).[401] As noted above, classical Trinitarian thought affirms that every work of God includes the work of the three persons. This must be the case because there is one singular work and will in the Godhead, so that there *cannot* be actions taken by one person to the neglect of the others. For Dukeman, however, there are three separate workings which not only are not singular, but *cannot* coexist with one another. Every act of God which involves the three persons, for Dukeman, has some kind of self-kenosis of one of the persons so that the other two persons are "allowed" to cooperate.[402] When the Father sends the Son and the Spirit to interact with creation, he limits his own power in order

---

[400] Ibid., 74–75.

[401] Vidu, *Same God*.

[402] Dukeman, *Mutual Hierarchy*, 80.

to make room for the other persons. This seems to present the Father, Son, and Spirit as three infinite beings whose powers are in a kind of competition with each other, so that each person must cease being infinite in order that the other two persons may act. It is difficult to see how this proposal can be anything *but* tritheism. If there is no unity in operation, the unity left is one of will between persons, and ultimate the submission of the wills of the Son and the Spirit to the Father. This, again, is the Arian position.

Moving beyond the economy, Dukeman further inserts his conclusions into the immanent Trinity. In his approach, the divine persons mutually constitute one another.[403] He is not speaking here merely of the acts of generation and procession as constitutive of the persons, as he argues that this mutual constitution is due to self-limiting.[404] There is something of an inequality here between the relations among the persons. Dukeman argues that the Father is closer to the Spirit than to the Son, thus creating an inter-Trinitarian mediation between Father and Son by means of the Spirit.[405] Within these inter-Trinitarian relations, Dukeman purports that there are distinct "properties" of the Father, Son, and Spirit. The Father has the "unique" properties of "leadership, grounding ability, and stability." The Son has the unique properties of "responsiveness, complementarity, and fostering completion." The Spirit has the unique properties of "intimacy, mediation, and fostering fellowship."[406] The problems here are numerous. First, this distinction between the divine essence and these properties is an explicit denial of divine simplicity. Second, this seems to posit some kind of temporal divine life of inter-Trinitarian actions which function like human relationships. This is clear in Dukeman's view that the Son "gradually limits his powers" in God's immanent life, which, apparently, has been temporalized.[407] Third, Dukeman's view has essentially erased any

---

[403] Ibid., 102.

[404] Ibid., 102.

[405] Ibid., 104–5.

[406] Ibid., 106.

[407] Ibid., 113.

sense in which the Son is really *homoousios* with the Father. With distinct powers, roles, wills, and properties, there is nothing left to unite the persons as sharing in one essence in any manner beyond three humans who happen to share a common nature. It is difficult to make any serious differentiation between Dukeman's view and a subordinationist tritheism.

As a pastor within the Lutheran Church—Missouri Synod, Dukeman professes adherence to the Nicene and Athanasian Creeds. He thus would not openly profess any kind of departure from the ecumenical creeds. Unless Dukeman is simply being dishonest (and I do not believe this to be the case), his arguments show a misunderstanding of the context and content of historic Trinitarian theology. This demonstrates a rather profound weakness on behalf of the general understanding surrounding the classical doctrine of God from within contemporary confessional Lutheranism. The fact that such a radical departure from historic orthodoxy could be written by a self-professed confessional Lutheran, and then endorsed by professors of confessional Lutheran seminaries, without there being any self-conscious discrepancy, shows that classical Trinitarianism is misunderstood among both pastors and professors. A retrieval of classical Trinitarian theology is vital.

Conclusion

This examination demonstrates that departures from classical Trinitarian orthodoxy have occurred within a broad range of theological schools and traditions. Moltmann rejects older realist ontologies for one in which the future is prioritized. As has been shown in prior chapters, this has shaped the Trinitarian thought of figures like Robert Jenson, Carl Braaten, and Wolfhart Pannenberg. The Trinity is no longer grounded upon eternal *ad intra* relations, but on the divine economy. The Father-Son relation is created by the events of the life of the historical Jesus (though this is explained somewhat differently in each thinker), and the relationship of these two persons with the Spirit is determined by the future. This raises the question of whether this can really be called Trinitarian theology at all, at least as the term has been historically understood.

But this departure is not present only in those thinkers who are influenced by Hegel, or the heirs of neo-orthodoxy. Dukeman is a confessional Lutheran who believes himself to be consistent with the Book of Concord and Martin Luther's own thought. This is a difficult claim to make considering how consistent his departure is. Nonetheless, it is demonstrative of how broad these misunderstandings have spread. In a similar fashion, many evangelicals have adopted a doctrine of eternal subordination and rejected the doctrine of eternal generation. It might be assumed that such ideas would not arise in the midst of a more historically rooted tradition like Lutheranism, but this is clearly not the case. It is an absolute necessity for the church to once again train its pastors and laity to confess that which is professed in the Athanasian Creed, and it can only do that by teaching the clear definitions of the classical terms and contexts used therein.

The alternate views presented, whether it is in the Hegelian model or a supposed evangelical or Lutheran one, do not have the same extensive explanatory power as the classical Nicene Trinitarian formulae. It is only the classical model which sufficiently defines a true tri-personality of the Godhead without deviating into a form of tritheism. Though social trinitarians do not intend to argue for a polytheistic approach to Christian theism, it is hard to escape such a conclusion in light of their premises. I contend, then, that we should not abandon the earlier view, as has often been done within the last hundred years. Let us heed the wisdom of those who have come before us.

8

Conclusion

This study has explored four tenets of classical theism (simplicity, immutability, atemporality, and impassibility), and has evaluated each of them in light of current critiques. With regard to each of these points, it has been demonstrated that newer proposals do not solve the problems they attempt to resolve, and they further create far more complications than the classical view. In this conclusion, we review the basic arguments for each of the four claims of classical theism, along with the reasons for accepting classical Trinitarian theology, and the flaws of the alternative views.

The first of the aspects of classical theism addressed in this work was divine simplicity. In a classical view, God's essence shares an exact identification with his attributes. There is no difference between substance and accidental properties in the divine nature. Further, as Aquinas noted, there is no distinction between God's essence and his existence. This doctrine defends the ontological priority of God above all beings, as he differentiates himself in having necessary being, whereas the existence of all other things is contingent. God's simple essence is the foundation for divine aseity, because if God were composed of anything other than himself, then those things that were part of his composition would be more ontologically basic than he is. Thus, God would no longer be self-existent, but would instead be dependent upon mutual relations to be what he is.

CONCLUSION

Critiques of simplicity are often driven by the desire to focus on the revealed nature of God in the text of Scripture, which does not delve into extensive detail about the relationship between the divine essence and attributes. The truth of this is to be granted. However, though divine simplicity is not a central concern of either the Old or New Testament authors, it is a theological and philosophical necessity in light of other clearly outlined biblical notions, such as God's self-existence, unity, uniqueness, and infinity. Alternative proposals require a redefinition of each of these ideas, and they do so with an unstable philosophical grounding.

The second aspect of classical theism explored in this book was God's immutability. God is to be differentiated from all creaturely existence in that while created things change, God does not. God's unchangeability does not only refer to his faithfulness or moral character, but to his very nature. While other things are composed of both act and potentiality, the divine nature does not move from potency to act. Instead, God is pure actuality. As pure act, God is not some kind of static or immovable object, but is instead infinitely active. He is thus far more active than anything else that exists. It is this ontological claim about God's nature which then is the necessary presupposition for a clear understanding of God's promises as similarly unchangeable.

More than perhaps any of the other attributes discussed here, the criticisms offered of the classical view are largely based on a misinterpretation. There is a continued conflation of immutability and supposed immobility, which is simply not an accurate representation of either Aquinas or the Protestant scholastics. Other critiques are dependent upon a strict reading of the texts of Scripture in which God appears to change his mind through his interactions with creation. These critiques would perhaps be compelling were it not for a variety of other texts which speak otherwise, and thus point the reader to an analogical reading of God's dealings with his people. Ultimately, the problem that none of the newer views are able to overcome is God's aseity. If God in any way is determined to be who he is by something outside of himself, he cannot be truly self-existent. This then challenges the most fundamental distinction between God and humanity.

The third aspect of classical theism explained in this work was divine atemporality. Existence within the confines of time is, by nature, a limitation. God, who is without limits, is not so bound. Atemporality is then an aspect of God's infinity. Divine eternality is strongly differentiated by the Augustinian tradition from the immortality partaken of by angels or the human soul. This is the case, not only in the fact that God's existence goes infinitely into the past as well as the future (which is not the case with any created thing), but in that God has a different relationship to time altogether. He exists outside of the boundaries of temporal moments and instead exists in one eternal present.

Criticisms of atemporality generally come from a rejection of the Greek philosophical tradition. It is uncontested that Plato, Aristotle, and other ancient philosophers were largely driven by questions of the relationship between time and timelessness. The very fact that it is a Greek concern does not, however, mean that it is inherently mistaken. Scripture, beyond simply speaking of God as eternal, often contrasts God's relationship to time with that of creatures. Further, as with the other attributes discussed, temporality cannot coexist consistently with aseity.

The final aspect of classical theism in this text is God's impassibility. The doctrine of impassibility addresses two specific concerns. First, the notion that God is impassible means that he is not capable of human emotions, as humans change from one emotional state to another. Contrary to many portrayals, this does not mean that God is totally unfeeling. Aquinas, Gerhard, and others who are committed to classical theism speak of God's eternal existence as one of pure joy, delight, and blessedness. In fact, these attributes are far truer of God than they are of creatures, whose emotions are a small picture of who God is. Second, God's impassibility means that he does not suffer. Human nature suffers physically, emotionally, and spiritually. God, as the one in whom there is no darkness, cannot suffer in this way.

Those who argue against impassibility, such as Jürgen Moltmann, often point to the centrality of suffering in the Christian message. At the heart of the gospel is the suffering of God through the cross of Christ. As opposed to Moltmann's claims, however, the cross does not necessitate a suffering of the divine nature in itself, but is instead to be placed under the mystery of the hypostatic union. Moltmann's conclusion leads him to contend that there is some kind of inter-Trinitarian rupture which creates the relationship between Father and Son. There is simply no biblical or historical basis for such a claim. The other common argument, that love necessitates some kind of co-suffering, is also baseless. There is no reason to assume that one must suffer in order to love. The greatest human need is not for one to suffer with us, but to overcome suffering. It is this that is overcome through the cross.

After our examination of each of these four tenets of classical theism, we then examined the phenomenon of social trinitarianism, which flows out of a rejection of the philosophical convictions of classical theism. Social trinitarians argue that God's unity is found not in a sharing of essence, but within divine community, through shared actions and wills between the persons. It was shown, however, that social trinitarianism results in a division of divine wills and actions from one another, and ultimately leaves no strong grounding for monotheism. A community of persons in social trinitarian constructions is simply a modified form of tritheism which is difficult to differentiate from beliefs like Mormonism, which affirms three distinct personages while denying the unity of one divine essence.

Why Does it Matter?

We end this study with a simple question: Why does any of this matter? It is here more than anywhere else that Christians tend to ask whether theologians simply create problems to solve that do not touch on the practical Christian life. Certainly, most individuals in the pew do not consider the relationship between God's essence and his attributes on Sunday morning. It is certainly not my contention that these (sometimes difficult) issues should be at the heart of all Christian preaching. Nonetheless, they do matter.

The nature of God is that which stands behind those things which are most practical for the Christian. While divine simplicity may sound abstract, God's unity does not. The notion that God is one is one of the most basic confessions that any Christian makes. Simplicity is therefore the working out of something which is known by all Christians. Divine immutability is that which gives us assurance that God's law continues to hold its demands over us, and that God's promises are as true in the future as they are today. We never have to fear that God will somehow go back on his word. Not only *will* he not do that, but if God is immutable, he *can't*! The promise that God gave you at your baptism, that you are his child, is just as unchangeable as the very being of God himself. Further, divine immutability assures us that God's standards do not change with the winds of culture. In the midst of a seemingly unendingly changing moral compass in the Western world, our views of what is good and right are anchored in an unchanging God.

God's atemporality assures us that in the midst of our fears of aging, death, and decay, there is a divine reality which has power over the sands of time. Time, which is often our enemy, is not the ultimate reality. It has no power over us who are in Christ. God instead holds time in his hands as a mere creation. Its negative effects are to be abolished one day by the one who created it. Finally, the impassibility of God comforts us with the reality that suffering is not of the very essence of things. God, the ultimate reality, does not and cannot suffer. Eternal life in union with God is also therefore a sharing in God's own eternal joy, delight, and blessedness. Our hope is in the beatific vision, in which we share in God's bliss forever, and suffering is no longer a present reality.

These truths, like any other that God has revealed, are given for our benefit. When they are lost, there is not merely some kind of abstract academic shift, but a practical one. As God's church, we are called to honor and worship him as he is, as the simple, unchangeable, atemporal, and impassible triune God who made us his own in the waters of Holy Baptism and feeds us richly with his word and the very body and blood of Christ until he comes again.

Bibliography

Ante-Nicene Fathers: The Writings of the Fathers Down to AD 325. Edited by Alexander Roberts and James Donaldson. 10 vols. 1885–87. Reprint, Peabody, MA: Hendrickson, 2004.

Allen, Diogenes. *Philosophy for Understanding Theology.* Atlanta: John Knox, 1985.

Anatolios, Khaled. *Retrieving Nicea: The Development and Meaning of Trinitarian Doctrine.* Grand Rapids: Baker, 2011.

Aquinas, Thomas. *Introduction to St. Thomas Aquinas. The Summa Theologica, The Summa Contra Gentiles.* Edited by Anton C. Pegis. New York: Random House, 1945.

———. *Summa Contra Gentiles. Book One: God.* Translated by Anton C. Pegis. London: Notre Dame, 1955.

———. *The Summa Theologica.* Translated by Fathers of the English Dominican Province. New York: Benziger Brothers, 1947.

Arand, Charles, Robert Kolb, and James A. Nestingen. *The Lutheran Confessions: History and Theology of The Book of Concord.* Minneapolis: Fortress, 2012.

Baines, Ronald S., Richard C. Barcellos et. al. *Confessing the Impassible*

God: The Biblical, Classical, & Confessional Doctrine of Divine Impassibility. Palmdale, CA: RBAP, 2015.

Barnard, L. W. *Justin Martyr: His Life and Thought.* Cambridge: Cambridge University, 1967.

Barrett, Matthew. *Simply Trinity: The Unmanipulated Father, Son, and Spirit.* Grand Rapids: Baker, 2021.

Barrett, William and Henry D. Aiken, eds. *Philosophy in the Twentieth Century: An Anthology.* New York: Random House, 1962.

Barth, Karl and Emil Brunner. *Natural Theology: Comprising "Nature and Grace" by Professor Dr. Emil Brunner and the Reply "No!" by Dr. Karl Barth.* Translated by Peter Fraenkel. Eugene, OR: 2002.

Bauckham, Richard. *Jesus and the God of Israel: God Crucified and Other Studies on the New Testament's Christology of Divine Identity.* Exeter: Paternoster, 2008.

Bavinck, Herman. *Reformed Dogmatics.* Vols I-IV. Translated by John Vriend, Grand Rapids: Reformation Heritage 2008.

Boethius. *The Consolation of Philosophy.* Translated by Henry Rosher James. Silchar, Assam: East India Publishing, 2022.

Boston, Thomas. *Human Nature in Its Fourfold State of Primitive Integrity, Entire Depravity, Begun Recovery, and Consummate Happiness of Mystery.* Reprint, Banner of Truth, 1964.

Boyd, Gregory A. *God of the Possible: A Biblical Introduction to the Open View of God.* Grand Rapids: Baker, 2000.

Braaten, Carl E. *The Future of God: The Revolutionary Dynamics of Hope*. New York: Harper & Row, 1969.

Bray, Gerald. "Impassibility in the Church Fathers: Why the Great Tradition Affirmed Impassibility," *Credo Magazine* 9, no. 1 (2019).

Calov, Abraham. *Systema Locorum Theologicorum*. 12 vols. Wittenberg: 1655–77.

Carter, Craig A. *Contemplating God with the Great Tradition: Recovering Classical Christian Theism*. Grand Rapids: Baker, 2021.

Cassidy, James J. *God's Time for Us: Barth's Reconciliation of Eternity and Time in Jesus Christ*. Bellingham, WA: Lexham, 2016.

Cobb, John B. Jr. and David Ray Griffin. *Process Theology: An Introductory Exposition*. Philadelphia: Westminster, 1976.

Cooper, Jordan B. *In Defense of the True, the Good, and the Beautiful: On the Loss of Transcendence and the Decline of the West*. Ithaca, NY: Just and Sinner, 2020.

——————. *Lex Aeterna: A Defense of the Orthodox Lutheran Doctrine of God's Law and Critique of Gerhard Forde*. Eugene, OR: Wipf and Stock, 2017.

Copleston, Frederick. *From Greece and Rome: From the Pre-Socratics to Plotinus*. A History of Philosophy, vol. 1. New York: Doubleday, 1993.

Craig, William Lane and J. P. Moreland. *Philosophical Foundations of a Christian Worldview*. 2nd ed. Westmont, IL: IVP Academic, 2017.

Davies, Brian. *An Introduction to the Philosophy of Religion*. 3rd ed. Oxford: Oxford University Press, 2004.

Dolezal, James E. *All That Is in God: Evangelical Theology and the Challenge of Classical Christian Theism*. Grand Rapids: Reformation Heritage, 2017.

———. *God without Parts: Divine Simplicity and the Metaphysics of God's Absoluteness*. Eugene, OR: Pickwick, 2011.

Dorner, Isaak August. *Divine Immutability: A Critical Reconsideration*. Translated by Robert R. Williams and Claude Welch. Minneapolis: Fortress, 1994.

Duby, Steven J. *Divine Simplicity: A Dogmatic Account*. T&T Clark Studies in Systematic Theology. London: T&T Clark, 2016.

———. *God in Himself: Scripture, Metaphysics, and the Task of Christian Theology*. Studies in Christian Doctrine and Scripture. London: Apollos, 2020.

———. *Jesus and the God of Classical Theism: Biblical Christology in Light of the Doctrine of God*. Grand Rapids: Baker, 2022.

Dukeman, Jeffrey A. *Mutual Hierarchy: A New Approach to Social Trinitarianism*. Eugene, OR: Wipf and Stock, 2019.

Eglinton, James, ed. *Bavinck: A Critical Biography*. Grand Rapids: Baker, 2020.

Evans, C. Stephen. *Exploring Kenotic Christology: The Self-Emptying God*. Vancouver: Regent, 2009.

Feser, Edward. "William Lane Craig on Divine Simplicity," *Edward Feser*, November 1, 2009. http://edwardfeser.blogspot.com/2009/11/william-lane-craig-on-divine-simplicity.html.

———. *Scholastic Metaphysics: A Contemporary Introduction*. Piscataway, NJ: Transaction, 2014.

Forde, Gerhard. *On Being a Theologian of the Cross: Reflections on Luther's Heidelberg Disputation, 1518*. Grand Rapids: Eerdmans, 1997.

Frame, John M. *The Doctrine of God*. A Theology of Lordship, vol. 2. Phillipsburg, NJ: 2002.

———. "Scholasticism for Evangelicals: Thoughts on *All That is in God* by James Dolezal." *The Works of John Frame and Vern Poythress*. 2017. https://frame-poythress.org/scholasticism-for-evangelicals-thoughts-on-all-that-is-in-god-by-james-dolezal/.

———. *Systematic Theology: An Introduction to Christian Belief*. Phillipsburg, NJ: Presbyterian and Reformed, 2013.

———. "Two Models of Divine Transcendence: Pure Being vs. Divine Lordship." *The Works of John Frame and Vern Poythress*. https://frame-poythress.org/two-models-of-divine-transcendence-pure-being-vs-divine-lordship/.

Gavrilyuk, Paul L. *The Suffering of the Impassible God: The Dialectics of Patristic Thought*. Oxford, 2006.

Gerhard, Johann. *Loci Theologici*. Edited by Johann F. Cotta. 20 vols. Tubingen: 1762–80.

Giles, Kevin. *The Eternal Generation of the Son: Maintaining Orthodoxy in Trinitarian Theology*. Downers Grove, IL: IVP, 2012.

Gunton, Collin E. *Act and Being: Towards a Theology of the Divine Attributes*. Kindle edition. Grand Rapids: SCM, 2002.

Hegel, G. W. F. *Early Theological Writings*. Translated by T. M. Knox. Philadelphia: University of Pennsylvania, 1971.

_____. *The Phenomenology of Spirit*. Translated by A. V. Miller. Oxford, 1977.

Hinlicky, Paul R. *Divine Simplicity: Christ the Crisis of Metaphysics*. Grand Rapids: Baker, 2016.

Hoenecke, Adolph. *Evangelical Lutheran Dogmatics*. 4 vols. Milwaukee: Northwestern, 1999–2009.

Hollaz, David. *Examen Theologicum Acroamaticum*. Rostock and Leipzig, 1718.

Jacobs, Henry E., ed. *The Lutheran Commentary Series*. 11 vols. Ithaca, NY: 2019.

Jenson, Robert W. *The Triune God*. Systematic Theology, vol. 1. New York: Oxford, 1997.

_____. *Theology as Revisionary Metaphysics: Essays on God and Creation*. Edited by Stephen John Wright. Eugene, Cascade, 2014.

Jenson, Robert W. and Carl E. Braaten, eds. *Christian Dogmatics*, vol. 1. Minneapolis: Fortress, 1981.

Johnson, Jeffrey D. *The Failure of Natural Theology: A Critical Appraisal of the Philosophical Theology of Thomas Aquinas*. Conway, AR: Free Grace, 2021.

Johnson, John F. "Analogia Fidei as Hermeneutical Principle," *The Springfielder* 36, no. 4 (1973), 249–59.

Juliano, Chance. "Divine Simplicity as a Necessary Condition for Affirming Creation Ex Nihilo." Digital Commons @ ACU, Electronic Theses and Dissertations. 2019. Paper 160.

Keating, John F. and Thomas Joseph White. *Divine Impassibility and the Mystery of Human Suffering*. Grand Rapids: Eerdmans, 2009.

Keller, Catherine. *On the Mystery: Discerning Divinity in Process*. Minneapolis: Fortress, 2007.

Kelly, J. N. D. *Early Christian Doctrines*. Rev. ed., 3rd printing. Peabody: Hendrickson, 2007.

Kline, Meredith G. *Kingdom Prologue: Genesis Foundations for a Covenantal Worldview*. Eugene, OR: Wipf and Stock, 2006.

Kretzmann, Paul E. *Popular Commentary on the Whole Bible*. http://www.kretzmannproject.org.

Kurtz, Ronni. *No Shadow of Turning: Divine Immutability and the Economy of Redemption*. Ross-Shire: Mentor, 2022.

Lamb, David T. *The Emotions of God: Making Sense of a God Who Hates, Weeps, and Loves*. Downers Grove: IVP, 2022.

Lenski, R. C. H. *The Interpretation of The Epistles of St. Peter, St. John, and St. Jude*. Minneapolis: Fortress, 1945.

Lister, Rob. *God Is Impassible and Impassioned*. Wheaton, IL: Crossway, 2012.

Little, Caleb J. "Emotions and the Divine Nature: Impassibility in the Greek Apologists and Iranaeus." *Channels: Where Disciplines Meet* 1, no. 1 (2016): art. 4.

Loy, Matthias. *The Augsburg Confession: An Introduction to Its Study and an Exposition of Its Contents*. Columbus: Lutheran Book Concern, 1908.

McInerny, Brendan. *The Trinitarian Theology of Hans Urs von Balthasar: An Introduction*. Notre Dame, 2020.

Minich, Joseph and Onsi A. Kamel, eds. *The Lord Is One: Reclaiming Divine Simplicity*. Leesburg, VA: Davenant, 2019.

Molnar, Paul D. *Faith, Freedom, and the Spirit: The Economic Trinity in Barth, Torrance and Contemporary Theology*. Downers Grove, IL: InterVarsity, 2015.

Moltmann, Jürgen. *The Church in the Power of the Spirit*. Translated by Margaret Kohl. San Francisco: Harper Collins, 1975.

_____. *The Crucified God: The Cross of Christ as the Foundation and Criticism of Christian Theology*. Translated by R. A. Wilson. Minneapolis: Fortress, 1993.

_____. *Theology of Hope: On the Ground and the Implications of a Christian Eschatology*. Minneapolis: Fortress, 1993.

Mortimer, Sarah. *Reason and Religion in the English Revolution: The Challenge of Socinianism*. Cambridge Studies in Early Modern British History. Cambridge, UK: Cambridge, 2014.

Muller-Fahrenholz, Geiko. *The Kingdom and the Power: The Theology of Jürgen Moltmann*. Translated by John Bowden. London: SCM, 2000.

Mullins, R. T. *God and Emotion*. Cambridge, UK: Cambridge, 2020.

Nakskow, Petrus Sachariae. *The Articles of Faith of the Holy Evangelical Church: According to the Word of God and the Augsburg Confession as Set Forth in Forty*

Sermons. Translated by J. M. Magens. Updated by Jordan Cooper. Ithaca, NY: Just and Sinner, 2021.

Oderberg, David S. *Real Essentialism*. London: Routledge, 2007.

Ogonowski, Zbigniew. "Faustus Socinus." In *Shapers of Religious Traditions in Germany, Switzerland, and Poland, 1560–1600*. New Haven: Yale University Press, 1981. 195–210.

Oliphint, Scott K. *God with Us: Divine Condescension and the Attributes of God*. Wheaton: Crossway, 2011.

Pannenberg, Wolfhart. *Jesus—God and Man*. Translated by Lewis L. Wilkins and Duane A. Priebe. London: SCM, 1968.

——————. *Metaphysics and the Idea of God*. Translated by Philip Clayton. Grand Rapids: Eerdmans, 1988.

Pauck, Wilhelm, ed. *Melanchthon and Bucer*. The Library of Christian Classics, vol. 19. Philadelphia: Westminster, 1969.

Peckham, John C. *Divine Attributes: Knowing the Covenantal God of Scripture*. Grand Rapids: Baker, 2001.

Pelikan, Jaroslav. *The Emergence of the Catholic Tradition*. The Christian Tradition: A History of the Development of Doctrine, vol. 1. Chicago: University of Chicago, 1971.

Pieper, Francis. *Christian Dogmatics*. 4 vols. Saint Louis: Concordia, 1950–57.

Pinnock, Clark H. *Most Moved Mover: A Theology of God's Openness*. Grand Rapids: Baker, 2001.

Poythress, Vern S. *The Mystery of the Trinity: A Trinitarian Approach to the Attributes of God*. Phillipsburg, NJ: P&R, 2020.

Preus, Robert D. *The Theology of Post-Reformation Lutheranism: A Study of Theological Prolegomena*. 2 vols. St. Louis: Concordia, 1970–72.

Quenstedt, John Andrew. *Theologia Didactico-Polemica sive Systema Theologiae*. Leipzig: 1715.

Renihan, Samuel, ed. *God without Passions: A Reader*. Palmdale, CA: RBAP, 2015.

Reynolds, Matt. "Christianity Today's 2022 Book Awards." *Christianity Today*, December 14, 2021. https://www.christianitytoday.com/ct/2022/january-february/christianity-today-2022-book-awards.html.

Richards, Jay Wesley. *The Untamed God: A Philosophical Exploration of Divine Perfection, Simplicity, and Immutability*. Downers Grove, IL: InterVarsity, 2003.

Ritschl, Albrecht. *Three Essays*. Translated by Philip Hefner. Eugene, OR: Wipf and Stock, 1972.

Ross, James. "Comments on 'Absolute Simplicity.'" *Faith and Philosophy: Journal of the Society of Christian Philosophers* 2, no. 4 (1985), art. 4.

Sanders, E. P., ed. *The Shaping of Christianity in the Second and Third Centuries*. Jewish and Christian Self Definition, vol. 2. Philadelphia: Fortress, 1980.

Sanders, John. *The God Who Risks: A Theology of Providence*. Downers Grove, IL: InterVarsity, 1998.

Sartre, Jean-Paul. *Existentialism Is a Humanism*. New Haven: Yale University Press, 2007.

Scaer, David P. *James, the Apostle of Faith: A Primary Christological Epistle for the Persecuted Church*. Eugene, OR: Wipf and Stock, 1994.

Schaff, Philip, ed. *Nicene and Post Nicene Fathers*. First Series. 14 vols. Buffalo: Christian Literature, 1886–89.

_____. *Nicene and Post Nicene Fathers*. Second Series. 14 vols. Buffalo: Christian Literature, 1890–1900.

Schleiermacher, Friedrich. *The Christian Faith*. Edited by H. R. Mackintosh and J. S. Stewart. London: T&T Clark, 1999.

Schmid, Heinrich. *The Doctrinal Theology of the Evangelical Lutheran Church, Exhibited and Verified from the Original Sources*. Translated by Henry Eyster Jacobs and Charles A. Hay. Philadelphia: Lutheran Publication Society, 1876.

Schreiver, Frederick. "Orthodoxy and Diplomacy: James I and the Vorstius Affair." *The English Historical Review* 85, no. 336 (July 1970): 449–74.

Schweitzer, Albert. *The Quest of the Historical Jesus: A Critical Study of Its Progress from Reimarus to Wrede*. Baltimore, MD: Johns Hopkins, 1998.

Scotus, John Duns. *Philosophical Writings*. 2nd ed. Translated by Allan Wolter. Indianapolis: Hackett, 1987.

Strauss, David Friedrich. *The Life of Jesus: Critically Examined*. Translated by George Elliot. Cambridge: Cambridge University, 2010.

Stump, Joseph. *The Christian Faith: A System of Christian Dogmatics*. Philadelphia: Muhlenberg, 1942.

Stump, Eleanore and Norman Kretzmann. "Absolute Simplicity." *Faith and*

Philosophy 2, no. 4 (1985): 353–82.

"Three Forms of Unity." United Reformed Churches in North America website. https://threeforms.org/canons-of-dort/.

Torrance, Thomas F. *The Christian Doctrine of God: One Being, Three Persons*. 2nd ed. London: A&C Black, 1996.

Vidu, Adonis. *The Same God Who Works All Things: Inseparable Operations in Trinitarian Theology*. Grand Rapids: Eerdmans, 2021.

Voigt, Andrew George. *Biblical Dogmatics*. Columbia, SC: Lutheran Board of Publication, 1917.

Volf, Miroslav. *God's Life in Trinity*. Minneapolis: Fortress, 2006.

Vos, Geerhardus. *Biblical Theology: Old and New Testaments*. Repub., Grand Rapids: Eerdmans, 1988.

Weidner, Revere Frankin. *God and His Works*. A System of Dogmatics, vol. 1. Ithaca, NY: Weidner Institute, 2022.

Wenthe, Dean O. "The Rich Monotheism of Isaiah as Christological Resource," *Concordia Theological Quarterly* 71, no. 1 (January 2007): 57–70.

Westphal, Merold. *History and Truth in Hegel's Phenomenology*. London: Humanities Press, 1979.

White, Thomas Joseph. *The Trinity: On the Nature and Mystery of the One God*. Washington, DC: Catholic University, 2022.

Whitehead, Alfred North. *Process and Reality*. Edited by David R. Griffin and Donald W. Sherburne. Free Press, 1979.

Williams, Rowan. *Arius: Heresy and Tradition*. Rev. ed. Grand Rapids: Eerdmans, 2002.

Wilson, Howard Allan. "The Doctrine of Mortification and the Opus Alienum Dei in Luther and Representative Lutheran Theologians," PhD Diss., (Edingburgh, 1964).

Wolfson, Harry Austryn. *The Philosophy of the Church Fathers, Volume One: Faith, Trinity, Incarnation*. Cambridge, MA: Harvard, 1956.

www.ingramcontent.com/pod-product-compliance
Lightning Source LLC
Chambersburg PA
CBHW030853170426
43193CB00009BA/596